Uncover the Hidden Power of Television Programming

Uncover the Hidden Power of Television Programming

...and Get the Most From Your Advertising Budget

Kevin J. Clancy, Ph. D.
David W. Lloyd, D. B. A.

Sage Publications, Inc.
International Educational and Professional Publisher
Thousand Oaks ▪ London ▪ New Delhi

For information:

SAGE Publications, Inc.
2455 Teller Road
Thousand Oaks, California 91320
E-mail: order@sagepub.com

SAGE Publications Ltd.
6 Bonhill Street
London EC2A 4PU
United Kingdom

SAGE Publications India Pvt. Ltd.
M-32 Market
Greater Kailash I
New Delhi 110 048 India

Printed in the United States of America

Library of Congress Cataloging-in-Publication Data

Clancy, Kevin J., 1942-
    Uncover the hidden power of television programming:—and get
the most from your advertising budget / by Kevin J. Clancy and
David W. Lloyd.
        p. cm.
Includes bibliographical references and index.
ISBN 0-7619-1581-8 (cloth: acid-free paper)
ISBN 0-7619-1582-6 (paper: acid-free paper)
1. Television advertising—United States. 2. Television
broadcasting—United States. 3. Television viewers—United States.
I. Lloyd, David W., 1949- II. Title.
    HF6146.T42 C49 1999
    659.14'3—dc21   99-6227

99 00 01 02 03 10 9 8 7 6 5 4 3 2 1

Acquiring Editor:	Harry Briggs
Editorial Assistant:	MaryAnn Vail
Production Editor:	Astrid Virding
Editorial Assistant:	Karen Wiley
Typesetter/Designer:	Danielle Dillahunt
Index:	Wally Wood

Contents

Preface

In his *Meditations,* written during lulls in his Gallic campaigns, Marcus Aurelius commented, "An arrow travels in one fashion, but the mind in another. Even when the mind is feeling its way cautiously and working round a problem from every angle, it is still moving onward and making for its goal."

Our goal when we began this investigation more than a decade ago was to report on a small library of research studies published over four decades that sought to understand the relationship between viewer involvement in television programs and advertising response. The genesis of our interest was the serendipitous discovery that the single best predictor of whether a person can recall television commercials is his or her attitude toward the program in which the commercial appeared. The more involved viewers are in a program, we found, the more likely it is that the advertising the program carries will imprint a message. Intrigued by this finding and encouraged by financial support from Dr. Elizabeth Roberts, we believed that like Aurelius's arrow, we would make straight for and quickly reach our mark.

We soon discovered that the issue is far more complicated than we thought. The literature on the topic is extremely rich but inconsistent, and one can approach the measurement of involvement and its effects in myriad ways. To better understand the relationship between involvement and advertising response, we designed and carried out two research studies of our own, one to measure the relationship between involvement and response to television programs; the other, a parallel study, for print publications.

Now, at the end of the process, we are comfortable in the knowledge that we have examined "the issue" cautiously and from every angle and that we most assuredly have reached our goal. We understand the link between television program (and print) involvement and advertising effectiveness and know how this information can be employed to make better, more cost-effective media decisions.

Many advertising and media theorists and practitioners played a significant role in helping this particular arrow reach its mark. The seminal thinking or pioneering research (or both) of David Aaker, Hans Baumgartner, John Bernbach, Leo Bogart, Gilbert Churchill, John Cronin, Stephen A. Greyser, Jerome Greene, Michael Houston, Chris Ingram, John Kennedy, Arthur Kover, Herbert Krugman, Clark Leavitt, Larry Light, Leonard Lodish, Herb Manloveg, Haim Mano, Ed Pappzian, Jon-Wong Park, Victor Principe, Lew Pringle, Harold Ross, Nicholas Schiavone, M. J. Schlinger, Horace Schwerin, Gary Soldow, Horst Stipp, W. A. Twyman, Tyzoon Tyebjee, Sonia Yuspeh, Bob Wachsler, Wayne Walley, Jerry Wind, and Judith Zaichkowsky all played an instrumental role in helping us think about the topic. Academic colleagues, including Paul Berger, Russell Haley, Donald Kanter, and George Miaoulis, helped frame our original research and commented on various aspects of our evolving monograph.

Henry Gamse, Peter Krieg, and Robert Shulman of Copernicus and Lisa Carter of McKinsey & Co. were very helpful in designing and carrying out the first of the two studies reported here. Steve Tipps and Sean Keller of Copernicus, Scott Heekin-Canedy and Jeff Shaffer of *The New York Times,* and Tom Nagle of The Strategic Pricing Group played critical roles in our print media study, which extended our original findings. We would like to thank Ami Bowen, David Clancy, Susan Clancy, Katherine Ives, and Elizabeth Shanley for their assistance in editing early drafts of the manuscript. We're especially grateful to Wally Wood, a brilliant business writer and editor, who transformed a work originally written as a technical research monograph for academics into a work that advertising practitioners can understand and enjoy.

KEVIN J. CLANCY, Ph.D.
Gloucester, Massachusetts

DAVID W. LLOYD, D.B.A.
Holden, Massachusetts

1

The Declining Effectiveness of Television Advertising

Television advertising has declined in effectiveness and efficiency over the past decade, and because it has, advertisers should be more interested than ever in making their advertising dollars work harder.

What are the symptoms of declining advertising effectiveness and efficiency? Among them, media fragmentation, television fragmentation, advertising clutter, zapping and zipping, rising costs, and ad copy with less impact.

Consider media fragmentation. In the mid-1960s, most people watched the three major television networks, read a relative handful of magazines, listened to AM radio, went out to the movies (or waited for them to show up on television), and read one or more daily newspaper. For consumers, there were no cable television networks, no video cassette players, no video games, no home computers, no Internet, no CD-ROM.

Today, the situation is so radically different that *Business Week* can run an article discussing "The Entertainment Glut" (February 16, 1998). Today, there are six broadcast television networks (ABC, CBS, NBC, Fox, WB, and UPN), almost 200 cable television networks, literally thousands of special interest magazines, hundreds of FM radio stations, thousands of video tapes, video games, and the Internet, which today (again literally) has more World Wide Web sites than one could visit in a lifetime. Perhaps, the only medium to have lost ground in the past 30 years is the daily newspaper, as both the absolute number of papers has dropped and average readership has fallen. But why not? The one thing that has not changed is the number of hours in a day.

TELEVISION AUDIENCE
FRAGMENTATION CONTINUES

Although there is no question that the video game and the home computer continue to grow (indeed, more and more people are playing video games on the Internet via the home computer), television remains the most important entertainment appliance in most homes. As daily set usage per home has risen from about 5 hours in 1960 to more than 7 hours in 1998, the number of channels available to the average American home has also risen from 5.9 to 43. In 1960, the average household watched what was available; according to A.C. Nielsen figures, the household watched 4.2 channels 10 or more minutes a week; by 1996, however, Americans were watching 10.3 channels 10 or more minutes a week (i.e., only about a quarter of the channels available). Consumers now spend on average about 9.5 hours a day with some form of media, and some observers feel the saturation point being reached.

Today, ABC, CBS, and NBC split less than half the television audience between them each night. Others watch new networks such as Fox (13%), WB, and UPN, as well as cable or satellite alternatives. One estimate is that in 1998, only 58% of American homes will be tuned in to broadcast TV (as opposed to cable or satellite) at some point during a typical 24-hour period. Industry observers forecast that the big three broadcast networks' share will sink well below 50% in 1998 because during the viewing season 1996-1997, only 49% of prime-time viewers watched the big three, according to Nielsen. The rest of the viewers are going to "wannabe networks" such as UPN and WB or to big cable companies such as TNT. By one estimate, TV is losing 1 out of 20 prime-time viewers every year.

> A News Corp. study estimates that with digital compression total channels available to the average TV viewer will grow from about 75 now to 1,000 by 2010.

Where is everybody going? They are watching more and more specialty channels (and some are surfing the Internet or playing video games). The greater the number of these channels (Home and Garden Television, the Golf channel, the Romance Classics network), the more fragmented the audience will become.

There are about 200 "unrated" channels around, cumulatively taking a bite out of traditional broadcast television. And there are more in the works: Fox, Tele-Communications, Cablevision Systems, and NBC have joined forces to launch Fox Sports Net. *Sports Illustrated* magazine and CNN are starting a CNN/SI sports channel. There are two new mini "networks" slated for launch, the 65-station Pax Net, targeted to women, and Barry Diller's broader interest network. Fox and NBC each launched all-news cable channels. If consumers aren't already overwhelmed, a News Corp. study estimated that with digital compression, total channels available to the average TV viewer will grow from about 75 now to 1,000 by 2010.

At the same time, the decline in network broadcast television audiences has not been reflected in the prices the networks charge advertisers. Robert Coen, who tracks advertising media spending for McCann-Erickson, estimates that the networks collected $14 billion in ad revenues in 1998, 5.5% more than in 1997. But total ad spending is pegged at a 6.8% increase (to $200 billion), so the networks are lagging slightly, whereas advertiser spending on cable is projected to grow by 13% (to $6 billion).

Fragmentation means that large blocks of demographically desirable viewers that advertisers want are becoming rare; to reach them, the advertisers must pay a premium. So although the networks' share of the mass market has shrunk, the cost of buying time on network programs has gone up faster than inflation in the past 15 years. This is because of the soaring value of commercial slots in the diminishing number of programs that pull in big crowds. Increased costs also means fewer advertising exposures per dollar invested; marketers are spending more and getting less.

CLUTTER, ZAPPING, ZIPPING, AND OTHER HURDLES

Besides raising their prices, the broadcast networks have added commercial time to their broadcasts. Ordinary viewers and advertising professionals feel too many ads crowd into television programs, and middle pods—the groups of ads that appear halfway through a half-hour program—have gotten too long. In 1986, for example, ABC aired about 6.5 minutes of ads per hour in prime time. Now, viewers get 9.5 minutes on average. But it isn't simply the 3 more minutes of advertising time spread through the hour; it may be as many as 12 or more added commercials. CBS made the 15-second spot official in August 1985, when the network announced that it would accept a 15-second buy as a stand-alone ad, not just as half of a 30-second buy. Today, television carries 60-,

30-, 15-, 10-, and even 5-second spots, all adding to the commercial clutter. Probably, every marketing expert in America agrees that increasing clutter contributes to declining advertising effectiveness.

To defend themselves against commercial onslaught, many television viewers hit the "mute" button or zap the commercials by changing channels during commercial interruptions with the remote control, which has become a standard feature. This, of course, was rarely done 20 years ago, when someone would have to get off the couch to change stations. Channel surfing is so universal and pervasive that it is the topic of the daily comics. And when women get together over coffee and complain about the strange behavioral rites of men, their guys' behavior with the TV remote is often a subject for discussion. Today, it is estimated that at least 30% of all commercials are zapped by male viewers and a significant but albeit lower percentage by women.

Another more serious form of zapping is zipping—fast-forwarding when viewing a prerecorded or rented videotape. Cronin and Menelly (1992) found in a laboratory study, and validated the findings by a field investigation, that zipping through commercials altogether was extremely common, with more than half the research participants skipping the commercials. They concluded,

> Zipping may be substantially reducing the size of commercial audiences . . . it's not the content of the commercial that causes it to be zipped but its very presence. . . . [and] almost all zippers practiced block zipping. . . . It is clear that many commercials never have a chance to grab the viewers' attention; each is merely one of several zipping past the viewer at high speed. (p. 1)

It might not make much difference for the advertiser if the viewers were to watch the commercials, because many of them are ineffective anyway.

Not that it might make much difference for the advertiser if the viewers were to watch the commercials, because many of them are ineffective anyway. "Today, the people who are paid to write advertising are not interested in selling," said David Ogilvy in an interview with Kenneth Jacobsen of *AdWeek* magazine almost a decade ago ("Fall TV Report," 1991), but the situation has not changed.

They consider advertising an art form. And they talk about creativity all the time. I'm a salesman. I don't care whether what I do is arty or clever. I want to sell products, but advertising people today, they want to win awards. They use advertising to promote themselves, so they can get better jobs and higher salaries. It's a scandal. (p. 4)

ADVERTISING EFFECTIVENESS CONTINUES ITS STEADY DECLINE

Substantial support for Ogilvy's position exists in the form of in-market studies that show declining advertising copy effectiveness. On-air related recall scores, for example, measure the proportion of people exposed to a television commercial who can play back something about it on an unaided or partially aided basis the next day. Whereas these scores averaged about 24% for a 30-second prime-time spot 20 years ago, our current estimate is an 18% average, representing a 33% drop in 17 years.

IPSOS-ASI, Stamford, Connecticut, one of the pre-eminent advertising research companies, measures advertising recall by recruiting consumers to watch a cable TV program in which advertising is embedded for testing. Dave Walker, IPSOS-ASI's director of research, reported to the authors in April 1998 that the mean average related recall scores for all commercials tested (:30s among women ages 18-65) by calendar year hit a 25.1% peak in 1986 and has shown almost steady decline to 20.0% in 1997, a 25% drop. The ASI recall scores use cable TV to simulate on-air exposure under controlled test conditions, with the same number of commercials in the same program positions for each test. "As such," says Walker,

> IPSOS-ASI recall should be less directly influenced by changes in the media environment during the period in question. Even so, the decline in recall levels appears to be real. The annual averages show a significant linear trend, implying a drop of about three and a half points over the 19-year period [1979-1997].

Another indication of declining advertising effectiveness comes from studies on awareness of new products and services heavily advertised on television. In 1985, if you bought 1,000 gross rating points (GRPs) on prime-time television in a single month you could expect an average level of total brand awareness of about 54% (unaided and aided). In 1998, awareness is closer to 41%—a 24% decline—and dropping. This finding is reinforced by a study conducted by

Research Systems Inc. of Evansville, Indiana, another high-powered advertising testing company. Five years ago, they reported that the sales effectiveness of TV commercials supporting the introduction of new products had declined 27% from the late 1970s to 1993. Meanwhile, the number of competing brands in the average category had increased 37% over the same time period. According to Research Systems, this combination of increasing new product introductions and declining advertising effectiveness means that average new-product advertising will produce "significantly less market share than it did in the late '70s," ("TV Ad Effectiveness," 1993, p. 1).

We reported another disturbing finding about the state of contemporary advertising in *Marketing Myths That Are Killing Business* (Clancy & Shulman, 1995). There, we reported a study we had done to measure advertising positioning penetration for the five leading brands across a broad range of product and service categories, such as ground coffee, financial services, airlines, copying machines, and personal computers. Although we wish that we had time-series data so that we could inform our readers how these numbers have changed over time, the findings themselves were startling enough to repeat them here.

> We found that fewer than 8% of the respondents could cite anything about the average leading brand that we would begin to call positioning.

Our intent was to measure the extent to which these leading brands were successful in registering a clear positioning strategy—a sense of what they stand for. When a buyer is at the point of sale, whether it be in a supermarket, discount store, or computer outlet, what he or she knows about the brand at that moment will have some impact on the purchase decision. This what researchers might describe as unaided positioning penetration and is measured by asking consumers without prompts what they know or think about a brand and how it is different from any other brand. We found that fewer than 8% of the respondents could cite anything about the average leading brand that we would begin to call positioning. This is not true in all product categories, of course. In high ad spending categories such as automobiles, beer, and soft drinks and in categories where there are relatively few dominant brands, unaided positioning penetration is higher—about 15%.

When we gave respondents clues, called *tracer elements,* such as a slogan or a positioning for the brand—the essential positioning statement—we improved the score. But even with clues as obvious as the positioning/message strategy, the slogan, or some dominant visual, respondents correctly identified the advertising with the positioning only about 16% of the time.

When we gave respondents the exact positioning or slogan and asked if they had ever heard it, not surprisingly we did better yet. "Have you ever heard Coke use the slogan 'It's the Real Thing'?" achieved 92% recognition, which was interesting because Coca-Cola has not used that slogan regularly for more than a decade. However, the average, fully prompted, completely clued positioning awareness score for the top five brands in most product categories was less than 30%.

The fact that fully aided measures of positioning awareness are considerably higher than their less-prompted and certainly unaided counterparts should be no surprise to anyone. It's a little bit like taking an uncommon word from the dictionary—*lubricity,* for example—and asking people to define it, then giving them some clues, like putting it in the context of a sentence, and finally asking people have they ever heard the word lubricity used to describe "oily smoothness, as of a surface, slipperiness." The proportion of the population that might get the meaning correct on an unaided basis is probably under 5%, but it would rise to 30% or more when given its complete meaning.

ADVERTISING MEASURES
LOOK FOR BIGGER NUMBERS

It is interesting to note that in the advertising research business today, a great deal of effort is going into campaign tracking that is measuring the performance of advertising campaigns over time, typically using a range of measures including indicators of unaided, partially aided, and fully aided measures of message registration (also known as positioning penetration). What concerns us as we've examined many of these studies in the past decade is that the emphasis more and more in analyzing these studies is shifting to the fully prompted measures. The reason for this is simple: The numbers are bigger and therefore more suggestive that the advertising campaign really works.

As we complete this book, we've had recent experiences where major advertisers, having spent many millions of dollars (a minimum of $25 million), have observed message communication scores close to 0%. The fully prompted recognition numbers, on the other hand, range from 20% to 45%. Clients and agencies focus on the recognition numbers, congratulating themselves for the strong performance of their campaign while virtually no buyers are walking around at point-of-sale with a clear message of what the brand stands for. Looked at from a different perspective, it could be argued that there is no analog in the real world buying process to a fully prompted recognition measure unless the package, or sales person, or shelf talker produces the recognition, thus simulating the research interview by reminding people of the brand's essential message, what it stands for. Because this rarely occurs in practice, it is further evidence for us of the declining effectiveness of advertising.

> The average campaign has a return of 1% to 4%, a number not significantly different than what one might obtain by investing the money in a Certificate of Deposit.

Let's move beyond survey-based measures of advertising effects and discuss advertising's effects on sales. What effect does advertising have? Our research shows the average campaign for an established product or service has a return on the advertising investment of 1% to 4%, a number not significantly different than what one might obtain by investing the money in a Certificate of Deposit. It is probably normally distributed. Most campaigns (plus or minus one standard deviation, or about 68% of them) are average; they follow the standard bell curve illustrated in Figure 1.1. This is not a new discovery. A decade ago, Peter Rogers (1988), executive vice president of Nabisco Brands, said about the money his corporation had spent on new products: "We would have done much better had we just taken our new product dollars to the bank and put them in an ordinary passbook savings account" (p. 17).

This is not to suggest that advertising cannot be effective. We know that advertising is much stronger for new products and services. We also know that if marketers and their agencies follow a serious process for developing and evaluating advertising performance prior to a real world introduction, they significantly improve the chances of a successful, profitable campaign.

With all the money going into television advertising, and given that television advertising needs to work so much harder than it ever worked before because it is fighting against promotion, fighting against brand proliferation, and fighting against clutter, one would think that advertisers would go out of their way to identify and select the most powerful campaigns that they could run before they

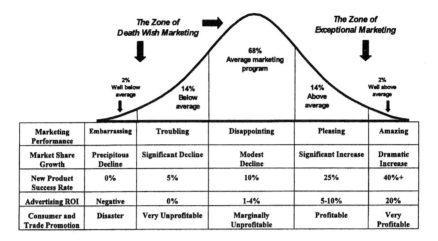

Marketing Performance	Embarrassing	Troubling	Disappointing	Pleasing	Amazing
Market Share Growth	Precipitous Decline	Significant Decline	Modest Decline	Significant Increase	Dramatic Increase
New Product Success Rate	0%	5%	10%	25%	40%+
Advertising ROI	Negative	0%	1-4%	5-10%	20%
Consumer and Trade Promotion	Disaster	Very Unprofitable	Marginally Unprofitable	Profitable	Very Profitable

Figure 1.1 The Marketing Performance Bell Curve
SOURCE: Rogers, P. (1988, March 28). Food marketers. Slow the "frenetic" pace of new product introductions. *Marketing News,* p. 17. Reprinted by permission of the American Marketing Association.

actually take them into the marketplace. Yet, most companies develop and run advertising campaigns without the benefit of any serious advertising testing—and the results show it. By *serious,* we mean research done among a reliable, representative sample of buyers using a methodology known to predict real world performance. Focus groups and "one-on-ones" are not serious.

There was a time not long ago when advertisers and their agencies could argue that copy testing produced numbers without any known relationship to sales. It was not clear that if Ad A beat Ad B significantly in a copy test, A would outperform B in the real world. But over two decades, advertisers and agencies have learned a great deal about copy testing. Today, a number of copy-testing firms can support a claim that their scores predict real world sales response. By testing more advertising campaigns, the probability of finding the blockbuster with exceptional marketing performance is increased.

Even when advertisers test, however, they may not follow the findings. Two years ago, a major advertiser asked us to test two different commercials developed by a top-10 advertising agency for one of their brands. We tested both and found them to be extremely weak. Neither communicated a clear message about the brand and why it would be superior to competitors. Not surprisingly, the needle, in terms of purchase interest, did not move. We reported this finding to the client and agency and expressed our belief that the campaigns were too ethereal, too image-oriented, and, although capable of winning a Clio or Cannes award for advertising creativity, they were unlikely to win a David Ogilvy award for advertising effectiveness.

The client, like many, was in a rush to judgment and insisted on picking one of the two campaigns and running it. The company spent $32 million on a television campaign over the next 6 months.

A year after the copy testing, we were invited back to the client's marketing war room to hear a presentation by a well-known advertising tracking company the client had commissioned to measure the campaign's performance in the marketplace. To the client's and the agency's surprise (and even to our amazement), the tracking report was staggering. Awareness of the positioning message in the marketplace after the $32 million investment was not 3%, or 2%, or 0.5%. It was 0%. It did not exist. The tracking firm found no one who could play back anything about the client's brand that reflected the advertising's positioning/message strategy. This is one of the cases that we referred to earlier.

The agency management supervisor then responded to this news with a comment worthy of a White House spin meister:

> If you remember, before we ran the campaign, copy testing suggested that this was a transcendental, image-laden execution. It did not pound home a message for the brand. This kind of advertising probably produces a subliminal, sleeper effect, in which case 0% awareness may be a good thing. It suggests that the campaign is really working.

No one laughed. As preposterous as these words were, some people in the room seemed to be taking notes, perhaps to look up *subliminal* and *sleeper effect* in the advertising dictionary back at the office. As disappointing as the results were in terms of awareness, attitudes, brand preference, and ultimately sales, the campaign continued to run for another year before the advertiser killed it.

> Even a casual television viewer knows that most advertising campaigns do not appear to be based on either a clear targeting or positioning strategy.

This is not an unusual story in modern American marketing. As even a casual television viewer knows, most advertising campaigns do not appear to be based on either a clear targeting or positioning strategy. The question we hear over and over again from clients, from MBA students, from friends and family, is "What were they thinking when they made that commercial?"

Even when companies put strong commercials on the air, they sometimes do not run them with enough frequency to have an effect. Because network television audiences have been declining and prices have been rising, it costs more than in the past to accomplish the same reach and frequency (although narrowcasting to a clear target may cost less). Even with an effective ad execution, a company must budget enough for the advertising to have an impact on the target audience. Because companies do not spend enough money to have an effect—which shows in flat sales—they switch to promotion, where there does seem to be a prompt response.

THE PROBLEM WITH THE COST PER THOUSAND

Beside fragmenting audiences and ineffective ads (and a shift of marketing dollars to promotion, which is beyond the scope of this book), there is another issue of interest. Virtually all television advertising is bought on the basis of the cost per thousand people exposed—CPM—and some crude demographics—sex and age, figures based on A.C. Nielsen syndicated audience data. Television media buyers tend to assume that programs are simply neutral carriers; if the demographics match, one program is much like another.

If (as we demonstrate in subsequent chapters) selection of program *carrier* is key to effective advertising, conventional program selection criteria can be shown to be deficient and inaccurate as well as a contributing factor in the declining role and effectiveness of network television ad campaigns.

Advertisers have bought television on the basis of CPM for 50 years because they have assumed that, for the most part, a viewer is a viewer is a viewer. The only number that counted was the total number of 18- to 34-year-old women, or 24- to 44-year-old men (or some other simple demographic) watching a given program.

But "we are beginning to discover these broad demographic descriptors just don't work any more," says George Hayes, senior vice president, media director of McCann-Erickson Worldwide, New York (Mandese, 1994, p. S-2). Indeed, there is almost no connection between demographics—sex and age being the most common—and product consumption. Men buy aftershave and women buy perfume, but that does not help a marketer very much, even if he sells aftershave or perfume.

"In the old days," says Hayes,

Tide was one big brand. It stood for clean, white clothes, and all women 18 to 49, whether they had kids or didn't have kids, washed their clothes. But now you have Tide with Bleach, Tide Ultra, Tide Unscented. And although each of these brands is still targeted at women 18 to 49, they are targeted at different *segments* of women 18 to 49. And it is those differences that you can't find by using demographics. (Mandese, 1994, p. S-2)

Once a company and its advertising agency go through the work of defining the target market and developing a media plan, "it drops off a cliff when we go in to negotiate with the networks," says Betsy Frank, senior vice president and director of television information and new media at Saatchi & Saatchi Advertising, New York. "Everything gets converted back to a broad, nondescript demographic." (Motavalli, 1989, p. 158)

WHAT IS A POTENTIAL SOLUTION?

Improving the effectiveness of television ad campaigns begins by understanding the factors that contribute to good advertising results. Few have acknowledged that choice of the *program carrier* may be as important and sometimes more important to advertising effectiveness than characteristics of the commercial itself, despite the results of advertising agency-sponsored studies and academic research spanning four decades that suggest this conclusion.

What is the effect of the television program carrier on advertising response? At one time, advertising and media researchers assumed that program content did not affect advertising test scores. We once tested a supposedly breakthrough Vicks Formula 44 cough medicine television commercial that produced exceptionally low copy-testing scores. Everyone was disappointed. Vicks had employed the "on-air" testing method, which we discussed earlier. Interviewers called about 200 people who had watched the program the night before to ask them about the commercials the program carried. The percentage of people who remembered something—anything—about the commercial was the "recall" score.

At that time, 24 was an average score. This particular Vicks Formula 44 commercial brought in a 13, which troubled advertising agency and client executives. What did such a low score mean? Based on their past experience and professional judgment, they thought it was a better commercial than the score indicated, so shortly later they tested it again. This time the score jumped to 45.

Thus, over a short period of time (with no intervening advertising), two tests of the same commercial generated both the lowest and the highest recall scores Vicks Formula 44 commercials had ever recorded. No one knew exactly what to do with that information except to say, "Well, clearly the commercial isn't as bad as the first test said it was."

> At one time, media researchers were more concerned with day and time slots and felt the program had little or no impact on commercial recall scores.

In those days, researchers routinely tested commercials without paying much attention to the program itself. They were more concerned with day and time slots and they felt the program had little or no impact on commercial recall scores. The Vicks Formula 44 finding was so intriguing to us that we asked several companies (e.g., Campbell Soup, BBDO Advertising, Procter & Gamble) who were major copy testers to provide us with as many examples as they could of commercials that had been tested twice in a relatively short period of time.

What we discovered when we looked at this data was that the reliability of on-air testing was not as high as we expected it to be. That is to say, the difference in scores between the same commercial tested twice was much greater than chance alone would predict. But we also discovered that often the programs on which the same commercials were tested twice were different. Indeed, the difference between the scores for the first and second airing of a commercial was far greater when the ad was tested on two different programs than when it was tested on the same program.

Could it be, we wondered, that programming itself has something to do with advertising effectiveness? Is it possible that the same commercial placed in two different programs that have the same viewership and the same audience profiles does not generate the same advertising response? Is it possible that viewer response to the commercial varies depending on viewer involvement in the program? If this is so, then a new, more efficient means for selecting media/programming could be devised that takes this into account.

What was required was a large-scale, state-of-the-science investigation to measure the impact of television programming on advertising response. If there is such an effect, and it is predictable, then resulting differential program impact or involvement scores can be used to adjust conventional program selection criteria and cost-efficiency calculations. If this is so, then the study could play at least a modest role in addressing the problem of declining television advertising effectiveness, which this chapter addressed.

The purpose of this book is to unravel this mystery and deepen our understanding of the relationship between television programming and advertising response. Our findings, we believe, will help uncover the hidden power of television programming and print editorial environment toward the end of improving advertising effectiveness. To the extent that this work finds ways to make television advertising (and print for that matter) more effective, our efforts may play some role in arresting and, perhaps reversing the declining power of television advertising.

2

Television Programming: Vampire or Standard Bearer?

For over 30 years, marketing and advertising researchers have engaged in intellectual warfare over the impact of television programming on advertising effectiveness. Although all agree that the extent to which viewers are involved in the program significantly affects receptivity to, and therefore the effectiveness of, television advertising, the point of contention is whether this involvement helps or hinders advertising effectiveness. Does an involving program suck the life out of the commercials it carries, perhaps because viewers resent the interruption—the vampire effect?

Or does an involving program actually help the commercials, perhaps because viewer involvement carries into the advertising—the standard-bearer effect?

The idea that commercials introduce an unwelcome and intrusive element into a positive or engaging program viewing experience leading to lower levels of advertising receptivity and response is intuitively plausible. Anyone who has been irritated by a commercial interruption will sympathize with the video vampire hypothesis. The evidence compiled to date, however, does not bear out this view. Rather, the vast majority of available, published studies have found higher levels of program involvement or liking to be accompanied by higher levels of advertising effectiveness. It would seem at this point that involving television programs act as standard bearers for the commercials they carry. Either situation, of course, has implications for the cost per thousand (CPM) method of buying television time.

THE 40-YEAR DEBATE

The literature on the relationship between television involvement and advertising effectiveness is bewildering because researchers use different concepts, different definitions of the same concept, different measures (i.e., operational definitions) of the same concept, and different research methodologies—all of which contribute to rampant confusion. Some researchers, as an illustration, focus on the viewing environment—the real world situation in which people watch a television program and the embedded advertising. Some consumers watch programs by themselves without many interruptions and without switching channels. Others view television programs in a social setting with family members or friends, eating dinner, munching popcorn, taking telephone calls, and periodically surfing. The circumstances surrounding the viewing experience, with its interruptions and diversions, play a critical role in the nature and extent of the viewer's exposure to programs and to commercials. Although we were intrigued by these differences in the viewing environment, our research studies this phenomenon only indirectly. Ours is not research into viewer environment. This is not a major limitation of the work reported here, however, because viewer environment is not a variable over which networks and their sponsors have any control. Therefore, although greater knowledge about this topic may enhance our understanding of the process, it is limited in terms of managerial implications.

> Some investigators have observed that higher levels of perceived tension induced by program material tend to be accompanied by lower advertising response scores.

A different tack undertaken by other researchers is to consider the program environment—the nature and type of programming to which viewers are exposed. The vast majority of investigations in this research have considered the program environment to consist solely of the programming material in which commercials are embedded. For example, some investigators have observed that higher levels of perceived suspense or tension induced by program material tend to be accompanied by lower advertising response scores.

Horace Schwerin (1960), a pioneer in the advertising research industry, conducted one of the earliest investigations into the advertising effects of the program environment. His research exposed respondents in a theater test environment to commercials embedded in one of three television programs: a quiz show, a musical, or a courtroom drama. Following exposure, respondents rated their reactions to the program content on a three-level scale—*relaxed, concentrated,* or *tense.* Schwerin concluded that recall of a given commercial was lower when the viewers rated themselves as tense than when they rated themselves as relaxed.

Although subsequent research frequently cites these conclusions, it never raises the possible limitations in the original research. Schwerin (1960) measured program content reaction in a judgmental and restrictive manner. The presence or absence of perceived tension reveals little about how program content affects commercial recall. This is true even if one assumes that all respondents interpreted the terms relaxed, concentrated, and tense the same way. As a consequence, one must question the integrity of the observed relationship between the reported tension and commercial recall. Schwerin does not appear to have analyzed whether this relationship was affected by differences in respondent characteristics, usage of the advertised products, television viewing preferences, or other possible contaminating factors.

> Others researchers have observed that more favorable reaction to program content tends to be accompanied by higher advertising response scores.

Others researchers—frequently those who define affective response in less specific terms, such as "liking" for program material—have observed the opposite: More favorable reaction to program content tends to be accompanied by higher advertising response scores. The resulting evidence has therefore become polarized into support for what may be termed the negative-effects hypothesis (the video vampire) versus support for the positive-effects hypothesis (the TV standard bearer).

The tendency among both groups, however, is to limit definition of program involvement to some form of one-dimensional, single-item, affective response to the program material directly surrounding the advertising. They do not include characteristics of the wider physical environment in which program and commercial exposure occurs—typical situational in-home distractions, for example—as part of the overall program environment. Celsi and Olson (1988) noted for example that "like most consumer researchers, we view *perceived personal relevance* as the essential characteristic of involvement." They argue that only when consumers see some link between their needs, goals, and values (self-knowledge) and their product knowledge (attributes and benefits) is there involvement; the authors say nothing about the physical environment. The environmental psychology literature offers evidence that the physical environment in which reception occurs significantly influences the effects of persuasive communications (Mehrabian & Russell, 1974; Rapaport, 1971).

Consumer behaviorists have studied both the viewing environment and programming environment factors. They have promoted a wider definition of the program environment and the influence of situational factors in the television reception environment on the processing of commercial messages (Baumgartner, Sujan, & Padgett, 1997; Cohen, 1983; Tyebjee, 1978; Webb, 1979; Wright, 1973). Baumgartner et al. acknowledge the need for testing—in this case program context effects on affective responses to commercials—"under realistic viewing conditions." The same is implied in involvement-oriented research by Park and Hastak (1994).

> Situational factors range from the physical environment surrounding reception to elements of the psychological environment in which reception takes place.

Situational factors range from elements of the physical environment (the effects of distraction and interruptions, etc.) to elements of the psychological environment in which reception takes place (effects of mood, attention state, and interest). Thus, much of the relevant advertising research literature misuses the term *program environment*. Researchers have often compared evidence of program content effects obtained from on-air testing in a natural, homelike reception environment directly to evidence obtained under a variety of more tightly controlled artificial testing environments with little (or no) consideration for the possible impact on advertising response of these very different conditions.

A third school of research focuses on program *involvement,* which we will tentatively define here as the degree of liking for, engagement with, or connection to a particular television program.

Mitchell (1979) described involvement as an individual level, internal state variable that indicates the amount of arousal, interest, or drive evoked by a particular stimulus or situation. Some researchers, such as Zaichkowsky (1985), urge the application of one definition of involvement in all circumstances where the involvement construct may be applicable. Although researchers have widely applied the concept of involvement in a variety of contexts, they have reached no clear consensus either in terms of the definition or measurement of the concept (Grunert, 1996; Laurent & Kapferer, 1985; Mackenzie & Spreng, 1992; Mano & Oliver, 1993; Rothchild, 1979; Tyebjee, 1978).

Clearly, one definition presents problems, but most advertisers and agency executives have acknowledged the importance of viewer involvement in programming. Many also recognize the importance of providing the correct overall program environment to achieve maximally effective advertising campaigns.

Program involvement, as we have begun to conceptualize it (keep in mind that the research this book reports goes a long way to clarify the confusion over the meaning of program involvement) cuts across both the viewing environment and the program environment that we have discussed. Viewers, for example, by our working definition of involvement as engagement with a television program, can be involved (or not) whether they are watching alone or in a group, relaxed or tense, doing nothing or eating a meal, watching a suspenseful drama or an amusing sitcom.

Program involvement, in contrast to viewer environment or program environment, is the subject of this investigation. It is a construct that in our view will be easier to measure than either viewer or program environment and should have clear management implications.

THE NEGATIVE EFFECTS POSITION

Forty years of research on this topic, however, has still not satisfactorily resolved the vampire (i.e., negative effects) or standard bearer (i.e., positive effects) hypotheses about the role of this variable in determining advertising effectiveness. Let us review some of the studies in support of each of these positions.

Observers have frequently cited two separate studies by Steiner (1963, 1966) to support the negative-effects hypothesis. In the latter, Steiner concluded that commercials could be considered objectionable interruptions of program material, particularly when the program is interesting or enjoyable. Later researchers may have misinterpreted this finding, however, as Steiner (1966) qualified this conclusion:

> When the average network commercial begins, fewer than one out of a hundred expresses strong annoyance. Four percent show signs of mild annoyance, and an additional 4 percent show pleasure or relief. The remaining 90 percent exhibit no overt reaction at all. This annoyance level is surprisingly low in view of the fact that annoying interruptions is a major criticism. (p. 272)

Steiner concluded that "only 5 percent show any signs of annoyance at onset [of the commercial break]; and during the commercial itself, more people have something good to say than something bad" (p. 272).[1]

It remains entirely plausible that many viewers consider commercials to be objectionable interruptions of a positive viewing experience. However, even if Steiner had found more persuasive evidence of this, he does not make clear whether the perception of commercials as objectionable also renders them ineffective and, if so, why.

Most researchers who have hypothesized a negative relationship between interest or absorption in program material and advertising effectiveness reason that commercials *do* represent an intrusion on an enjoyable or interesting viewing experience and are, therefore, filtered out or perceived negatively. Schumann and Thorson (1990), for example, speculated in their model of the influence of viewing context that although recall measures may be greater with liked programs, "attitudes towards commercials (and the products advertised) may be negatively affected by these highly popular programs."

These studies, however, do not explain whether and how the transition from program to commercial might precipitate an alteration in viewer perceptual processes or behavioral state in such a way as to impede commercial message reception. More recent research, which includes affective, emotional, memory-based, involvement-oriented, and information processing-based investigations into advertising response, has suggested insights into these relationships—and the link between programming and ad response. (We will discuss these in the next chapter's exploration of the program involvement construct as mediator of advertising response.)

> Kennedy hypothesizes that commercials will be less effective in programs where the viewer's drive for closure is higher.

Kennedy (1971) is one of the few investigators who reports evidence supporting the negative effects hypothesis and provides a theoretical rationale for the effect. He argues that viewing a television program can be considered a commitment to a task in which the principle of closure is operative. The strength of a viewer's drive for closure is determined by, among other things, characteristics of the program, such as the plot or story line. We would add to this program involvement—again interest in, engagement with, or connection to the program itself.

Kennedy hypothesizes that when a commercial break interrupts a program in which the drive for closure is strong, the break is particularly unwelcome because it frustrates this drive. This, in turn, impedes the processing of what the viewer considers irrelevant or annoying commercial material. As a result, commercials will be less effective in programs where the drive for closure is higher (defined as a suspense-thriller program) than if placed where the drive for closure is presumed to be lower (a situation comedy).

Although Kennedy's (1971) hypothesis is entirely plausible, his findings do not clearly substantiate it: His study has some of the same limitations apparent in Schwerin's (1960). Kennedy also limited consideration of the program environment to immediate program content without examining whether different viewing conditions affect a drive for closure. Furthermore, although Kennedy conceptualizes program content reaction in an interesting way, the definition is constraining. Kennedy assumes that the nature of program content effects on commercial performance is a function of a difference in the strength of drive for closure; this strength differs by program, whether judged to be suspenseful or not.

Although Kennedy (1971) observes differences in reported drive for closure between the two program types, he does not indicate how that drive was measured in the sample beyond a summated rating scale. (A summed rating scale requires respondents to express their agreement or disagreement with attitude-related statements, usually along a 5- or 7-point scale. A study assumes that all statements reflect elements of a common subject, such as attitudes toward a television program's individual attributes. The researcher sums up the scores for each individual statement, creating a total score for each respondent.)

Also, Kennedy (1971) provides no basis to compare how the drive for closure activated in the study compares with some absolute or average drive levels activated by typical programming. Furthermore, one must question whether drive for closure adequately represents the larger construct—program content effects. Finally, as in Schwerin's (1960) study, some question remains as to whether one may attribute the observed effects solely to the concept of closure or if they are due in part to variation in uncontrolled factors. Although Kennedy apparently achieved samples matched on demographic characteristics, it is possible that uncontrolled differences in respondent usage of advertised products or television viewing habits may have contaminated his findings.

> Researchers found evidence of lower recall scores in the suspenseful program, but the way they defined program environment render the evidence suspect.

Soldow and Principe (1981) conducted a very interesting study among a cross-section of employees from a single business organization. Two programs were selected for this research: one judged to be suspenseful and the other nonsuspenseful. The researchers then divided their sample of 87 into three treatment groups of 29 members each. One viewed the suspenseful program, the other, the nonsuspenseful program, and the third constituted a control group. Soldow and Principe found that in most cases the advertising was less effective in the suspenseful—and presumably more involving—program. Although demographically matched, a total sample of 87 respondents recruited from the same business organization with only 29 respondents per cell calls into question the ability to generalize the findings, if not their validity. That the audience exposure took place under artificial conditions further weakens this research's external validity.

Another study by Tavassoli, Shultz, and Fitzsimons (1995) explored the relationship between program involvement and both ad memory and attitudes toward the ads. Although the authors develop the intriguing hypothesis first postulated in the consumer behavioral literature by Kroeber-Riel (1979)—that there is a curvilinear relationship between arousal intensity (read involvement) and advertising effectiveness—the study has many of the same limitations of work on inverse effects. These limitations include sample size and representativeness (86 university students in one class) and its measures of television programming involvement (only one program, a summary of the first half highlights of a World Cup soccer game followed by the entire second half and a postgame show). The involvement measures confounded involvement with the program with involvement with soccer as a game; one item, for example, asked students how much they agree or disagree with the statement, "I can play soccer well." Finally, the research was apparently done in a highly artificial exposure environment that allowed the researchers, for one of their treatment conditions, to preempt the game with commercials, thus almost certainly provoking annoyance.

Despite the study's limitations, the authors discovered an intriguing inverted U-shaped relationship. Advertising effects were highest for the moderately involved subjects and lower for the least and most involved subjects. Given the nature of their soccer-enthusiast sample, it could be argued that the subjects who scored highest in involvement represent "soccer-obsessing aficionados" who are unlike the consumers who fall into the highest levels of program involvement in most product categories. Certainly, they are very different from the people scoring highest in program involvement in the research studies we have reviewed and will review in this chapter. Thus, if we exclude from the analysis of Tavassoli et al. these hyperenthusiasts for the game, we are left with evidence (albeit with the same limitations of sample size, etc.) of a positive effect. This comment notwithstanding, we suspect that the work may help explain some findings reported in the literature.

Brock and Shavitt (1983) provide one more perspective on the negative-effects hypothesis in their review of cognitive response theory in advertising communications. Like Kennedy (1971), they offer a well-reasoned and plausible theory for the inverse relationship between an interesting or absorbing program viewing experience and advertising effectiveness, but they provide no new evidence as support. In much the same vein as Kennedy, they posit that an intense program viewing experience (defined as preoccupied and involved with program material) preceding advertising will impair integration of the commercial message into memory because active cognitive processing will remain displaced toward the program material. Similarly, renewed processing of intense programming material that follows advertising also impedes cognitive processing of the commercial material. They conclude by suggesting that the ideal environment to foster favorable cognitive responses toward advertising would seem to be placing the advertising before unengaging programming that is reminiscent in some ways of the advertising.

> Although the video vampire hypothesis has a level of intuitive plausibility, the supporting evidence must be considered equivocal.

Although the video vampire hypothesis has a level of intuitive plausibility, the supporting evidence must be considered equivocal. It is perhaps significant that in each study finding support for this hypothesis, measurement of the program content effect was accomplished using a single, constraining, judgmentally selected dimension of program involvement. Stated differently, it is often the researchers who decided judgmentally that the program was involving or engaging, tension-filled or insightful. It is not apparent that respondents interpret concepts such as *tension* and *suspense* similarly or that they adequately represent the basis for, and nature of, their attitudes toward program material.

THE POSITIVE-EFFECTS POSITION

A substantially larger body of evidence suggests that a positive reaction to the program content improves advertising effectiveness. Investigations in which this conclusion is drawn (although, in many cases, subject to their own methodological limitations) differ from those concluding negative effects in three fundamental ways:

1. The effects of program content are measured with simple unidimensional scales, such as 0-to-10 "liking" scales, and a number of others, but they are evaluative scales and not judgment scales like those restricting respondents' program content reactions by limiting response to, for example, tense, relaxed, or concentrated.

2. Most of these investigations employ larger and more representative samples who were exposed to programming and advertising in a generally natural viewing environment.

3. In most of these studies, the measurement of advertising effectiveness is limited to various forms of commercial recall rather than the broader array of measures characteristic of works in the "negative effects, forced-exposure" tradition.

> Smith found clear evidence of a positive relationship between enhanced viewer attention levels and an increased ability to recall advertising in those programs.

Smith (1956), using a sample of over 800 females in the Tuscaloosa, Alabama, viewing area, carried out one of the earliest investigations lending support to a positive-effects hypothesis. Based on data from diaries kept by sample respondents regarding their in-home television viewing behavior, and on periodic follow-up interviews, Smith found clear evidence of a positive relationship between enhanced viewer attention levels toward, and liking for, programs and an increased ability to recall advertising in the program carriers.

The numerous independent investigations that major ad agencies and research firms conducted during the 1960s provide the bulk of the evidence in support of the positive programming effects hypothesis. Because few of these studies about positive effects were published, the studies concluding a negative relationship between program intensity or involvement and advertising effectiveness were unable to review this evidence.

A 1970 Benton & Bowles, Inc., internal report looked at a large number of program environment studies undertaken by several advertising agencies and marketing research firms between 1961 and 1968. The stated purpose was to determine the effect, if any, of television program environment on the selling effectiveness of a large packaged goods firm's television commercials. The overall conclusion drawn from this comprehensive review was that individuals who have a positive attitude toward a program will have greater commercial recall than the average viewers of that program.

The findings extracted from these studies, as reported by Benton & Bowles (1970) were:

1. Two investigations, one conducted by Foote, Cone, & Belding during 1961-1962 and the other in 1963 by Needham, Louis, & Broby, demonstrated that housewife viewing and presence in the room during commercials varied significantly with [perceived] program performance. Attentiveness to the commercials was 10% and 24% higher, respectively, during the higher-rated programs than during lower-rated programming.

2. A 1967 W. R. Simmons study reported that the number of women paying full attention to commercials was 11% greater during high-rated programming.

3. A number of studies reported higher commercial recall scores among women viewing higher-rated programming. This ranged from 10% greater in a 1962-1963 Gallup & Robinson investigation to a full 50% higher in a 1968 L. E. Hooper study.

4. A summary of Home Testing Institute, Inc., Favorites studies (discussed below) found TvQ scores to be, on average, 50% higher for higher-rated shows compared to lower-rated ones.

5. A 1965 N. T. Fouriezos study commissioned by the Bureau of Advertising indicated that greater interest and involvement in programs tends to improve recall of commercials. They found advertising recall was 64% higher among those liking a program much more than average compared with those who had an average attitude.

The Benton & Bowles (1970) report summarizes the evidence culled from these investigations into the relationship between program interest or liking and advertising effectiveness by observing

We point out that the above findings are all consistent in that conclusions drawn from the various studies are at least directionally in agreement. Further findings— notably those regarding commercial recall by program type and commercial position—are "inconsistent" in that conclusions drawn lack consensus.

> Commercial performance does not vary significantly by type of television program; rather, it varies significantly by specific shows.

This statement is significant not only for its conclusions regarding the nature of program environment/content effects but also for its conclusion regarding a general relationship that conventional wisdom held to exist between the viewing of types of programs and advertising effectiveness. There is a definite possibility that some studies concluding negative program effects, in assessing advertising response to suspenseful programs (operationalized as thrillers) versus nonsuspenseful programs (operationalized as musicals or sitcoms), were at least partially measuring differential reaction to program types. Following a comprehensive investigation sponsored by J. Walter Thompson, Inc., Yuspeh (1979) concluded that commercial performance does not vary significantly by type of television program. Rather, it varies significantly by specific shows.

A 1968 Home Testing Institute, Inc., review of 14 investigations conducted internally and by other organizations provided further evidence substantiating the positive-effects hypothesis. The overall conclusion drawn is virtually identical to that drawn in the Benton & Bowles review:

> All of these studies strongly suggest that people who say a program is a favorite and claim to like the program tend to pay more attention to the program, are more likely to see the commercials contained therein, and can recall more brands and/or sales messages than a non-favorite or a person with a low opinion of the program.

In appraising this evidence supporting positive effects, it is important to remember points made earlier about the methodological characteristics common to most of these studies, which contrast with those employed in studies concluding negative effects. It is clear that the differences in sample composition, exposure environment, the operationalization of program involvement, and other details play an important role in the drawing of opposite conclusions.

Several additional studies have also concluded that a positive relationship exists between commercial effectiveness and positive attitudes toward programming expressed in terms of greater liking for programs. A study by Clancy and Kweskin (1971), looking into the apparent lack of reliability in on-air recall scores, is noteworthy for its scope (it involved over 6,000 respondents) and for revealing the relative significance of program attitudes in explaining the troublesome variation in on-air recall scores. Clancy and Kweskin point out that testing the same commercial twice often results in scores that are almost as different as scores from testing two completely different commercials.

However, their research also revealed that program attitudes (measured using the IPSOS-ASI, Inc. standard 5-point rating scale, ranging from *my favorite program* to *a poor program*) are the single best predictor of day-after recall and have significantly greater explanatory power than factors such as demographics and usage of advertised products. Because television programming is not systematically controlled in on-air testing, they argue, and because programming has an effect on recall scores, the source of the unreliability problem is at least partially if not fully explained. Twyman (1974), Yuspeh (1979), Krugman (1983), and Rust (1987), and more recently, Murry, Lastovicka, and Singh (1992), Stipp and Schiavone (1990, 1996), and Baumgartner et al. (1997), present further evidence of a positive relationship between favorable program attitudes and enhanced commercial effectiveness.

We will discuss the two former studies later in the chapter, but the recent Stipp and Schiavone (1990, 1996) research is of interest for several reasons. It treats the positive program involvement and environment effects on advertising as a virtual given and hence, goes on to related issues, while demonstrating the positive-effects position. Stipp and Schiavone present results of a study that substantiates our primary hypothesis, although only as a secondary consideration. In this case, their chief concern is whether program-induced positive program-response effects are shown to enhance commercial receptivity (taken for granted) at two levels: first, toward the details of expected viewer positive response to the advertising, and second (and central to the study's main hypothesis), whether these effects led to clear evidence of positive attitudes and attributions toward the advertisers—hence, clear evidence of a positive sponsor "source effect."

The test advertising spots were embedded in program coverage of the 1992 Olympic games in Barcelona. The authors state that this environment provides "extraordinary benefits" to sponsors in the form of advertising and communications effects including "unprecedented reach" (90% of U.S. homes); the editorial content effect on advertising (positive) due to the high regard in which viewers hold the Olympics; and the "uniqueness" of the advertising—many sponsors create superior ads just for the games. In this context, the authors postulate another factor that may be important: "the value of Olympic sponsorship, i.e., to be recognized by the audience as a supporter of a worthwhile cause" (Stipp & Schiavone, 1990).

The study, conducted by SRI, Inc., using the results from a heavy schedule of airings of a test commercial of an unidentified, but well-known company, found support for all the authors' hypotheses and contentions. They report that "quality is important . . . those who liked the ads were more likely to hold positive opinions about the sponsor." The "second and third factors," they state, "are responsible for the added value [and added insights into the relationships of interest] which can be derived from Olympic sponsorship" and, presumably, other types of special events. A huge number of Americans hold the Olympics in great esteem with "very positive attitudes which can 'rub off' on an Olympic sponsor." However, "this kind of 'halo effect' can only occur" if the sponsor has visibility during the Olympics.

This suggests a prominence in the media possessing a salience-building effect on viewers in conjunction with the heightened popularity and the various "social functions" that communications researchers associate with the social use of involving television programs (particularly when they carry quality advertising). This theoretic view suggests, therefore, that the combination of high involvement programming, advertising, and viewership, with the highest possible level of reach among target viewers, is a prescription for advertising and campaign effectiveness.[2]

Note that in none of the studies mentioned in this chapter was there clear evidence of this positive relationship, suggesting that enhanced interest in, or involvement with, the program material carried directly over into the commercial break, producing an enhanced interest in the commercials.

> The more people like a program, the more likely they seem to pay attention and remember the commercials carried by the program.

Rather, the evidence has led to theories that interesting or well-liked programs arouse a general attentiveness in viewers that does not appear to diminish fully with the onset of commercial messages. Twyman (1974) has termed this "a state of enhanced behavioral attention." Viewers thus affected are more likely to stay in front of their television sets during the commercials, remaining receptive to media-produced stimuli, including commercials. As Clancy and Kweskin conclude, the more people like a program, the more likely they seem to pay attention and remember television commercials carried by the program.

The apparent explanation for these conclusions is that characteristics of the program carrier (compelling story line, emotional content, characterization, and role portrayal, to name a few), as subjectively perceived by the viewer, produce enhanced attentiveness and receptivity to the program material. The viewer is motivated to minimize both the potential attraction, as well as distractions associated with competing activities present in the viewing environment. Then, rather than abruptly ceasing as the commercials begin, this enhanced attentiveness remains active to some extent when the commercial message begins, resulting in a higher-than-normal receptivity to commercial stimuli and a positive effect on commercial performance. With program-involved viewers, in other words, the disinclination toward distractions and the heightened receptivity to media-produced stimuli does not dissipate entirely with the onset of the commercial break. Such viewers are, therefore, more likely than disinterested or uninvolved viewers to be exposed to, recall, and be persuaded by the commercials. As Krugman (1983) states, "When an interesting show is interrupted by an interesting commercial the momentum of aroused interest does carry over" (p. 21).

PLACING ADVERTISING WITHIN CONGRUENT PROGRAMS

This perspective on the placement of commercial material, intended as theoretical support for the negative-effects hypothesis, rekindles interest in research that is not only directly related to program environment effects but appears to be an initial step toward the positive-effects hypothesis. The idea of placing advertising with program content and congruity in mind is finding renewed acceptance and widespread practical application, making some discussion of this parallel research important. The idea that advertising effectiveness could benefit from a level of congruity between program content and commercial content is not new. Several investigators (Crane, 1964; Horn & McEwen, 1977; Stanton & Lowenhar, 1977) pursued it in the past, but the results were largely inconclusive. More recently, however, advertising practitioners have been giving the ideas originally put forth by Crane and others a great deal of attention. This renewed interest rests on the premise that ad content and programming should be reminiscent in some ways of each other.

The theory, in brief, suggests that advertising may be more effective when there is some level of thematic consistency between commercial material and the program carrier. Walley (1989) provides an example, quoting an agency executive, "A fragrance commercial in wrestling might give you the gross rating points you want, but it doesn't give the right impression for the product. A fragrance commercial in *Body Heat,* however, could reinforce the image" (p. 47).[3] This has led to the quest for seamless advertising and commercial breaks and to lengthy periods between the onset of a program and the first commercial break, which is designed to build involvement in the program. Although not all broadcasters attempt this with program/ad congruency, one evening in front of the set will reveal a few attempts at both seamless breaks as well as congruency (albeit not at the level of niche cable programming and infomercials). But returning to the initial point, a commercial for glamorous fashion apparel featuring Sharon Stone in an ornate drawing room setting would be more effective if placed in an episode of, say, *Cybil* or *Caroline in the City* than if placed in a typical episode of *Frasier* or *ER.*

The success of such an approach is as dependent on engaging programs— programs with holding power—as it is on quality advertising with product/ program congruency. As a result, advertisers have demanded and have had some success in obtaining greater influence, not only on programming created with commercial congruency or sponsorships in mind, but for control over the entire production process in order to create product-related programs (MacDonald, 1986; "Star Wars," 1997; "Un-seamly," 1997; Zachary, 1995). Meanwhile, advertisers have taken other less drastic measures, from program sponsorship to commercial-promotional tie-ins.

> Advertisers expect that a clear level of congruency between commercial and adjacent editorial context produces a form of carry-over effect.

Whether the approach is blatant or subtle, advertisers expect that a clear level of congruency between commercial and adjacent editorial context produces a form of carry-over effect: Viewer interest in the program material often transfers to adjacent commercial material. This is, of course, old news to magazine advertisers (Appel, 1987; Crane, 1964). From a broadcast television perspective, however, it appears that much remains to be tested and learned. It may be reasonably easy to present a product or service in a manner more congruent with the surrounding program environment. Congruency between program and advertising might range from commercial production formats identical to the typical program production format, to actors sponsoring products in ads within their own shows, to the infomercial, where the program is the commercial and vice versa.

Although this theory is intuitively appealing, supporting evidence tends to be anecdotal rather than based on published empirical research. Greene (1984) suggests, for example, that a positive synergistic effect could be expected from the placement of an ad for batteries to power a toy jeep within an episode of the old *Rat Patrol* series. He goes on to provide insights into programming circumstances where continuity effects could be expected to be either positive, negative, or insignificant and remarks on the generally predictable nature of these circumstances. These insights represent what may be termed conventional agency wisdom, however, rather than the results of empirical research.

An investigation by Cannon (1982), on the other hand, provides the necessary empirical basis but offers evidence that only partially supports a continuity or congruency effect. Cannon hypothesizes that such effects result from a similarity between the values expressed by the program material and accompanying commercial material. Although his findings support this hypothesis, he fails to demonstrate effects on specific dimensions of advertising response and acknowledges limitations on the ability to generalize his findings. Thus, although both commonsense and contemporary practice support continuity or congruency effects, from a purely empirical basis, the results of research into this issue must be considered inconclusive.

The notion that it is possible to achieve the beneficial aspects of program/commercial congruity in the midst of unengaging programming is, however, wholly unsupported at present. Furthermore, the generally questionable nature of the evidence reviewed and cited by Brock and Shavitt (1983) in support of advertising placement within unengaging or low-intensity programming would seem to argue against their theory.

VAMPIRE OR STANDARD BEARER: WHAT WE KNOW TO DATE

It is interesting to report that there is a sizable literature supporting both the negative and positive hypotheses. As an aside, the congruency argument—that similarities in commercial and programming content may foster a positive relation—does not explain the debate. Never in our experience, or in the experience of several outside readers of this chapter, has an academic/published literature used such dramatically different methodologies to support contradictory findings. Among the most significant findings to emerge from the literature are that virtually all published research concluding positive effects apparently employed natural environment/on-air designs; and that the measurement of advertising effectiveness was confined, in most studies, to recall.

In fact, those studies concluding negative effects tended to use highly controlled, artificial forced-exposure designs and employed a greater range of advertising response measures. In addition, we found rather precise methodological differences between studies drawing contrasting conclusions; from sample composition and operational definitions of the involvement construct, to the type of stimuli used (Lloyd, 1987).

Table 2.1 summarizes these contrasting methodological characteristics, reinforcing the evidence that the nature and direction of program environment effects

TABLE 2.1 Comparison of Typical Methodological Characteristics

	Negative Effects	*Positive Effects*
Exposure technique	Artificial laboratory design. No distractions	On-air design. Natural in-home viewing environment
Operationalization/ measurement of program environment effect	Constraining and judgmental. Examples: difference in ad response between those viewing one of three types of shows and rating viewing as either "tense, relaxed, or concentrated." Difference in response—those rating program as either "suspenseful" or "nonsuspenseful"	"Liking" scale. TvQ Score. Attention scales. ASI "Favorites" scale Single affect-dimension scale (5-point; 0-10)
Sample	Usually smaller convenience samples. Often students	Large representative samples of the population. Often adult women
Stimuli	Thirty-minute program videotapes. Ads embedded or as carried by vehicle. Shorter program segments occasionally used; often only clutter reels	Natural on-air
Criterion variables	Early studies: recall only. Later studies: full range of advertising response measures	Recall only, in the majority of studies
Validation of independent variable	None published	None published
Tests of the integrity of observed effects	No results of tests for possible contaminants published. Some pre-exposure demographic matching reported	Known limitations associated with on-air designs and correlations analysis

on advertising response depends on the testing methodology used. Because, therefore, the nature of program effects findings seems almost systematically related to the copy-testing methods and measures employed in the various studies, it seems appropriate to examine this topic in more detail.

First, virtually all studies concluding positive effects involved on-air testing among large samples of 1,500 or more respondents and limited advertising response measurement to various categories of commercial recall. Thus, the testing environment is rightly considered natural and, therefore, as with most on-air designs, highly representative of the actual viewing experience. In addition, the large samples enhance the ability to generalize the findings. It must be recognized, however, that although viewers are exposed to advertising in their natural home environment, with distractions present, enhancing the likelihood of observing representative effects, studies have criticized the on-air methodology itself for providing findings of questionable reliability (Clancy & Ostlund 1976; Schlinger, 1982; Young 1972; Yuspeh 1979). These critics point out that on-air scores may reflect variation in external, biasing factors such as viewer characteristics, program preferences, and program content reaction as much as variation in advertising recall. The lack of control over the testing procedure, therefore, permits the pollution of true scores by a variety of uncontrolled factors.

> It is essential for a realistic understanding of the nature of program environment effects that researchers make every effort to simulate a natural viewing environment.

For example, there remains the possibility, as Twyman (1974) suggests, that the positive program content-reaction effect may mask artificial effects due to differences in the characteristics of viewers. Yuspeh's (1979) admonition in support of some means to ensure controlled testing is well-taken, therefore. It is nevertheless essential for a realistic and actionable understanding of the nature of program environment effects that researchers make every effort to simulate a natural viewing environment in their investigations, while at the same time recognizing the need for (unobtrusive) controls over the viewing experience, when required.

At one end of the commercial testing spectrum are the various forms of artificial, forced-exposure test environments. In the natural exposure environment, respondents are often far from being glued to their sets, either for programming or commercials. They leave the room, succumb to distractions, and in many ways periodically break their attention toward the TV and the program.

In contrast, artificial, forced-exposure takes place in a theater, or often an austere test facility, employing all too frequently forced, attentive exposure to unrealistic stimuli, using small, nonrepresentative samples. Respondents are placed in front of a screen, enjoined from conversation or inattention, and placed in a position to evaluate commercial material by researchers who, it would seem, have created a test environment as foreign to natural viewing as possible.

We demonstrate the results of such testing in Chapters 6 and 9, but as to the issue of artificial versus naturalistic testing methods, one comment by Krugman (1988) is worth a dozen papers on the topic: "There may be few limits on what people can see and remember having seen when politely forced to attend" (p. 43).

There is always the question, in artificial, forced-exposure test environments, whether the measurements reflect respondents' true reactions to the commercials, reactions biased by the artificiality of the exposure environment and required attention, or an interaction between the two (Aaker & Myers, 1987). True, extraneous elements can be controlled, but this cannot offset the artificiality of the test environment and hence the impact on advertising effectiveness scores.

This raises two additional methodological issues, treated in greater detail in Chapter 3. First, as Yuspeh (1979) notes in her study of contextual effects by program type versus individual program, commercial response measurement should not be confined to a single criterion. Although the majority of the on-air investigations examined more than one category of commercial recall, measurement was still generally restricted to recall/memorability.

> Research into program environment effects should employ criteria representing a more complete range of advertising effects.

Today, it is widely accepted that recall alone is an insufficient basis for assessing total commercial performance. It must also be questioned whether the measurement of program content-reaction in studies concluding positive effects is accomplished sufficiently using simple, largely unidimensional scales. As in the case of the negative-effects studies, therefore, researchers must consider whether such measures adequately reveal the nature of program content effects on advertising effectiveness. Numerical ratings scales, indices of liking for programs, and measuring program content-reaction in terms of favorite to least-liked shows do not suffer the same interpretation and measurement constraints. Compared with the more judgmental and reaction-restricting measures some negative effects studies have used, these methods are more likely to assess—with at least face validity—summary attitudes toward programs. Thus, research into program environment effects should employ criteria representing a more complete range of advertising effects.

Second, and of demonstrable importance in the pursuit of generalized effects of the reception environment, including the effect of program involvement on commercial performance, we encourage a more appropriate approach to the operationalization and measurement of the program environment. The presence and nature of a more fundamental or revealing relationship is inadequately assessed when the measurement of program environment or content effects is constrained to a single, and what must ultimately be considered arbitrary, element of reaction such as tension or suspense. That responses along these subdimensions of program reaction are spoken of in terms of involvement only serves to further cloud the nature of program environment effects. As we will demonstrate shortly, there is every reason to believe that involvement is a multifaceted construct.

Thus, adequately assessing the effect of program involvement or program attitudes on commercial performance requires multiple measures of cognitive and affective response to program material across programs rather than types of programs. Operationalization in terms of program type assumes that the nature of program response depends on categories of programming. There is no evidence, however, to suggest the existence of a systematic relationship between reaction to types of programs and response to commercials under natural viewing conditions.

Based on this review of the evidence, it seems likely that disagreement concerning the direction of program environment effects on television advertising performance is the result of a failure by many investigators to

1. Operationalize the program environment in a manner that recognizes the potentially interactive nature of viewing conditions and program content reaction on advertising response
2. Measure program content reaction along a sufficiently broad spectrum of potentially relevant attitudinal dimensions
3. Use research methods that are amenable to an interstudy comparative assessment of evidence

Our hypothesis is that a research study that overcomes these problems will put to rest the video vampire (negative effects) versus standard-bearer (positive effects) controversy, providing advertisers and their agencies with new concepts and measurement tools for media planning purposes.

NOTES

1. Reprinted by permission of the University of Chicago Press.
2. Reprinted by permission of the American Marketing Association.
3. Reprinted with permission from the September 29, 1989, issue of *Advertising Age*. Copyright Crain Communications Inc., 1989.

3

A New Model
of the Effects of
Television Programming

Our review of the literature on television demonstrates that the model of how programming may affect advertising is incomplete. The measures researchers used to assess program content reaction or "involvement" are inadequate for the task.

We propose an expanded model of the program environment (illustrated by Figure 3.1), on the theory that both the program and the advertising in the program determine advertising effectiveness. At the same time, this expanded model argues that the surrounding viewing conditions directly and interactively act as filters and therefore must be considered in any measure of advertising effectiveness.

This expanded model constitutes the true program environment in terms of its measured effects on advertising response. This model makes plain the advertiser's need to extend the measurement of program content reaction from single dimensional scales (which have been highly specific and judgmental or overly general) to multidimensional measures that capture a more complete range of people's responses to television advertising.

The rationale for this expanded model draws heavily on evidence in related disciplines. These range from environmental psychology and mass communications theory to the determinants of television program preference structure.

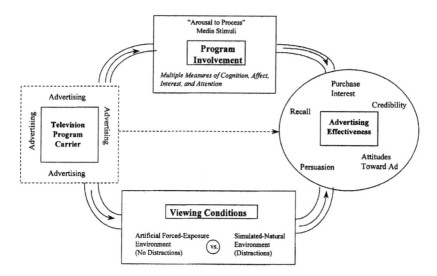

Figure 3.1. An Expanded Model of the Effect of Television Programming on Advertising Effectiveness

As anyone who has ever watched television knows, the typical television commercial is vulnerable to loss of viewer attention due to any number of competing activities, under natural viewing conditions. How viewers receive television is affected by the level and intensity of cognitive arousal (physiological and emotional state, attitudes, and the like) and by the opportunity to process incoming stimuli (stimulus complexity and the level of distraction present).

We argue for a broader view of distraction, the competing activities typically present in which in-home television viewing ordinarily occurs. These activities are almost completely absent in the artificial forced-exposure test environment in which much of the program environment research has been carried out but to adequately appraise the program environment effects requires a model that takes into account differences in surrounding exposure conditions.

Program-content reaction measures must capture a broad range of responses, as well as any form of involvement "carry over" to commercial material. The measurement dimensions must cover a reliable and validated range of response dimensions, from the core feeling/affect to program-related beliefs on a cognitive level, and program-to-advertising carryover of feelings, moods, beliefs, and evaluation.

Some of the same dimensions found to underlie television program preferences—such as personal relevance and entertainment value—underlie attitudes toward commercials.

Our model of the program environment includes viewing conditions (representing the opportunity to process media in the presence of typical distractions) and program involvement level (representing the degree of arousal to process media as reflected by viewer cognitive and affective response to program content).

> The effects of program involvement level on advertising response measures will vary depending on the degree of artificiality or realism in the viewing environment.

The model will demonstrate that the effects of program involvement level on advertising response measures will vary depending on the degree of artificiality (no distractions) or realism (typical in-house distractions) in the viewing environment.

In examining the relationship between program environment and advertising effectiveness we tested five primary and two secondary hypotheses.

The first hypothesis states that program content involvement, or program attitude, is a multidimensional construct requiring multiple measures of attitudinal response.

The second hypothesis states that advertising effectiveness varies significantly with differences in the environmental conditions surrounding program exposure. As viewing conditions become more artificial and less representative of natural conditions, average response scores will increase. This is a product of artificial test conditions.

The third states that the more positive the program attitudes, or the more interesting and involving the viewing experience, the more effective the advertising the program carries will be.

The fourth states that the effects of program involvement on advertising response will vary depending on viewing conditions. Specifically, the positive effects of program involvement on advertising response will be clearly delineated under exposure conditions that simulate a natural, in-home environment.

The fifth states that the multidimensional, multi-item approach to measuring program involvement more completely assesses the nature of viewers' program involvement than single-item affect scales. The multidimensional measure more accurately reflects the impact of program involvement on commercial response and is more closely related to advertising effectiveness than typical unidimensional measures.

The sixth begins with the premise that if program involvement enhances advertising effectiveness, then the greater the viewer's involvement in a program, the stronger the effects of the advertising shown in that program. If this is true, and if involvement means more than simply viewership—which we believe it does—then the cost per thousand people *involved* in a program (CPMI) is different from cost per thousand people *exposed* to a program (the traditional CPM).

Finally, the seventh and last hypothesis states that simulating the physical details of the natural program environment will yield lower advertising response scores (i.e., lower recall, lower levels of pre-post behavioral intentions, change, etc.) than a traditional artificial, forced-exposure environment. As a result, the simulated natural environment should have greater face validity and greater ability to discriminate between commercials tested.

The rest of this chapter expands on these points.

AN EXPANDED MODEL OF THE PROGRAM ENVIRONMENT

Under natural viewing conditions, the typical television commercial is vulnerable to loss of viewer attention due to any number of competing activities. Some viewers look on a commercial break, often a predictable interruption, as an opportunity to leave the room. Others engage in distracting activities, such as talking or glancing at newspapers or magazines, during both program and commercial. Understanding the program environment's impact on advertising response, therefore, requires considering more than the impact of program content involvement in isolation.

One viewpoint gaining increasing recognition and acceptance, and based largely on work in environmental psychology, suggests that the effectiveness of a commercial communication depends considerably on the nature of the total reception environment. As we noted in the last chapter, Wright (1973, 1974) and Tyebjee (1978) undertook seminal efforts to extend a psychological concept of the communications environment to advertising research. The result was a pattern that divided the elements of the television reception environment into two categories:

1. Environmental elements affecting the level and intensity of cognitive arousal, such as physiological and emotional state, attitudes, and so on
2. Environmental elements affecting the opportunity to process incoming stimuli, such as stimulus complexity and the level of distraction present

According to this dual-level concept, Tyebjee (1978) provides a straightforward interpretation of Wright's original: The reception environment is appropriately modeled "in terms of the level and type of arousal it engenders in the receiver and the opportunity it provides to process message stimuli." Thus, efforts to assess the effects of the reception environment on the effectiveness of commercial messages must consider environmental influence at both levels.

Webb (1979) proposed an even more detailed model of environmental influence. It was composed of numerous elements logically suspected to affect TV commercial processing. The practical utility of such highly detailed models may be limited, however. The number and variation of environmental elements included, as well as the apparent complexities involved in accounting for and testing their separate and interactive effects, has discouraged efforts to investigate and validate some of these models. One also questions the value of detailed findings relating to highly specific elements over which the marketer has little or no control. At present, the primary value of these models lies in their contributions to advertising theory and our understanding of how advertising works.

Nevertheless, the original models of Wright, Tyebjee, Webb, and others have significant implications for efforts to resolve the uncertainty and disagreement surrounding the issue of program environment effects on advertising response. Tyebjee (1978) suggests that message stimuli may involve several types of arousal, from physiological to attitudinal arousal and involvement, findings that have been substantiated by more contemporary researchers such as Mano and Oliver (1993) and Baumgartner et al. (1997). Tyebjee acknowledges the ill-defined nature of involvement but suggests that most interpretations agree that involvement reflects the capability of a stimulus to "orient a receiver's attention towards that stimulus and thereby enhance the likelihood of cognitive responses about the stimulus." Similarly, he suggests the need to identify concepts associated with the opportunity to process commercial stimuli, such as the rate at which they arrive (or information load) and the environmental distractions present.

TABLE 3.1 Proposed Versus Traditional Involvement Measurement

	Number of dimensions	
	Two or more	*One*
Items per dimension *Two or more*	The research reported in this study	Little published research
One	Little published research	The traditional approach based on a great deal of published research

> We take "arousal to process" to reflect the programming's capacity to influence the individual viewer's internal psychological state.

In adapting this dual-level concept of the commercial reception environment, we have made certain assumptions regarding the representation of "arousal to process" and "opportunity to process." We take arousal to reflect the programming's capacity to influence the individual viewer's internal psychological state. We assess it primarily in terms of attention to and attitudes toward the program carrier rather than toward the commercials. Implicit in the adaptation is idea of arousal as a multidimensional measure of program content involvement. Table 3.1 contrasts our proposed involvement measures with the traditional research.

We take the opportunity to process to reflect the presence or absence of environmental distractions and their influence (with arousal, or attitudes, toward the program carrier) on commercial response measures.

VIEWING CONDITIONS:
THE PRESENCE AND ABSENCE OF DISTRACTION

To place this pivotal element of the expanded model of the program environment into a wider research perspective, it is instructive to look at the concept of distraction that researchers in another related research context found to be an influential mediator of advertising response (Festinger & Maccoby, 1964; Gardner, 1970; Venkatesan & Haaland, 1968; Wright, 1973).

These studies examined distraction with a different objective in mind than ours. They focused on the manner by which specific forms of behavioral and visual distraction interfered with subjects' tendencies to counter or argue with the content of persuasive communications (a device familiar to advertising researchers and copy writers, who use it in attempts to counter negative feelings or attitudes toward the object or content in commercials). These studies did not consider distraction terms relating to the presence or absence of naturalistic television viewing conditions, nor was television necessarily present in the experimental stimuli. Nevertheless, these studies influence our thinking and conception of an appropriately expanded model of the program environment.

We argue for a broader and more fundamental view of distraction, a summary term for the competing activities typically present when someone ordinarily watches television at home. These activities are almost completely absent in the forced-exposure test environment in which much program environment research has been carried out. We therefore define distraction as the two opposite exposure conditions that copy research uses most frequently: a simulated natural testing environment constructed with attention to the details that permit replicating as closely as possible natural home viewing conditions and a typical forced-exposure environment. The experimental alternatives differ markedly in terms of the opportunities present to engage in typically available alternative activities within the overall television viewing context.

The research design employed a third viewing condition, essentially another highly artificial cell in which respondents were given hand-held meters to register program/commercial reactions at regular intervals. This artificial exposure condition has primary value in the pursuit of separate research objectives but has potential secondary value in the present research context as it represents: (a) an exposure condition that has found very limited application in previous program environment research, and (b) a potential intermediary distraction condition. Including this condition, however, implies a distraction continuum. However, there is no clear conceptual basis or support from subsequent analyses for this position. As a result, primary interest revolves around the two polar viewing/distraction conditions.

These alternative activities include the opportunity to leave the room, converse, read, or engage in other competing activities. The opportunities are either (a) fully present (closely simulating the typical in-home viewing environment) or (b) fully absent (similar to the artificial laboratory exposure environments used in many previous investigations of program environment effects).

> Researchers have typically ignored the fact that a program's influence on advertising response varies by reaction to its content as well as viewing conditions.

Our dual-level program environment model (measured program involvement and exposure conditions surrounding reception) suggests that the tendency of previous investigators to disassociate the program from its broader environment is an inappropriate approach to measuring program environment effects. The program is one of two elements of the reception environment. Researchers have typically ignored the fact that a program's influence on advertising response varies not only with the reaction to its content, but with surrounding viewing conditions as well. As Tyebjee (1978) points out, however,

> Arousal [program attitudes, or program content involvement] provides the motivating drive to process information. However, several factors in the environment may thwart this drive. For this reason, opportunity to process information is included as a major determinant of cognitive responses.

A more realistic portrayal of the impact of viewing conditions on program involvement and advertising effectiveness recognizes that there are innumerable disruptive elements in the typical viewing environment—from a telephone ring to a comment from a fellow viewer. Each is a threat to engaged, interested, or involved viewing, which may be fully suspended, partially suspended, or virtually unaffected, depending on the nature or strength of viewers' involvement in the program and the strength of their motivation to recapture or sustain the original state of attention toward the television.

Adequate appraisal of program environment effects, therefore, requires a model that takes into account differences in surrounding exposure conditions and accompanying differences in the opportunities to process media stimuli. Given that the dispute in the literature over the direction of program environment effects appears neatly divided between those researchers conducting their tests under artificial, forced-exposure viewing conditions and those testing under more natural, freely motivated conditions, this need is more compelling.

ASSESSING PROGRAM CONTENT INVOLVEMENT

Just as the program environment models of Wright, Tyebjee, and Webb demonstrate inaccuracies in previous attempts to account for the program reception environment, they also indicate the inaccuracy in measuring program content reaction. Tyebjee's (1978) multiple levels of arousal, for example, encourage recognizing program-induced attitudes (or content involvement) as multidimensional. This view is supported by those who have sought to define the central, response-evoking concept of involvement.

Krugman (1965) refers to involvement as personal connections made by the viewer in response to stimulus material (in this case, programming). In other words, involvement consists of "spontaneous bridgings" between the material's content and the viewer's personal life experiences "expressed in his immediate post-exposure replay of thoughts."

Subsequent definitions considered involvement as a multifaceted construct that reflected increased attention and orientation of perceptual processes toward a stimulus. Myers (1968), for example, refers to involvement as a manifestation of the "psychological, social, or economic stake" an individual perceives in relation to a particular activity or stimulus. Wright (1974) relates involvement to "levels of motivational arousal." Despite the variation in definition, researchers seem to agree that involvement in a stimulus cannot be imputed from responses measured along a single response dimension.

Laurent and Kapferer's (1985) efforts to devise an inclusive and valid approach to measure this frequently indistinct theory substantiated this idea. Based on a review of the literature, they conclude involvement to be a "causal or motivating variable with a number of consequences on the consumer's purchase and communications behavior" (p. 41). Furthermore, consumers differ not only in their level of involvement in (or intensity of arousal toward) a particular stimulus, they differ in the type of involvement (emotional, rational, attitudinal, etc.). The authors provide persuasive evidence critical of any assessment of involvement obtained from a single continuum and argue instead for involvement-profile assessment. Such a profile's primary dimensions are those most consistently cited in the literature: importance (personal meaning or relevance), symbolic value (psycho/social, conceivably connected with enduring personal values), and hedonic value (emotional appeal, ability to provide affect). A true picture of involvement results from measuring the level of intensity along each of these dimensions.

Zaichkowsky (1985) also attempts to develop a single, comprehensive measurement scheme for involvement, one that would eliminate the need for different methods and measures to assess different types of involvement (for example, involvement with ads, involvement with products, involvement with attributes, etc.). As she examines varying measures associated with different types of involvement, she points out that researchers used divergent measures in each situation and notes that when they obtain conflicting results, one cannot know whether this is due to the different measures or to the different behaviors.

Zaichkowsky (1985) also notes that many of the scales used are single-item measures that may not capture the total involvement concept: "Current multiple-item measures have not been tested for internal reliability or validity. Hence, a standardized, general, valid, and multiple-item measure of involvement should be used" (p. 341). Chapters 5 and 6 will demonstrate that our technique for measuring program involvement meets these requirements.

This is a call for a multiple-item measure of involvement that is just as sensitive and valid for measuring, say, involvement in a small appliance purchase decision to involvement in a television program. These involvement-measurement requirements, according to Zaichkowsky (1985), are satisfied by some rather vague and apparently limited categories suggested by Bloch and Richins (1983) and Houston and Rothschild (1978):

1. *Personal*: inherent interests, values, or needs that motivate
2. *Physical*: characteristics of the object that cause differentiation and increase interest
3. *Situational*: something that temporarily increases relevance or interest toward the object

We believe that although a universally applicable involvement scale may be an important goal for research into consumer behavior, it appears more appropriate to build a custom-tailored or domain-specific program involvement measurement tool, drawing on applicable sources.

Although we found scant evidence of studies devoted to examining involvement and its operational potential, much has been published on the elements of involvement under specific—usually advertising-related—conditions. Researchers have found these elements instrumental in explaining, contributing toward, and sometimes codetermining the outcome of a multitude of studies.

We concluded early in our research that component emotive responses—feelings, if you will—necessarily precede liking.

Murry et al. (1992), for example, examine the impact of program-elicited feeling and program liking simultaneously on evaluations of television commercials. They maintain that research in these two areas has been conducted independently and thus propose to determine, as one goal, whether a "liked" program eliciting negative feelings would enhance or diminish the performance of the commercials the program carries. But, as we concluded early in our research (and as substantiated by Morris, 1995), component emotive responses—feelings, if you will—necessarily precede liking. Liking is a composite response that could not exist without prior or simultaneous feelings. Considerable evidence exists, merging into commonsense, that feelings and liking are either/both antecedent and resultant parts or simultaneously-processed, interrelated elements of involvement. However, we already know that feeling-based liking is a strong correlate of involvement and hence contributes to the program-content response and ad reaction.

This is especially true of ad-related involvement (Baumgartner et al., 1997; Grunert, 1996; Morris, 1995; Park & Hastak, 1994). But despite the importance of establishing the emotive dimensions of feeling and integrating them into the concept of liking (and then into involvement), it is only in combination with involvement's elements that we see feeling-based concepts and liking becoming powerful predictors of program content and ad content reactions. Published evidence concludes that both feelings and liking are strongly interrelated elements of the dominant affective component of involvement (Baumgartner et al., 1997; Lloyd, 1987; Lloyd & Clancy, 1991; Morris, 1995; Park & Young, 1986, among many others).

Murry et al. (1992) did not find that program-elicited feelings carry over or influence viewer ad evaluations, but these feelings undoubtedly influence viewers' program liking. The authors found that only program liking influenced attitudes toward ads and brands.

The effect of program liking [on attitudes towards the brands] only emerged as a mediating effect, through attitudes toward the advertising. Hence, program liking is an antecedent of attitudes toward the ad, but it is attitudes toward the ad that ultimately influences attitudes toward the brand. . . . Ad managers concerned about the effect of programming on attitudes toward their ads and brands should concern themselves with the program liking variable rather than with the specific feelings that programs elicit.

Callcott and Phillips (1996) arrive at similar conclusions. They maintain that likable spokespersons "generate attention to the ad and positive feelings toward the brand that can potentially affect purchase behavior." But their message—that liking can culminate in advertising effectiveness if one pays attention to the relevant stimuli and transfers this attentiveness to positive feelings toward the advertising—is an oversimplification of the way viewers process advertising (Grunert, 1996).

Murry et al. (1992) refer to the liking variable as the "overarching liking construct," taking in "intrinsic satisfaction," and "enjoyment" of the experience, "arousal," "fantasy, and feelings." Our measure makes it clear that liking is a core element of the overarching involvement construct. In other words, there is more to program involvement, program involvement effects, affective response, and similar forms of involvement than liking. Liking does remain a key composite concept of the program content effect. Involvement implicitly considers a full range of emotional and affective dimensions of attitude, as well as its cognitive, and evaluative elements. In fact, Morris (1995) states that recent evidence supports a three-dimensional approach for modeling emotional response (as did Mehrabian & Russell, 1974; Russell, 1989, above). These are (a) pleasure/displeasure, (b) degree of arousal, and (c) dominance/submissiveness. This PAD model, although conceived and developed to measure emotional response to advertising simply and directly, goes beyond the purely emotive to belief states in its over 100 dimensions of emotional response.

> Program-content reaction measures need to capture a broader range of response, as well as any form of involvement "carry-over" to the commercials.

Program-content reaction measures, on the other hand, must take more into consideration. We need to capture a broader range of response, as well as any form of involvement carryover to the commercials. Thus, the basic measurement dimensions must cover a range of response dimensions, each item-analyzed, reliable, and validated. These dimensions range from the core feeling/affect toward program-related beliefs on a cognitive level to the program-to-advertising carryover of feelings, moods, and beliefs.

In this context, the study by Baumgartner et al. (1997) is worth mentioning for its recognition of the importance of the overall test environment to accurate measurement. The research starts off by investigating "moment-to-moment" patterns of response to ads, particularly ways by which various affective and emotional reactions to commercials might lead to enhanced liking for, or overall positive judgments of, ads. The researchers employ what they refer to as "more realistic viewing conditions" in the experimental design: We would consider these conditions halfway between the wholly artificial and the simulated natural viewing environment on the testing continuum. In the process, they found that advertising containing clear emotional content is "naturally viewed with particular interest because it generates affective involvement (findings attributed to Park & Young, 1986). Our findings might be expected to replicate in environments in which participants can turn their attention away to other tasks."

In other words, in a naturalistic program reception environment, involvement with the advertising found in involving programs, if imbued with appropriate emotional or "affective dimensionality," stands a greater chance of generating positive ad responses than would uninvolving ads in uninvolving programming. Baumgartner et al. (1997) find empirical substantiation for hypotheses involving greater "ad liking," "brand liking," and cognitive measures such as recall accompanying more positive "affective response patterns" evoked by the advertising and its reception environment.

Two additional and related research areas are particularly valuable in helping us arrive at a similarly multidimensional but more specifically relevant measure of program content involvement: The literature exploring the behavioral and attitudinal correlates/determinants of television program preferences and viewing habits and the literature relating to measuring attitudes toward advertising. It is quite reasonable to assume that many of the same cognitive, emotional, mood-oriented, and value-based factors and dimensions found to explain program preferences or attitudes toward commercials will also help explain program-induced attitudes.

DETERMINANTS OF TELEVISION PROGRAM PREFERENCES

Companies have conducted a great deal of research searching for what determines television program reactions and preferences. Several factors repeatedly emerge in studies explaining the apparent social and psychological motives and rewards underlying viewer preferences.

In his examination of the appeal of entertaining programming, Tannenbaum (1980) concluded that such programming provides viewers with a "vicarious emotional experience." When viewers separate themselves momentarily from the "world of reality" in response to entertaining programming, they receive a "significant emotional input in return." Because of this emotional arousal due to the program's "dramatic content," Tannenbaum reasons that viewers become participants. The reward is diversion from "their other daily worries."

> Eastman conducted a comprehensive investigation into television's uses, providing a list of 11 factors that underlie reaction to, and preferences for, TV programs.

Comstock (1977) observed a "personal relevance" dimension—explained as content pertinent to the viewer—that he saw as central in explaining viewing habits. Eastman (1979) conducted a comprehensive investigation into television's uses, providing a list of motives that remains currently applicable. Based on her own and other research, she hypothesized 11 factors to underlie reaction to, and preferences for, television programs:

1. *Arousal*: Indicates emotional arousal functions; "touching one's feelings"
2. *Pleasure*: Entertainment function
3. *Information*: Information-seeking to assist in daily life; other researchers refer to this as a "surveillance" function
4. *Conversation*: Associated with the use of story, characters, or theme as a conversation medium
5. *Social substitute*: Substitute for social interaction; may be associated with vicarious experiences
6. *Distraction*: Predominantly emotional/tension release and capacity to "cheer up when sad;" that is, linked with the same functions as Escape, below
7. *Modeling*: Behavioral guide/role model function; associated with a number of related elements, variously labeled in other studies the social learning function (assistance in daily life); socialization (inculcation of "correct" values in children

through commentary, permitted viewing, etc.); personal identity (personal preference, reinforcement of personal values, reality testing); and relational (relate to characters, problems and circumstances)

8. *Pass time*: A positive use in the sense of an actively sought leisure pursuit

9. *Background noise*: Structural function; structures the day; provides accompaniment for other activities; in other research, companionship

10. *Escape*: Escape problems, everyday concerns; vicarious experiences in other research

11. *Boredom*: Pass time in negative sense; detached, indifferent

More recently, Lee and Lee (1995) investigated television viewership patterns and determinants to assess the idea that interactive TV would soon eclipse traditional television. Their research indicates this to be highly unlikely, "at least to the year 2001." But the primary value of their research to us is in the emotional, attitudinal, and motivational concepts, as well as specific whys and hows that prompt TV viewing. Often, we can consider these as direct measures of program reaction dimensions and program content-involvement.

Many of the reasons and uses Eastman (1979) uncovered appeared equally significant in the Lee and Lee (1995) study. This lends strong support to the reliability and consistency of the factors that determine viewing. It also supports several component elements of our program involvement measure and the dimensions tapped. For example, Lee and Lee labeled one of the eight factors explaining why people watch television Routinization of Viewing, which appears to contain Eastman's Pleasure and Pass Time factors. Although they noted the wide diversity of channels available, Lee and Lee found that 66% of their sample had watched specific programs before and that 54% said they always watched a specific program.

Substantiating these findings, Lee and Lee (1995) cite somewhat parallel findings obtained from a Times Mirror (1994) national survey, where 61% of the sample claim to tune into a program they know will air at a particular time, rather than skipping around to see what might be on. A clear majority (66%) reported that they did not use their remotes to change channels frequently as they watched television. As reported by Lee and Lee, Eastman (1979) and Eastman and Newton (1995), who observed remote users, found the greatest amount of "grazing" occurred not during the programs, but between them. Taken together, these findings would indicate that the power of "routinized viewing behavior" could be a substantial obstacle to new uses of the television set.

> It appears that television viewing still occurs most frequently in a social context—roughly two thirds of prime-time viewing is in the company of others.

Another factor, viewing as a social activity, remains strong in explaining viewership; it is a factor that influenced our conceptualization of the program environment measure. Despite multiple-TV households and the individuality that a myriad of viewing alternatives makes possible, it appears that television viewing still occurs most frequently in a social context. Lee and Lee (1995) found that "roughly two thirds of prime-time viewing is done in the company of others."

Their factor, Social Grease, is also related to the often neglected social side of TV viewing. Respondents were found to value programs as the basis for current and future conversation. The findings substantiate an earlier survey by Bruskin, Inc. (Tooley, 1989), which found that TV programs are one of the most popular topics of conversation, among both men and women. Furthermore, people watch programs they know will be talked about.

But this is simply one broad-based example. Other factions within the conversational viewing segment could exist, ranging from soap operas to specific news programs and newscasters, from episodes of highly successful programs such as *Seinfeld* and *Frasier* to numerous age or special-interest programs (some with commercial spinoffs) such as *The Power Rangers, Star Trek: The New Generation, Leno,* and *Letterman.* It would be short-sighted to assume that conversation is limited to the program without some reference to the advertising. This is particularly true if an ad is imbued with a unique execution or has a story line relevant to members of a particular conversational viewing segment.

Viewing as a solitary activity has two different motivations. In the first, Lee and Lee (1995) say, the gratification sought is associated with the "desire for undemanding relaxation, [personal] involvement in engrossing stories, and the enjoyment of a routinized activity" following a strenuous day. Here, viewing is the sole activity and concentration is high, seemingly ideal circumstances for program involvement with a heightened likelihood of advertising receptivity.

In the second case, Lee and Lee (1995) name one factor, An Engrossing World, where pure escapism transports the viewer into a life altogether different from his or her own. Examples would be programs that place viewers in Africa chasing antelopes or under the sea in a quest for sunken treasure. Under these circumstances of high program environment, conventional and plausible reasoning might forecast the likelihood that involvement in the program would carry over to positive ad receptivity and response would be weak.

But from the evidence and anecdotal material we have seen, the exact opposite is more probable. The viewer would be more likely to remain firmly attached to the focal stimuli, including the commercials, waiting for the program to resume. This might be easier to accept among advertisers and agency people, who have finally been persuaded to accept the idea (and have experienced the benefits as a result) that advertising reminiscent of, or similar in context to, the program in terms of style, theme, pace, and actors is more likely to meet with a favorable impression than advertising that is very different from the program.

These concepts of preference-forming, motivational television usage dimensions emerge so frequently in the communications literature (as well as in other cross-disciplinary investigations such as marketing and consumer research), they go a long way toward explaining viewing habits and preferences. It is perhaps intuitive that program content involvement may result, in part, from the viewers' appraisal of a program's performance in terms of those television usage dimensions salient to them. It is not unreasonable to suggest, therefore, that incorporating similar dimensions into program involvement and attitude measures will contribute to understanding true program environment effects.

DETERMINANTS OF ATTITUDES TOWARD ADVERTISING

The literature concerning the determinants of attitudes toward advertising is also useful in attempts to improve measures of program involvement, as we discussed earlier. It is significant that some of the same dimensions found to underlie television program preferences have been found to underlie attitudes toward commercials. Researchers have repeatedly identified the concepts of personal relevance and entertainment value, for example, as two of the most significant factors underlying attention to, and liking for, commercials. In a study of viewer reactions to over 500 commercials, Aaker and Bruzzone (1981) discovered four factors that explained 75% of the variance in attitudinal response to commercials. The most significant factors were entertainment (amusing, imaginative, lively) and personal relevance (informative, interesting), followed by dislike (phony, irritating, silly) and warmth (appealing, gentle, well done).

Similarly, Wells (1964), Leavitt (1970), Wells, Leavitt, and McConville (1971), and Schlinger (1979) found factors relating to entertainment value, or the ability to provide affect, and personal relevance to be the two most significant items to explain commercial reactions. Additional factors found to be significant include empathy and alienation (Schlinger, 1979), irritation (Leavitt, 1970; Wells et al., 1971), and humor (Bartos & Dunn, 1976; Gelb & Pickett, 1983; Wells et al., 1971).

Arnold and Bird (1982) reviewed over 50 studies relating commercial recall to various behavioral and attitudinal factors. The factors most consistently related to higher commercial recall scores include:

1. *Involved:* empathy or identification with characters, situation, products
2. *Entertained:* amusing, not boring
3. *Moved:* feeling, sensuousness
4. *Interested:* imaginative, informative, curious, unbelievable
5. *Captured attention:* looked, listened

Mackenzie and Spreng (1992) examined the ways motivations moderate the impact of information processing on the formation of attitudes toward brands and purchase intentions. Much of the research appears to treat involvement as analogous to, if not synonymous with, arousal and motivation (for example, Kamp & MacInnis, 1995, and Mano & Oliver, 1993, greatly subsume the construct's meaning). Nevertheless, in Mackenzie and Spreng's conceptualization and findings, "motivation increased the impact of both negative and positive 'central processing' on advertised brand attitudes," and "increased the impact of brand attitudes" on their measure of purchase intentions.

Mano and Oliver (1993) envision involvement as a "product relevance" device—need fulfillment, value expression, interest, and so on. However, in parting with traditional expectancy-value and cognitive processing models, they maintain that because there is much overlap between their concepts of utilitarian instrumentality and hedonic judgment, it is deficient as a means to assess attitudes. Furthermore, they maintain the view that involvement cannot be considered an evaluative dimension.

Mano and Oliver's (1993) findings are somewhat at odds with this posture, however. The correspondences between involvement and the Need/Value (Utilitarian) and Interest/Positively/Appealing (Hedonic) dimensions of their conceptualization were found to be significant. They conclude by remarking that "a major premise of this study was that involvement would emerge as an influence on affective space. . . . As is clear . . . the effect of involvement is to enhance virtually all of affective experience."

> Liking, overall brand rating, and measures of overall affective reaction to commercials are the best predictors of advertising or campaign effectiveness.

Despite the contributions of this research, it is mainstream advertising research and copy testing that have made some of the most significant contributions to our understanding of attitudes toward advertising. Briefly, the team (co-author Kevin Clancy is one of them) behind the 5-year ARF Copy Research Validity Project (Haley, 1990a; Haley & Baldinger, 1991) revealed a great deal about attitudes toward ads, not only in terms of involvement, but in terms of the measuring overall advertising effectiveness. Liking, overall brand rating, and "measures of overall affective reaction to commercials" were found to be the best general predictors of advertising or campaign effectiveness. The accompanying diagnostics (individual items) ranging from "This ad doesn't give any facts, it just creates an image" to "This ad was funny" or "This ad was clever" were especially sensitive measures.

VIEWER ATTITUDES AND PROGRAM-INDUCED MOOD

Axelrod (1963) provides a final perspective on the importance of multiple dimensions in the measurement of viewer attitudes toward television programs and related stimuli. He hypothesized that viewer attitudes toward products were influenced significantly by their moods and the manner in which their moods were influenced by the environment surrounding product/commercial exposure. According to Axelrod, mood is multifaceted and cannot be constrained in measurement, as had been done in the past, to lie along a single pleasant-unpleasant continuum. Such an approach places serious limitations on the sensitivity of the instrument as well as on the nature of the diagnostics and conclusions that can be drawn from the results. Consequently, Axelrod employed nine semantically differentiated dimensions of mood, shown in psychological research to measure separate mood effects.

Axelrod (1963) measured respondents' mood along the nine dimensions prior to, as well as immediately following, exposure to a "highly emotional" program (*The Nuremberg Trials*) to determine whether they considered various products (presented in a print ad context) to be either consistent or inconsistent with their mood at the time. His findings indicated the existence of a systematic relationship between attitudes toward various products and pre-post shifts in separate mood-aspect measures.

These findings hold important implications for program involvement/attitude assessment. A unidimensional measure of mood would enable testing the existence of a relationship between mood and product attitude in a pre-post design. It would not, however, demonstrate whether a systematic and predictable relationship existed. This would require demonstrating that a particular relationship holds across the several known dimensions of mood, each of which could vary independently of the others. (Certain mood-aspect changes could lead to more favorable attitudes toward certain products, whereas others could lead to negative attitudes, all in response to the same stimulus.) Axelrod's (1963) findings illuminate which components of product attitudes were affected by changes in individual dimensions of overall mood.

Unidimensional measures of program attitude or content involvement in the present research context are similarly limited. It is not unreasonable to suggest that these attitudes are also multidimensional, given that program preferences and attitudes toward advertisements were found to be multidimensional. Thus, determining whether a systematic relationship exists between program-induced attitude and advertising response requires that the former be assessed with respect to its several, potentially independently varying dimensions across several programs within the appropriate viewing environment. As we will demonstrate, determining these dimensions has depended substantially on evidence provided in the literature.

A PROPOSED EXPANDED MODEL
OF THE PROGRAM ENVIRONMENT

Two central elements in the proposed remedial (and expanded) model of the program environment suggest the primary hypotheses of this research:

1. *Viewing conditions* representing the opportunity to process media stimuli in the presence of typical distractions in the reception environment
2. *Program involvement level* representing the degree of arousal to process media stimuli as reflected by viewers' cognitive and affective response to program content

According to the model shown in Figure 3.1, the effect of the program environment on advertising response must consider the impact of surrounding viewing conditions that afford differential opportunities for processing media stimuli, not just that of program content reaction or involvement level alone and in isolation.

This model further asserts first that program content reaction is a multidimensional construct, defined as program involvement. It reflects the potentially diverse cognitive and affective connections between media stimuli and a given viewer, which determine the program involvement level for that viewer. A single judgmental affect dimension or summary affect scales improperly (or inadequately) measure the nature of such involvement.

Second, when program involvement level is measured in a manner that recognizes a more complete range of potential attitudinal response dimensions to programs, and when advertising effectiveness is also measured in more realistic multidimensional fashion (i.e., a composite made up of several advertising response dimensions), our model posits that program involvement level is positively related to advertising effectiveness.

> Failure to consider the interaction between viewing conditions and advertising response may be the source of the dispute over involvement's effect.

Third, explicitly incorporating viewing conditions into the model will demonstrate that the effect of program involvement level on advertising response varies depending on the degree of artificiality (no distractions) or realism (typical in-house distractions) in the surrounding viewing environment. We consider the failure of previous investigations to consider this probable interaction to be a primary source of the dispute in the literature over the true direction of advertising reponse to program environment, whether involvement in the program hurts or helps the commercials.

We tested five hypotheses in this examination of the relationship between program environment and advertising effectiveness. The first of these was pivotal, as it decides the relevance of testing the remaining hypotheses. We devote Chapter 5 to this first hypothesis. In Chapter 6, we examine the next four hypotheses and two secondary hypotheses, each designed to test the practical applications of findings associated with the primary hypotheses.

Hypothesis 1: The multidimensionality of program involvement. Previous re-searchers have defined and measured program involvement (or attitudes) as single-dimension constructs despite the probable multidimensional nature of viewers' reactions to program content. The first hypothesis states therefore:

> Hypothesis 1:   Program involvement (also known as program attitude or program content involvement) is a multidimensional construct requiring multiple meas-ures of attitudinal response.

This asserts the multidimensional nature of program involvement but not necessarily the inclusive measurement of all the facets of attitudinal response toward, or involvement in, programs. Measures of program involvement must reflect the multiple forms of involvement or arousal potentially engendered by program material. Furthermore, such an approach will result in responses that are more representative of the true nature of viewer reactions to program content than those using unidimensional measures. This assertion is based on recent evidence attesting to the multidimensionality of the involvement concept (Laurent & Kapferer, 1985; Lee & Lee, 1995; Mano & Oliver, 1993; Sawyer & Howard, 1991; Zaichkowsky, 1985) as well as on extensive evidence in related research. We will confirm the multidimensionality hypothesis by subsequent analyses, if we are able to extract multiple factors from the inventory of items used to operationalize program involvement and by subsequent item and internal con-sistency tests.

Hypothesis 2: Artificial viewing conditions inflate advertising response scores. The literature on program environment effects includes studies that have been conducted in highly artificial, forced-exposure laboratory environments, at one end, and those conducted with on-air testing under natural viewing conditions, with typical in-home distractions, at the other. Comparisons of these metho-dologically disparate investigations have ignored the potential effects of viewing environment on commercial response. Therefore,

> Hypothesis 2:   Advertising effectiveness varies significantly with differences in the environmental conditions surrounding program exposure. As viewing condi-tions become more artificial and less representative of natural conditions with typical distractions or competing activities available, average response scores across all advertising response measures will increase. This is considered to be a product of artificial test conditions and an attendant increase in the opportunity to process experimental stimuli in the virtual absence of the competing stimuli typically present in the natural viewing environment.

The second hypothesis calls for a significant main effect of the viewing conditions factor on the advertising response criteria. The direction of this effect is hypothesized to be negative in the sense that higher levels of environmental distractions will be accompanied by lower advertising response scores. Of greater initial importance, however, is confirmation that advertising response varies significantly with the opportunity to process focal stimuli, as provided by the conditions surrounding television exposure, and not simply with program content reaction or involvement, measured, as it were, in isolation.

This hypothesis is consistent with findings reported by Venkatesan and Haaland (1968) and Gardner (1970) concerning the effects of divided attention on message communicability and with Aaker and Myers's (1982) summary of the evidence regarding the effects of distraction on the cognitive processing of advertising stimuli.

Commercial test scores obtained under artificial, forced-exposure laboratory conditions may not represent the true nature of viewer responses to advertising.

If confirmed, this hypothesis leads to wide-ranging implications for commercial testing. It suggests, as many advertising researchers have long suspected, that commercial test scores obtained under artificial, forced-exposure laboratory conditions may not represent the true nature of viewer responses to advertising and are probably systematically inflated. We therefore expect a significant main effect of the viewing conditions factor on all, or the majority of, the advertising response criteria.

Hypothesis 3: Program involvement is positively related to advertising response. An assumption (not a hypothesis) is that advertising effectiveness is a multidimensional construct including (a) attitudes toward the advertising, (b) unaided and aided name and message recall, (c) copy credibility, (d) purchase interest, and (e) behavioral intentions change (i.e., persuasion). Thus,

Hypothesis 3: The higher or the more favorable involvement in a television program, or the more interesting and involving the viewing experience, the more effective embedded advertising will be across advertising response measures.

Advertising effectiveness is assumed to be, like program involvement, a multidimensional construct constituting a range of response dimensions from attitudes to persuasion. It is hypothesized, therefore, that when the effect of a more complete and representative range of involvement dimensions is assessed against a more complete and representative range of advertising effectiveness dimensions, this effect will emerge as significant and positive. This hypothesis reflects the theory that when one removes fundamental operational constraints from program environment effect measures, higher levels of program-induced involvement will be equated with enhanced receptivity and attentiveness toward media-produced stimuli. The enhanced receptivity will remain activated to some degree during commercial breaks, resulting in higher commercial response scores the more involved the viewer is or the more favorable the viewer's program-induced attitudes.

Confirming this hypothesis requires a significant, positive effect of program involvement on the advertising response criterion as measured along the significant dimensions found during the testing of Hypothesis 1.

Hypothesis 4: Simulated living room environments produce more sensitive results. We theorize that the formation and effects on advertising response engendered by program involvement will differ depending on the environmental conditions surrounding the exposure. Involvement in a program is self-motivated to a greater extent under naturalistic viewing conditions, where the viewer must constantly resist competing activities and distractions to sustain involvement. On the other hand, in the absence of these distractions, enhanced attentiveness is in large measure a function of the testing environment. Thus, under naturalistic conditions, we expect a more pronounced (positive) response differential between viewers with low program-involvement levels and those with high program-involvement levels. Due to the radically different characteristics of the forced artificial environment, this response differential is expected to be less pronounced. Therefore,

> Hypothesis 4: The effects of program involvement on advertising response will vary depending on surrounding viewing conditions. More specifically, the positive effects of program involvement on advertising response will be clearly delineated under exposure conditions that simulate a natural, in-home environment.

This hypothesis calls for a significant interaction of program involvement with viewing conditions on advertising response. Under simulated natural viewing conditions, we suspect a pronounced, monotonically increasing relationship between the level of program involvement and measures of advertising effectiveness. When viewing an engrossing program, the viewer takes conscious efforts to suppress the effects of distractions and resists the temptation to engage in competing activities. To some extent, this strong, self-willed orientation toward stimuli, induced by positively perceived program content, then carries over into the commercial break.

We have no hypotheses regarding program involvement effects within the artificial treatment conditions. In light of the operational and methodological differences between our research and the typical artificial forced-exposure laboratory study (which most frequently lead to negative-effects conclusions), such hypotheses would be based largely on conjecture. We will make a detailed comparative analysis of findings within the focal simulated natural and the artificial exposure conditions, however, with confirmation of Hypothesis 4.

We initially thought that an experimental environment involving hand-held meters offered the possibility of functioning as an intermediary distraction, as suggested earlier. This was supposed on the basis of the presence and task of operating the meter, while maintaining a level of viewer involvement in a less stridently controlled exposure environment. A detailed comparison of the criterion variable response means for each exposure environment (see Chapter 4), laid to rest the issue of incorporating this response condition into the research design. In only one instance, involving the comparison of several measures of advertising response across each of the three environments, could we find even the most remote support for any intermediary status of the metered environment.

> Much of the dispute can be attributed to concluding negative effects on the basis of artificial testing conditions, positive on more representative conditions.

Assuming we confirm these hypotheses, we will undertake a more detailed investigation into the various origins and manifestations of the dispute over the direction of program environment effects. The inquiry will proceed from the theory that much of the dispute can be attributed to the tendency to conclude negative effects on the basis of artificial testing conditions and to conclude positive effects on the basis of more representative samples and test conditions. The present inquiry takes the form of a detailed comparative analysis of findings within the artificial, no-distractions condition and the simulated natural condition.

Confirming these hypotheses would also suggest clear promise for testing Hypothesis 5. If we prove it, we will furnish strong evidence that attests to the practical application of the proposed multidimensional measure of program involvement, while rendering feasible the testing of two important secondary hypotheses.

Hypothesis 5: Multidimensional measures of program involvement produce more reliable and valid findings. Most earlier studies, and some contemporary syndicated services that examine the effect of television programming, employ a unidimensional (usually single-item) measure to gauge program involvement. Can the new multidimensional (multi-item) measure of program involvement proposed here be shown as superior to the simple tools used in most previous research?

It is reasonable to accept that people's attitudes toward programs often involve complex, multifaceted constructs, such as mood and emotion, as well as seemingly straightforward concepts, such as entertainment and information. By the same token, it would appear myopic to think that a single-item scale, even one backed by a phalanx of normative data to support the results, could adequately measure the range of sentiments and attitudes many programs evoke. This, of course, includes their differential impact on the ads. Such a measurement methodology is akin to personality inventories that use only a single item to measure each major characteristic. It is similar to an automobile tester who would measure performance solely on the basis of miles-per-gallon, comfort by the seating arrangement, and quality of construction by the thunk! of a closing door.

As long ago as 1972, Young expressed the sentiments of many copy researchers by concluding that only multiple measures of effectiveness, not one measure in isolation, could adequately capture an ad's performance potential. Clearly, it is past time to acknowledge the shortcomings of single-item/unidimensional measures of more complex and potentially significant determinants of advertising effectiveness. It is time we recognized that multidimensional attitudes and responses require multidimensional/multi-item measures. This is not intended to make media planning more difficult. It is based on the notion of finding the best homes for commercials where the audience composition, count, and involvement level enhance the probability of receptivity and exposure.

Based on this, therefore, we propose a fifth hypothesis:

Hypothesis 5: The multidimensional, multi-item approach to measuring program
     involvement, more completely assesses the nature of viewers' involvement than

single-item affect scales. The multidimensional measure will, therefore, more accurately reflect the impact of program involvement on commercial response and will be more closely related to advertising effectiveness than typical unidimensional measures.

We assume that the relationship observed between program involvement and the advertising response criteria is uncontaminated to any significant degree by respondents' demographic characteristics or other extraneous factors. Given the remedial methodological steps this study has taken, including sample composition and matching and analytical improvements, we will demonstrate this assumption of uncontaminated effects as reasonable. At any rate, we will conduct the relevant tests for extraneous influence when appropriate and report the results in later chapters.

We theorized earlier that the proposed multidimensional measure would reveal more about the specific elements underlying program involvement: the actual characteristics of programs and people's reactions to them. The value of this information in a media buying context, if valid and reliable, could be reason enough to assert the practical superiority of this new measure. It is necessary, however, to first demonstrate that the measure is statistically more significant and closely related to advertising effectiveness than the unidimensional measures traditionally used.

Thus, although the superior diagnostics afforded by the multidimensional measure lend a degree of practical relevance, confirmation of Hypothesis 5 will depend on the results of parallel analyses conducted using the new measure and two unidimensional measures commonly used.

Hypothesis 5 will be confirmed if the results of these analyses demonstrate that the multidimensional measure more closely correlates with the advertising effectiveness criteria. Furthermore, if the multidimensional measure has greater explanatory significance, while remaining free of contamination from extraneous variables to a significantly greater extent than the rival summary-affect measures, it will provide strong additional confirmation for Hypothesis 5.

COST PER THOUSAND . . .
OR COST PER THOUSAND INVOLVED?

To the media planner, CPM has been the standard indicating the efficiency and soundness of media buys. In many ways, the CPM may be considered the analog of the price-to-earnings ratio, which financial analysts use to indicate the soundness and efficiency of a firm's stock. Yet, whereas many other quantifiable tools are available and usually brought to bear in financial considerations, media planners, in the majority of cases, stand solidly (albeit reluctantly, at times) behind the inviolability of the single CPM criterion.

Simply stated, the syndicated measurement services supply the sample-generated audience counts, which reflect the number of viewers tuned to and presumably watching a given program. The higher the estimate (CPM denominator), the higher the cost of the program buy (CPM numerator).

Syndicated television audience counts may, in many cases, come closer to target exposure opportunities, which are quite different from actual exposure.

Unfortunately, the value of these estimates is problematic. The figures reflect audience or target size counts (or both), which may not accurately represent the number of people actually viewing the program or commercials. These audience counts may, in many cases, come closer to target exposure opportunities, which are quite different from actual exposure. As Chapter 9 will explore, this distinction is highly significant. Audience counts that merely reflect the opportunity for exposure fail to take into consideration contemporary viewing behavior and the shortcomings of current audience measurement methods and technology. The result: The advertiser may be paying for viewers who do not exist.

What do the issues of audience measurement and ratings have to do with our central theses of program attitudes and involvement? We can state the answer as our sixth hypothesis:

Hypothesis 6:   If program involvement enhances advertising effectiveness and if involvement means more than simply viewership, then the greater the viewer's involvement in a program, the stronger the effects of the advertising shown in that program. Therefore, CPMI is different from CPM to advertising, and the former measure should replace CPM as the tool of choice for media selection decisions.

Hypothesis 6 implies that, with rare exceptions, the syndicated measurement services fail to distinguish between exposure opportunities and actual exposure in their audience size counts and, with very few exceptions, fail to distinguish between involved, attentive exposure and restless, fleeting exposure.

> "The precisely wrong approach to evaluating a media plan is to just count the potential exposures. . . . In almost every case this is a precisely wrong methodology."

Thus, as Lodish (1986) states, "the precisely wrong approach to evaluating a media plan is to just count the potential exposures." Furthermore, "many media planners and media buyers prefer to judge the effectiveness of their media planning and buying by how low their cost per thousand audience . . . is [in relation to] alternative media schedules. In almost every case this is a precisely wrong methodology."

Lodish (1986) reasons that factors affecting viewer response to commercial material may differ for alternative schedules having the same audience figures or gross ratings points. Just because a person is counted as being in the audience for a particular program does not mean that person saw any given commercial (or program segment), and one of the primary factors affecting what an individual sees is the program environment. As Lodish states, "The environment in which an ad appears may have a significant effect on the reader or viewer"; this media (or vehicle) environment effect may be caused by viewer attitudes toward the vehicle, the mood engendered in the viewer by the vehicle, or the degree of involvement of the audience member.

Because the program environment—including commercial material and at-home viewing conditions—has an effect on audience attitude, mood, and program involvement, it is inappropriate to blame the syndicated services for all inaccuracies in audience counts and program ratings. Advertisers and their agencies have also played a role in creating the program environment and have thus contributed, to some degree, to inaccuracies that may exist in the data used to create the CPM.

Confirming the previous hypotheses would make it appropriate to create what may be termed the *involvement index value* associated with programs by means of a simple equation. This value would then be used to adjust the CPM denominator to reflect the more valuable proportion of the audience watching and involved in the program. The results could mean more accurate cost-efficiency ratios for the media planner, accomplished by means of a simple, straightforward adjustment to existing syndicated data. We describe the procedure for executing these analyses in Chapter 9.

Hypothesis 7: Simulated-living room test environments generate more discriminating advertising response scores. Hypothesis 7 maintains that a simulated natural program exposure environment will yield greater response differences to advertising stimuli tested (i.e., produce more discrimination) than will traditional artificial forced-exposure methods.

Most tests of television program effects and most copy tests (that is, tests of different commercial treatments) have traditionally employed artificial, forced-exposure designs. In a typical study, 100 to 300 respondents, who are not necessarily representative of any particular group within the population, are recruited to watch a program or advertising (or both) under artificial conditions. Not surprisingly, these tests not only yield high scores on the various measures of advertising effectiveness used—only natural because respondents are forced to pay attention—but often, researchers find, they yield nonsignificant differences between treatments. Therefore,

> Hypothesis 7: Close attention to simulating the physical details of the natural viewing environment as well as rigorous adherence to remedial methodological details, including sample, methods, measures, setting, and stimuli, will yield lower advertising response scores (i.e., lower recall, lower levels of pre-post behavioral intentions, change, etc.) but with greater face validity and ability to discriminate between commercials tested in contrast to traditional forced-exposure testing.

Hypothesis 7 proceeds from a general consensus that forced-exposure testing produces inflated response scores and artificial discrimination scores between executions due to the forced attention levels and the absence of natural competing stimuli that may occur in the home environment. Furthermore, although respondents may be voluntarily recruited for the forced-exposure test, this does not mean that the nature of the typical viewing experience was voluntary. This threatens the objectivity with which the basic task is undertaken and, of course, its validity.

Although most copy testers will say that they require reliability, validity, and ability to discriminate in their systems, rarely have they gone to extraordinary efforts to ensure the presence of these criteria. The goal in the typical artificial test is either to determine "the best" execution out of several or to gauge reaction to a single execution. Our position is that this methodology will mislead the advertiser in either task.

It might be reasoned that the higher forced-attention levels under forced-exposure conditions produce a similarly higher degree of perceptual selectivity than would occur under more realistic viewing conditions. Mean recall, for example, will be higher because of the greater opportunity for attention. It may be more variable between executions because there is more effective (artificial) exposure to them. This increased validity, in turn, could heighten the probability of greater individual selectivity between respondents in what they retained from the ads based on their differential reactions to advertising content.

An equally valid argument could be advanced, however, stating that lower levels of variability, and hence discrimination, within as well as between commercial executions is to be expected under most artificial, forced-exposure testing conditions. The comparatively high level and consistency in response scores may yield a concomitantly lower level of variability and ability to discriminate. However, this may be due not only to the forced-attention artificial exposure environment but also to the stimuli and methods of presentation frequently employed, such as "clutter reels" or short, often ambiguous program segments surrounded or punctuated with commercials (often only "roughs").

In the simulated natural program environment, on the other hand, we can expect lower but more realistic advertising response scores as we remove much of the task orientation and artificiality of the test. Interestingly, this may result in enhanced discrimination between executions in the simulated natural environment. The exposure environment and the program environment may interact with one another showing a particular ad as a strong performer in one instance and a weak performer in the next: The primary culprit may as often as not be the intervening impact of program involvement.

4

How the Program Involvement Study Was Conducted

Television program involvement research, as we discussed in Chapters 2 and 3, has been plagued by methodological problems for more than three decades. We designed our research to overcome these methodological shortcomings so that we could truly determine the effect of the program environment on television advertising. The bulk of this book describes our research on television; Chapter 10 reports on additional research to extend these findings from television to print. Those readers with the interest will find the methodological details of the study in the Appendix.

To provide more valid measurement and to allow us to generalize a greater number of conclusions from our findings, we included a larger, more representative sample of adult consumers (not college students) exposed to programs and commercials in three very different viewing environments; better methods for selecting highly involving versus less involving programs; and improved measures of program environment, including a detailed reliability and validity assessment for these measures. In addition, we tested the effects of multiple programs and commercials using a battery of measures of advertising response and employed an analysis of covariance to tease out the "true" effects of our design from spurious effects traceable to random differences between test samples in product usage patterns, television viewing behavior, and demographics.

Prior to program exposure, respondents completed a questionnaire that collected demographic data, television viewing habits, attitudes toward television, and product usage behavior. Respondents were then exposed to one of the four test programs. Following exposure, respondents completed another questionnaire, recording their commercial responses as well as responses to a variety of program-related measures including the program involvement item inventory and alternative measures of program-content reaction.

The resulting program attitude inventory indexes four basic response dimensions: entertainment value, relational connection, values congruency, and an escape/diversion dimension. The authors included responses to two other measures of program content reaction in this study to test the convergent validity of the proposed multidimensional measure, the IPSOS-ASI, Inc., Favorites measure and a liking scale measure.

> This study used five measures: unaided proven recall, aided copy-point recall, commercial credibility, purchase interest, and behavioral intentions change.

This study used five dependent measures to capture the multidimensional nature of advertising effectiveness: unaided proven recall, aided copy-point recall, commercial credibility, purchase interest, and behavioral intentions change.

To examine the relationship between the program environment and commercial effectiveness, we employed multivariate analysis of variance (MANOVA). We did so because, to assess the impact of the program environment on advertising effectiveness more completely, we used multiple commercial response measures, and because among its advantages is the unique multivariate test of factor effects, which permits tests of factor-level differences on the overall response construct. We can draw conclusions regarding overall commercial performance based on statistically accurate testing and need not infer them from univariate analyses on each criterion individually and in isolation. Other advantages include reporting closely related analyses and statistical tests.

FEATURES OF THE STUDY'S DESIGN

To provide more valid measurement and to allow us to generalize a greater number of conclusions from our findings regarding program environment effects, we incorporated several features into the study design. These include:

1. *A larger, more representative sample.* Most television program effects studies, in the negative-effects tradition in particular, were conducted among convenience samples (typically students) of fewer than 150 respondents.

This study's sample consists of 470 women, ages 18 to 49, representing a demographically heterogeneous cross-section of the female residents of a large Midwestern metropolitan area. This sample permits cell sizes in each of the three individual treatment conditions that exceed the total number of respondents used in many of the previous investigations. Furthermore, the issue of validity associated with student samples is not a problem as in some previous investigations (Morgan, 1979; Soley & Reid, 1983). Together, this sample's size and mix provide significant improvements to internal validity and findings that can be generalized.

2. *Improved operating definition of the program environment.* Most television program research limits measurement of the program environment to a single item or a one-dimensional measure of program content reaction under artificial viewing conditions, or under uncontrolled conditions, as in the typical on-air study.

In contrast, this study employs a multiple-treatment experimental design with appropriate levels of controlled conditions, from the obvious to the unobtrusive, including a unique, simulated natural viewing environment as well as the traditional artificial, forced-exposure condition. The measurement of program content reaction is multidimensional within each environment. The study design offers several significant advantages:

a. We are able to expand the operating definition of program environment from a solitary focus on program content effects to include effects of the surrounding reception environment in which the program is viewed.

b. It is possible to make direct comparisons between results obtained under artificial and natural viewing conditions, within the same study.

c. In contrast to most uncontrolled on-air, natural environment testing, this study's measurement of a wide range of respondent personal attitudes, product usage patterns, and TV viewing characteristics allows detailed testing of findings within cells for any significant effects of these potential covariates on the central relationships we examine.

3. *Improved measures of program involvement.* We believe it very unlikely that one can adequately assess the true nature of program content reaction effects on advertising response using a single and frequently heavily judgmental content-response dimension/measure such as "tense" versus "relaxed." Relevant find-

ings in related research areas appear to bear out this contention. Analyses of the attitudinal determinants of TV program preferences as well as analyses of affective responses to advertisements have revealed the multidimensional nature of consumer attitudes. We also believe that many of the same dimensions associated with attitudes in these contexts are of explanatory value in our research as well. As defined in this investigation, therefore, program attitude is multidimensional, measured in part along dimensions found to be significant in related research—particularly those found to explain the variability in viewer program preferences.

4. *Reliability and validity assessment.* We have taken considerable effort to establish the reliability and validity of the unique program attitude measures we employ in this investigation.

5. *An improved set of stimuli.* Several previous program environment studies have involved the forced exposure of respondents to a single artificially constructed program segment in which similarly artificial commercials were embedded. The researchers then drew conclusions concerning the nature and direction of program environment effects, in the majority of cases without considering the potential reactivity associated with such manipulations.

This study exposed respondents to one of four different full-length episodes of popular one-hour network programs (the program plus commercials). Actual commercials not previously aired in the test area were embedded into the programs at natural program breaks, and realistic program fade-in and fade-out occurred at the beginning and end of the program and at commercial breaks during the program. In addition, we took steps to simulate an in-home setting in the natural environment condition. These steps were intended to produce greater response variability while significantly enhancing our ability to generalize the findings.

6. *Multiple measures of advertising response.* Many previous studies of program environment effects employed a single advertising effectiveness measure, usually some variant of commercial recall. Consistent with current theory and practice, this investigation acknowledges commercial response as multidimensional, and we measure it using a range of standard industry approaches from recall to persuasion. Restricting advertising response to single dimensions (such as recall), albeit with several different measures of the same dimension, can be expected to provide a misleading impression of actual commercial performance (Young, 1972) and may limit the conclusions that one can draw concerning the relationship between program environment and advertising effectiveness (Clancy, 1990; Haley & Baldinger, 1991; Lloyd, 1996; Yuspeh, 1979).

7. *Analysis of covariance on observed effects.* Following the primary analysis, we have used covariance analysis to determine whether observed effects reflect the impact of the independent variable alone, uncontaminated by respondent differences.

> These seven features provide the means to investigate the origins and probable causes of the disagreement in the literature over the direction of program environment.

These seven features provide the basis for more valid testing of key program-environment research hypotheses while facilitating findings that are more general than previous studies. Equally important, they provide the means to investigate the origins and probable causes of the disagreement in the literature over the direction of program environment effects.

WHO MADE UP THE SAMPLE

The sample used in the experiment consisted of 470 female heads of households, ages 18 to 49, living in a major Midwestern metropolitan area. We chose women because prior research had shown them to be the primary purchase decision makers for the product categories represented in the test commercials. Future research should extend this work geographically, to men, and to both under-18 and over-50-year-old consumers. We recruited respondents using a random-digit dialing probability procedure and offered a monetary incentive for their participation. During the recruitment process, we collected basic demographic information from each potential respondent to assure that

1. The total sample would represent area residents demographically
2. We could randomly assign respondents to one of the three day-parts during which testing was conducted
3. We could randomly assign respondents to one of three treatment conditions and one of four TV programs in such a way as to ensure that demographic variability would be relatively constant within each cell.

A subsequent follow-up call to each potential respondent confirmed her participation and assigned her a time to report to the test facility. We scheduled appointments over a period of several days and evenings and conducted the experiment at a suburban test facility.

THE BASIC DESIGN OF
THE TELEVISION STUDY

We have asserted that to accurately assess a relationship between program environment and commercial effectiveness requires expanding the operational definition of program environment to include a separate factor that represents differences in surrounding program viewing (and testing) conditions. This argument is made more compelling, given that a principal source of the disagreement concerning the direction of program environment effects may be systematic differences in observed effects depending on whether measurement occurred under artificial or naturalistic testing conditions.

Thus, a fundamental methodological requirement was the ability to assess not only the effect of basic differences in viewing conditions but to compare program attitude effects observed in the typical artificial test environment with those observed in an environment representative of natural viewing conditions. This is best accomplished within a research design that incorporates appropriate controls over sample and method variation, stimulus presentation, respondent differences, and so forth—in other words, a controlled laboratory design (unobtrusive in the naturalistic treatment, with multiple experimental treatment or exposure conditions).

The alternative—for example, to use an on-air test to measure natural environment effects and a separate forced-exposure theater test to measure artificial environmental effects—would contribute little toward resolving the basic issue. Other alternative designs providing the necessary controls were not feasible. This is apparent when one considers the level of control needed to make a meaningful contribution toward resolving the disagreement. To conclude that observed effects within treatment conditions cannot be reasonably attributed to extraneous factors requires controlled exposure to, in this case, one of three viewing conditions and one of four programs such that similar proportions of demographically matched respondents within each of the exposure conditions view the same programs and commercials.

TABLE 4.1 Experimental Design by Day-Part

	Program				
Day Part	One	Two	Three	Four	Total
Morning	40	42	37	37	156
Afternoon	39	42	38	38	157
Evening	41	41	37	38	157
Total	120	125	112	113	470

Respondent assignments first called for dividing the sample by day-part (morning, afternoon, and evening sessions) and test program (one of four), maintaining constant demographic variability within each of the resulting 12 cells. This design ensured an approximately equal number of respondents for each of the three day-parts and for each of the four test programs, about 40 respondents per day-part, per program, with constant demographic variability (Table 4.1). This procedure controlled for possible viewing-time effects on results while ensuring adequate representation of working women in the sample.

In addition to day-part and test program assignments, we assigned respondents to one of three exposure conditions:

1. An artificial, forced-exposure viewing condition with no distractions present
2. A hand-held commercial rating device for registering reaction to commercial and program material
3. A simulated natural viewing condition with typical in-home distractions present and characterized by freely motivated viewing (see Table 4.2)

TABLE 4.2 Experimental Design by Viewing Condition

	Program				
Viewing Condition	One	Two	Three	Four	Total
Artificial (no distractions)	37	43	38	40	158
Artificial (with hand-held meter)	41	42	37	41	161
Simulated-natural (real world distractions)	42	40	37	32	151
Total	120	125	112	113	470

TABLE 4.3 Stimulus Materials

A. Test Programs	
Program	*Impact Rating*[a]
1	High
2	High
3	Low
4	Low

B. Commercials		
Viewing Order	*Commercial*	*Test or Clutter*
1	Trash bags	Test
2	Credit card	Clutter
3	Mouthwash	Test
4	Soft drink	Clutter
5	Mustard	Test
6	Corporate advertiser	Clutter
7	Light bulbs	Test
8	Home video game	Clutter

a. Impact index scores are based on viewer responses to two questions reflecting their reactions to program content and indexed to a scale of 0 to 100.

STIMULUS MATERIALS
THE STUDY EMPLOYED

To ensure a sufficient level of response variability and to enhance our ability to generalize the findings, we used four very different programs as commercial carriers in the experiment, each a popular prime-time weekly show. They included a comedy, a drama, a mystery, and a Sunday evening news program. Four major broadcast television networks were represented in the group of programs selected. We did not take any formal steps to ensure that the programs constituted a representative sampling of prime-time network fare, as the intention was simply to provide a reasonably diversified mix of programs.

> We chose examples of involving and noninvolving prime-time programs, based on a proprietary television program impact study that rated the programs.

Nevertheless, we did take steps to provide examples of what could be considered involving and noninvolving prime-time programs. Selection according to this criterion (Table 4.3) was based on a proprietary television program viewing study undertaken among a cross-section of more than 1,000 adult consumers. Two of the programs were rated as high impact and two as low impact.

Had the study's objectives included the ability to generalize about the performance of specific programs as commercial carriers, it would have been appropriate to include several episodes of each program in the experiment. This would have been necessary to reflect the significant variability found in viewer ratings, episode to episode, in the case of certain programs (Yuspeh, 1979).

As our objective was, however, to test whether higher levels of viewer involvement in programming were accompanied by higher advertising effectiveness scores, this level of experimental complexity was unnecessary. A sufficient level of response variability and ability to generalize requires only that an attempt be made to provide some diversification in program audience and content. Then, if commercial effectiveness can be shown to vary with viewer involvement, the next step is to determine whether programs systematically vary in their ability to involve the viewer over individual episodes.

A total of eight 30-second commercials were inserted into each program at natural program breaks, retaining realistic program fade-out and fade-in at the beginning and end of each break. Each program carried the same eight commercials in the same order. Although commercial order rotation would have been desirable from a methodological standpoint, other considerations rendered rotation impractical here. Although only four test commercials were used, proper rotation would require 24 different combinations. Dividing the total sample (470) by 24 order combinations would leave fewer than 20 respondents per combination and 5 respondents per position, which would have eliminated any meaningful testing for position effects and made it impractical to assign respondents by day-part.

Furthermore, this research focuses on overall commercial response rather than response to individual commercials or the effects of their position within programs. As a result, more immediate considerations outweighed the need to incorporate controls for these factors. For example, we took steps to ensure a constant level of demographic variability within the 12 experimental cells while providing an equal number of demographically matched respondents per program, per day-part.

All four test commercials advertised consumer packaged goods, and each represented a new campaign not previously aired in the area.

Each break contained two commercials: one test commercial and one clutter commercial for a total of four test and four clutter ads (Table 4.3). All four test commercials advertised consumer packaged goods, and each represented a new campaign not previously aired in the experimental area. Two of these campaigns represented established brands, and two represented new brands. Of the clutter commercials (all of which had been aired for a year or more), only one advertised a consumer packaged good. The others were for a financial service, a consumer durable, and a corporate image spot.

The primary function of these clutter commercials was to provide commercial breaks with realistic, diversified content. Although we collected some advertising response measures for each of these ads, there was no intention of including the resulting data in the primary analysis. The reason is that the criterion measures used, as well as the testing methods themselves, have traditionally found application in packaged-goods testing. Applying these methods and measures to a corporate image or financial service product campaign, for example, may be inappropriate because it encourages direct comparison of a corporate image ad's performance with that of a packaged goods ad along the same dimensions.

THE PROCEDURE OF THE TELEVISION STUDY

All respondents who were scheduled to arrive at the test facility at any given time had been assigned to the same exposure condition. Arrival and departure times were scheduled to prevent contact between departing respondents and new arrivals. When a group of respondents had assembled, a research supervisor reiterated the purpose of the research (when initially recruited, respondents had been told that the researchers were interested in their attitudes toward television programs and consumer products) and provided general instructions. They then ushered the respondents into a testing room, which had been set up in advance, in groups of 15 to 20 (groups were somewhat smaller in

TABLE 4.4 Experimental Procedure Flow

ORIENTATION AND GENERAL INSTRUCTIONS
Pre-Assigned Test Conditions

Artificial forced-exposure environment *(No distractions)*	Artificial viewing conditions *(Hand-held meter)*	Simulated-natural environment *(Real world distractions)*

Supervised, Self-Administered Pre-Exposure Questionnaire

- Demographics
- TV viewing habits
- TV attitude inventory
- Product usage behavior
- Pre-constant sum measure[a]

TEST PROGRAM RESPONSE (with 8 commercials embedded)
Supervised, Self-Administered Post-Exposure Questionnaire

Post Questionnaire A	• Unaided (proven) recall[a] • Post-constant sum measure[a]
Post Questionnaire B	• Partially and fully aided commercial and copy-point recall[a] • Commercial (copy-point) credibility • Attention measure • Unidimensional industry content reaction measures • Multidimensional program involvement inventory • Fictive purchase inventory[a] • Miscellaneous

a. Criterion measures described in chapter.

the case of the simulated natural environment condition). Table 4.4 summarizes the procedure flow.

Those assigned to the artificial, no-distractions condition were led into an undecorated room with folding chairs arranged in a semicircle directly in front of a video monitor. They were instructed to view the entire program/commercial tape without conversing with fellow respondents.

Those assigned to the other artificial condition were similarly situated and instructed but were given a wireless hand-held device with which to register their moment-to-moment reactions to the stimulus material throughout the treatment. These hand-held units were linked to a computer that simultaneously recorded all responses from each viewer.

(We said in Chapter 3 that we initially considered this to be an intermediary distraction condition. This presumption proved to be unfounded, as our analyses showed that people assigned to this treatment group exhibited scores on most measures that were not different statistically from those in the other artificial, forced-exposure condition.)

Finally, respondents assigned to the simulated natural environment condition were brought into a room about 12 by 20 feet in size, which had been converted to simulate a typical in-home (living room) viewing environment. The room was furnished with a comfortable sofa, several arm chairs, carpeting, and a large coffee table on which were a variety of popular magazines and local newspapers. A 27-inch color video monitor was placed on a television stand in a corner of the room, and a table holding a coffee maker and refreshments was at the rear. Respondents assigned to this treatment condition were encouraged to avail themselves of the refreshments provided, to look through the magazines or converse with others in the room at any time and, in general, to watch television as they might at home. Unobtrusive observation by the authors confirmed that respondents assigned to this room intermittently engaged in all the distractions available.

> A pre-exposure questionnaire collected demographic data and information on television viewing habits, attitudes toward television, and product usage behavior.

Respondents completed a supervised, self-report questionnaire prior to program exposure in each of the treatment conditions. This pre-exposure instrument collected demographic data as well as information on respondent television viewing habits, attitudes toward television, and product usage behavior. A pre-exposure behavioral intentions change constant sum criterion measure was also administered at this time. This consisted of the *pre* measure for the *pre/post* measurement of any change in behavioral intentions toward the test brands after viewing advertising for them. Respondents were then exposed to one of the four test programs, according to cell assignment. (One group in each treatment condition viewed each of the four programs.)

Following exposure, respondents completed another questionnaire in two parts recording their commercial responses as well as responses to a variety of program-related measures including the program involvement item inventory and alternative measures of program-content reaction, such as the IPSOS-ASI Favorites measure and a standard 0-to-10 rating scale (discussed in the following section). Other measures recorded self-reported attention to program material, whether or not the respondent had previously seen either the program or the episode, and whether the test program viewed was a preferred program.

OPERATIONAL DEFINITION OF PROGRAM ATTITUDES

As we have discussed, a basic problem with the available evidence on program environment effects is the ambiguity surrounding the principal independent measure: self-reported program content reaction. It has been labeled, defined, and measured in a variety of ways, but there have been few formal efforts to validate the measures used to specify the domain of content embraced by the labels used.

Mindful of these shortcomings, we established a thorough a priori procedure to ensure the content validity of the multidimensional program involvement measurement scheme this study employs. Briefly, this procedure involved the following steps:

First, we took efforts to specify the domain of content of the construct, program involvement (or the effects of the editorial context, as it has been labeled). This involved a thorough content analysis of the program environment literature and related research, most notably the communications literature dealing with determinants of television program preference and the literature concerning attitudes toward advertisements.

Second, we outlined the principal elements of this domain of content, culminating with an inventory of about 100 items. We then screened these items and selected those that met the following criteria:

- ◈ Repeated explanatory importance across studies
- ◈ The persuasiveness of the theory supporting the association of each element (with program preference formation or commercial attitude formation) including relevant empirical evidence
- ◈ The apparent relevance and applicability of each element (with supporting theory and evidence) in the program involvement context

A logical assumption guiding selection was that key items satisfying these criteria in explaining the origins of program preferences directly correspond to the primary dimensions along which antecedent program attitudes are formed.

Those items satisfying the criteria were then transformed into a 30-statement measurement inventory. Individual items in the inventory were constructed with straightforward, uncomplicated wording, for example, and, in several cases, positive and negative versions of the same item were included with appropriate spacing to disguise the repetition. Responses to each item were recorded on a standard 4-point, forced-choice scale: 1 = *strongly disagree,* 2 = *somewhat disagree,* 3 = *somewhat agree,* and 4 = *strongly agree.*

(We omitted a neutral position—*neither agree nor disagree*—as a potential source of response-style bias. In our research experience, a significant percentage of respondents select the neutral position on attitude scales for reasons other than true neutrality, that is, to get through the interview quickly without thinking. Respondents who volunteered that they "Didn't know" or "Couldn't decide" whether they agreed or not were assigned that neutral position—or a 2.5 if you will—for the purposes of data processing.)

The resulting program attitude inventory indexes four basic response dimensions:

1. *Entertainment value.* This is the fundamental, general element determining program preference and viewing behavior, in keeping with Comstock's (1980) observation that before all else, "television is predominantly entertainment." A similarly general interest-entertainment dimension was found to be particularly significant in explaining program preferences and attitudinal reaction to commercials. Entertainment value is considered to be measured best by several individual but closely related elements. Together, these elements index basic involvement with or attitudes toward programs: general emotional and cognitive impact, self-reported levels of program interest, concentration, and involvement. To neutralize forms of response set (bias), items constructed to measure this, as well as the other dimensions, were presented in positively and negatively worded versions.

2. *Relational connection.* As with the remaining dimensions, this criterion represents a more specific and distinctly separate measure of viewer involvement. It reflects the highly significant personal relevance factors repeatedly found to underlie both program preferences and, in an altered context, attitudes toward commercials. As defined here, the relational dimension reflects Comstock's (1977) definition, namely, program content is considered pertinent by the viewer in terms of related personal experiences and identification with the characters and situations depicted. Comstock (1980) suggests that this criterion also indicates the instructional role of programming: "Television entertainment is particularly likely to function as instruction where persons portrayed are perceived by viewers as somehow similar to themselves" (p. 92). Theory suggests that empathy and feelings of affiliation as well as vicarious involvement

inspired by program content are related reactions and will also be indexed by this dimension.

3. *Values congruency.* This dimension is based, in part, on the multi-aspect modeling or personal identity element that Eastman (1979) found to be a significant explanation for program preferences; it was variously labeled by other researchers. By direct extension of the underlying theory, substantiated and extended by Lee and Lee (1995) in terms of their Social Learning dimension, these studies suggest that reaction to program content is closely related to an individual's personal outlook, and to any parallels "picked up" between program content, actors, and so forth, in terms of the way program elements either reinforce or reject viewers' values, ethical standards, and convictions. Program preferences have also been expressed in terms of a somewhat related socialization function.

By implication, it is logical to suggest that values congruency may be evaluated not only in regard to the self, but with respect to children. The suitability of program material for children's viewing in terms of both social learning and the inculcation of correct values may be of dominant importance in assessing the values congruency aspect of program attitudes for many adults. Because a large percentage of network prime-time programming is accessible to children, adult attitudes toward programs—including the decision to view certain programs—may be partially expressed in terms of reaction to program elements, such as language, violence, sexual content, and theme or story line, from the perspective of perceived suitability for children's viewing. Thus, the hypothesized values congruency dimension of program attitude is designed to assess general value-based reaction ("I wish there were more people in real life like the 'good guys' in this program—it would make the world a better place to live in"), as well as child-oriented value reaction ("This show teaches young people poor values").

4. *Escape/diversion dimension.* Tannenbaum (1980), Levy (1978), Eastman (1979), Lee and Lee (1995), and others found this popularly perceived use of television viewing to be a significant determinant of program preference. Going beyond general entertainment, this dimension is hypothesized to reflect the ability of program content to distract viewers from their everyday problems and worries, to provide a diversionary tension-release, and to alter the viewer's current mood. While it is possible that program content could alter the viewer's mood negatively, as in terms of fear or alienation, it is more likely that in typical network programming, this effect will be manifested in mood elevation and a lifting of the spirits.

> Whether a program that triggers involved viewing does so through a personally positive or negative theme or plot, there is still involvement in program content.

We therefore captured this dimension of program attitudes with items such as, "Programs like this put me in good spirits and make me laugh" and "This is one of those uplifting programs that helps you forget about your own problems." We should note that several consumer researchers consider, and have substantiated, that "involvement is involvement." In other words, whether the program that has triggered involved viewing has done so through personally positive or negative, pleasant or unpleasant characters, theme, or plot, it is still involvement in program content, with similar dimensionality and with similar enhanced receptivity toward the program break contents.

Furthermore, in what can only be viewed as a single dimension of related support, LaTour, Snipes, and Bliss (1996) found, in the specific case of fear appeals, that advertiser reluctance to employ this device was for the most part misplaced. Examining the use of, and testing the impact of, fear appeals led the authors to conclude that they can be every bit as effective, if not more so, than more common types of appeals. Although distant and distinct from our research, the findings nevertheless provide a level of correlative support to our primary contention here.

We carried out additional tests to determine the validity of these procedures for measurement of program attitudes during the preliminary data analysis stage (Chapter 6).

ADDITIONAL MEASURES OF PROGRAM ATTITUDES OR INVOLVEMENT

We included responses to two other measures of program content reaction in this study to test the convergent validity of the proposed multidimensional measure and to test Hypothesis 5's new measure. (This is the hypothesis that multidimensional measures of program involvement produce more reliable and valid findings.) These additional measures are:

1. *IPSOS-ASI, Inc., Favorites* measure was used for subsequent convergent validity tests and in comparative explanatory significance testing to confirm Hypothesis 5. Content reaction is assessed by responses to the following question along a 5-point scale: "Do you consider the program _____ to be: 1) Your Favorite, 2) One of Your Favorites, 3) Good, 4) Fair, or 5) Poor?"

2. *Liking scale* measure (in this case based on an 11-point, 0-10 scale) is similar in intent to those used in many previous on-air tests of program environment effects and was used here both in convergence testing and testing of Hypothesis 5. Content reaction is assessed in response to the following question and scale: "For the episode of _____ that you just watched, please give your personal rating based on a scale from 0-10 where . . . "

OPERATIONAL DEFINITION OF ADVERTISING EFFECTIVENESS

Advertising effectiveness is assessed against multiple criteria both for well-documented theoretical reasons and for reasons specifically related to the objectives of this study.

For example, the question of whether advertising effectiveness is more appropriately measured in terms of recall or persuasion has been the subject of well-known debate for years within the advertising industry (Blair, 1987; Clancy & Shulman, 1995; Gibson, 1983; Haley & Baldinger, 1991; Haskins, 1964; Lloyd, 1987; Ross, 1982; Young, 1972).

A recent study that addresses the role of recall versus persuasion was reported by Lodish et al. (1995) and involved an analysis of 389 real world split-cable television advertising experiments. In contrast to the work of Blair (1987) and Haley and Baldinger (1991), this study found no clear relationship between either recall or persuasion scores and sales effects. Commenting on the Blair study, which had reported a "perfect relationship" between persuasion scores and test success, Lodish et al. say they were unable to replicate these results. The inconsistent findings from copy-test research studies over this long period of time, coupled with the knowledge that the authors in some cases are the owners/managers of firms marketing copy-testing services (not the case of Lodish et al.), results in continuing confusion about what works and what does not work.

An increasingly prevalent viewpoint, however, is that measuring commercial performance must involve evaluation against a number of different yardsticks because the individual measures frequently used are not synonymous—they do not tap the same dimensions of response. Similarly, there is no evidence to suggest the superiority of any one measure over all others in an accurate assessment of a commercial's effectiveness (Ernst & Verlag, 1978; Kover, Goldberg, & James, 1995; Rossiter & Eagleson, 1994; Wind & Denny, 1974; Yuspeh, 1979).

It is also generally acknowledged that different measures, assessing different dimensions of advertising response, may be appropriate depending on the nature of the commercial. In her landmark examination of copy-testing methods and measures, for example, Young (1972) concluded that recall measures may be adequate for assessing the communications value of explicit or factual advertising but are inappropriate for implicit or image-related copy. For these less explicit commercials, higher order response measures such as persuasion and purchase interest are considered more appropriate for gauging commercial performance. In our research, we used commercials with both explicit as well as implicit copy.

The use of multiple criteria was also motivated by practical considerations more closely aligned with the objectives of this study. First, it is clear that commercial performance can be more thoroughly and accurately assessed using multiple response dimensions. Second, to make the conclusions reached more meaningful, the measures selected should be representative of a range of currently accepted commercial testing criteria. Finally, to facilitate comparative discussions, some of the response dimensions used should be equivalent to those employed in previous program environment effects studies.

> Five dependent measures of advertising effectiveness represent both the recall-related dimensions of advertising response as well as the behavior-related.

In this study, we have used five dependent measures to define advertising effectiveness. Those measures represent both the memory function, or recall-related, dimensions of advertising response as well as the so-called higher order, or attitude and behavior-related, response dimensions. All are standard industry measures of advertising effectiveness. Responses for computing these measures were collected for each of the test commercials, as well as a more limited number for the clutter commercials, and in the case of some of the measures, for additional product categories not represented by the embedded advertising. The measures and their derivation are as follows:

1. *Unaided proven recall.* For each respondent and test commercial, spontaneous proven audiovisual and main point playback are measured. To prove recall of a test commercial, the respondent was required to have played back, unaided, the name and at least one of the key, unique execution or copy elements appearing in the advertisement in response to the following questions: "Write down everything you remember *seeing* and *hearing* in this commercial," and, "What was the main point of this commercial? What were they trying to tell you about the product?" This general measure has an extensive history of use in advertising research (Arnold & Bird, 1982) and has been found to be related to subsequent purchase of the advertised brand (Bogart, Tolley, & Ornstein, 1970; Stewart, 1986).

2. *Aided copy-point recall.* Respondents were presented with a series of copy statements, true as well as fictitious, that might have been in the test commercials. Respondents were then asked to indicate, for each brand separately, those statements they remembered having been made in each ad. Respondent scores were calculated as the ratio of actual (i.e., true) copy points recalled with prompting to the total copy points recalled for each test brand, averaged over the four test commercials. Again, aided copy-point recall is one of the most fundamental and accepted measures of commercial evaluation; together with proven message playback, it represents two of the most frequently used measures of commercial effectiveness in advertising research and in the more specialized area of program environment effects research.

3. *Commercial credibility.* After indicating aided copy-point recall, respondents were asked to indicate for the same sets of true and fictitious copy statements, those that they believed concerning the test brands. Respondent scores were computed as the ratio of true statements believed to the total number of true statements for each test ad, averaged across the four test brands. Measures of the believability of copy points routinely appear on practitioners' lists of key commercial evaluation measures (Dunn, 1984) because it has been suggested that eliciting meaningful emotional responses to message material may depend on the believability of the execution (Aaker & Myers, 1982). More recently, the notion of credibility has taken on importance as a significant concept in brand equity research (Aaker, 1996; Herbig & Milewicz, 1995).

4. *Purchase interest.* We gave respondents a shopping list of 10 different product categories and brands widely available locally. In each case, the brands on the list represented 80% or more (often 95% or more) of the sales of these product categories in the market in which the research was conducted. The categories represented a mix of the test brand categories, clutter brand categories, and "filler" categories designed to keep the respondents guessing as to what the research was all about.

A postexposure count was made of the number of times respondents indicated the test brand as the brand they intended to buy the next time they made a purchase in the product category. Responses were elicited by the question, "The next time you make a purchase in each of the product categories listed below, which *one brand* will you buy?" Measures of "the brand you intend to buy on the next purchase occasion" are also extensively documented in the wider literature as part of a class of behavioral measures designed to measure how much interest the advertised brand has stimulated (Aaker & Myers, 1982).

5. *Behavioral intentions change.* Constant sum scales representing a mix of test brand, clutter, and once again "filler" product categories were administered to each respondent both prior to and following program exposure. As before, the brands within each category represented the lion's share of sales in each category in the research market. On the pre-exposure measure, respondents indicated the number of times they had bought various brands, including test brands, during the last 10 purchase occasions. On the identical postexposure measure, a respondent indicated the number of times out of the next 10 purchase occasions she planned to buy the same brands. Each respondent's score on this measure was an average of the pre-post difference in test brand constant-sum ratings across the four test brands. Previous research has shown the constant sum scales to be a stable predictor of actual purchase behavior (Achenbaum, 1966; Axelrod, 1968; Haley & Case, 1979). True, the post-only with control group approach is generally considered superior for assessing attitude (or behavioral intention) shift, rather than the pre-post measure employed here. Because that approach was not feasible in this experiment, however, pre-exposure measurements were taken as a control for pre-exposure attitudes.

One measure of advertising response that the first study did not capture, and that we realized in retrospect would have improved our criterion variables considerably, is consumer attitudes toward the commercials. The Advertising Research Foundation's Copy Test Validity study (Haley, 1990a, 1990b) heightened awareness of the importance of this dimension; hence, we incorporated this potential predictor of ad effectiveness into our most recent media impact study, reported in Chapter 10.

We present the tests of our hypotheses and analyses in the next five chapters, with additional notes on methodologies in the Appendix. As will be evident, we used multivariate analyses of variance (MANOVA) and multivariate analyses of covariance (MANCOVA) to explain each of the hypotheses described in Chapter 3. We made a detailed comparison between the forced-artificial and simulated natural viewing environments. Our goal was to provide insights into the probable origins of the dispute in the literature concerning the true direction of program environment effects, whether program involvement helps or hurts the commercials.

We used MANCOVA to determine whether the observed effects of program involvement varied to any significant extent with differences in respondents' demographic characteristics (age, education, and family income), frequency of purchase of brands in test-brand product categories, and attitudes toward the value of TV viewing.

Furthermore, because we assume that results obtained in the simulated natural environment will be more representative of actual in-home viewing effects than those obtained from artificial forced-exposure testing, examining the comparative explanatory capabilities of the two measurement approaches (Hypothesis 5) is more appropriately conducted in the simulated natural viewing environment.

Before we tested this hypothesis, however, we analyzed the integrity of the relationship between program involvement and advertising effectiveness observed within the simulated natural environment via MANCOVA. The objective was to ensure that the observed relationship was uncontaminated to any significant extent by extraneous factors.

CHAPTER

5

Measuring Program Involvement on Several Dimensions

In virtually every chapter thus far, we have asserted that program involvement is a multidimensional construct that requires measuring program reaction along thoroughly researched, multiple dimensions of cognition and affect (Hypothesis 1).

Our preliminary stage analyses confirmed that first hypothesis: Program content or program attitude is indeed a multidimensional construct requiring multiple measures of attitudinal response, which earlier studies failed to adequately reveal.

Our results will demonstrate that the key determinant of program content attitude may be termed Program Involvement, itself a multi-aspect measure that includes emotional impact, entertainment value, identification, affiliation, and information functions.

The results also provide strong evidence of the content as well as construct validity of a first dimension, indicating the potential for further item development and testing to establish the validity of the secondary or more specialized dimensions of program involvement.

Our findings provide strong intuitive support to the basic contention that a simple constraining concept, such as the degree of tension or suspensefulness induced by program material, incompletely assesses program involvement.

Similarly, the findings suggest that unidimensional summary-affect measures such as "liking" or "favorites" scales may inadequately reveal the nature of content reaction.

Finally, we divided respondent standardized program involvement scale scores into low, moderate, and high involvement levels on each of the three program involvement dimensions to facilitate the application of analysis of variance models during the analysis stages of investigating relationships between program environment variables and the commercial effectiveness criteria.

THE DIMENSION OF PROGRAM INVOLVEMENT

To reach these results, we factor-analyzed the multi-item program involvement inventory to detect the presence of underlying dimensions of program content involvement. Although we anticipated four dimensions (factors), we ultimately extracted only three, together explaining about 60% of the variance in respondent involvement in the program viewed (as measured by the item inventory). This solution, unlike the four-factor solution, achieves a higher level of clarity of interpretation.

The initial item composition of each of these factors (prior to the results of item analysis), together with basic descriptive statistics, appears in Table 5.1. The items selected load exclusively or predominantly on the factor under which they are listed.

The first program attitude dimension extracted may be thought of as a comprehensive representation of the overall value of television programming to the viewer, expressed by Comstock (1980) as entertainment. Due to the rather all-encompassing nature of this factor—itself multidimensional—and for reasons of clarity of analytical exposition (as we will demonstrate shortly), we have labeled this dimension Program Involvement.

The individual viewer, of course, subjectively defines this concept across a variety of elements ranging from theme and story line to characterization. It is measured in terms of the ability of program material to influence recognized indicators of the effects of these multiple elements, specifically: emotional and informational impact/value and interest, involvement, and concentration levels. In this, the first factor conforms to an originally hypothesized entertainment value dimension.

Consequently, a primary dimension of program content involvement is expressed, not surprisingly, in terms of the program's capacity to perform its

TABLE 5.1 Item Composition of Program Involvement Factors

Factor 1: Program Involvement		Factor 2: Values Incongruency	
Factor loading	Item (Abbreviated)	Factor loading	Item (Abbreviated)
.82	The characters in story true to life and very believable	.87	So much sex and violence that I wouldn't want children to watch it
−.81	Never got involved in this program like I do when watching a really good show	−.84	Language acceptable even for children
.80	Parts in this show really touched my feelings	−.82	If this were a movie, it would receive a "G" (general audience) rating
−.79	I never became too interested in program, too easy to predict ending	.75	Too much adult material for a prime-time show
.79	Program was cut above average; thought provoking as well as entertaining	.62	This show teaches young people poor values
.78	Show had ability to make me feel some of same things as characters at times	.58	Some of the humor a bit tasteless

Factor 3: Mood Enhancement	
Factor loading	Item (Abbreviated)
−.75	Some of the scenes were farfetched and unrealistic
.73	I was really involved in the program. I wish it had lasted longer
−.72	The attempts at humor in program were forced and silly, not funny
−.71	I didn't relate to any of the characters in this program
−.71	If were watching at home, I would have switched channel
.68	One of those programs that really makes you concentrate
−.67	This program didn't affect my feelings.
.67	I would be disappointed if missed another program like this
.59	Really understood how characters felt–have been in situations like that myself
−.56	Can honestly say I learned nothing new or interesting
−.54	Was interested in program for first few minutes, didn't pay much attention after

Factor 3 items:

.72	This was one of the funniest shows I've ever seen
.67	Programs like this put me in good spirits and make me laugh

primary function—to entertain the viewer. (This factor explains more than two thirds of all explained variance.)

Of additional interest is the finding that personal reaction to the characters in the program is a dominant aspect of program involvement. We define and measure these personal reactions in terms of relational and affiliational sentiments aroused by identification with character(s), the circumstances they confront, and the feelings they express.

It is apparent that these two dimensions, entertainment and character identification, originally hypothesized as separate, are in fact components of the same dimension. This is again consistent with Comstock's perspective on television entertainment as having informational as well as entertainment value in a wide range of possible perceptual and attitudinal aspects. When, for example, viewers identify with a character or perceive people portrayed as being somehow like themselves, or how they would like to be, entertainment performs an instructional or aspirational role function.

This factor is, therefore, reminiscent of the dominant entertainment and personal relevance dimensions that both program preference and advertising attitude researchers have found, and it is consistent with the spirit of Krugman's (1983) definition of involvement as "personal connections" between viewer and stimulus elements. Furthermore, as in the Arnold and Bird (1982) study, the most significant commercial factor found to be associated with higher commercial response scores was termed "involved," the principal elements of which were empathetic reactions and identification with stimulus elements.

THE DIMENSION OF VALUES INCONGRUENCY

The second factor, interpreted as Values Incongruency, resembles the personal values-oriented personal identity and socialization dimensions that were strong factors found to underlie program preferences in the mass communications literature. As hypothesized, this factor seems to suggest that adult viewer concerns about the appropriateness of program material for younger viewers aired during prime-time hours are a significant part of program attitudes.

Values Incongruency is essentially a negative dimension that reflects a disconnect between program material and viewer values, particularly those values they consider desirable for children. Although this factor is significant according to the factor-analytic criteria and does account for 22% of the explainable variance, it is clearly secondary in importance to the Program Involvement dimension.

> Values Incongruency is worth further development in light of the "New Puritanism" that has motivated attempts to lobby against "distasteful" elements.

This Values Incongruency dimension is worth further development, however, in light of the so-called "New Puritanism" that has motivated many viewers/groups to attempt to lobby against the sex, violence, offensive language and other "distasteful" elements to be found in much of television's prime-time programming. This movement has gathered momentum during the past 8 to 10 years, resulting in potential congressional intervention on behalf of these petitioners. For now, however, major program carriers (with the exception of NBC) have agreed to a multilevel content-rating system to be displayed in association with their programming (Fitzgerald, 1997). Knowing the nature and underlying motives of movement members, whether they are self-oriented, protectionist, sociocultural, or prompted by some fundamental changes in audience agenda, would be of great value to programmers and advertisers.

Interpretation of the third factor, Mood Enhancement, is somewhat conjectural due to its comparatively weak factor structure. This is due in part to the factor's ability to account for only 8% of the explained variance. As this factor currently stands, there are relatively few item loadings, and of these, two items are somewhat shared with one of the other factors, indicating a less than desirable interdependence and a rather murky interpretation.

> The factor indicates a nascent Mood Enhancement dimension, suggesting that viewer involvement may be based somewhat on the material's ability to lift the spirits.

Furthermore, average intercorrelations among the items that make up this factor are comparatively low. Nevertheless, the factor is intuitively and strongly indicative of at least a nascent Mood Enhancement dimension, suggesting that viewer involvement with programs may be based in some measure on the material's ability to lift the spirits. Although this function is obvious and expected, it is not directly apparent that this factor is, as originally hypothesized (based largely on the findings of Eastman, 1979; Lee & Lee, 1995; and others) a clear escape/diversion dimension. The last two items listed in Table 5.1, which appear to reflect an escapist reaction ("One of those uplifting programs . . . " and "Part of the fun in watching a show like this . . . "), exhibit marginal factor loadings, and the two high-loading items relate more to the perceived humorous qualities of program material. Thus, this third factor provides some evidence for an incipient Mood Enhancement dimension to program involvement but will require additional item development and testing.

Factor analysis results, therefore, confirm the hypothesized multidimensional nature of program attitudes or content involvement. The resulting factor structure differs somewhat from the specific form we originally hypothesized, but it still strongly supports our contention that most other researchers have inadequately assessed program attitude or program content involvement. Not only do our findings demonstrate the highly restrictive nature of perceived tension or suspensefulness as measures of program attitude, the results also lend support to the contention that summary affect measures such as multipoint program-liking scales fail to provide an adequate understanding of the specific determinants of program involvement. Given a significant relationship between program involvement and commercial effectiveness, we need this information to understand why a television commercial performs more effectively in one program than in another.

ITEM ANALYSIS AND VALIDATION

A persistent problem with the available evidence on program environment effects is the ambiguity surrounding the principal independent measure: involvement or self-reported program content reaction. Individual researchers have defined it in a variety of ways but evidence of the validity of the operational definitions and measures they introduce is relatively weak.

It is partly with these shortcomings in mind that we undertook the extensive a priori item-analysis procedures discussed in the Appendix, to establish the content validity of the multidimensional program attitude measurement approach used in this study. Following the preliminary factor analysis, we reverse-coded the negative items and computed standardized scores for all items in Table 5.1. We then undertook item analysis in an effort to arrive at separate item combinations, one representing each of the original factors, yielding maximum

TABLE 5.2 Reliability Analysis Results for Three Program-Involvement Factor Scales

| | | Viewing Condition | | |
	Full Sample (n = 451)	Artificial Forced-Exposure Treatment 1 (n = 155)	Artificial (Hand-held meter) Treatment 2 (n = 156)	Simulated Natural Environment Treatment 3 (n = 140)
Program Involvement				
Coefficient alpha	.92	.91	.92	.92
Alternative forms alphas	.88 .82	.87 .79	.89 .82	.88 .83
Correlation between forms	.82	.80	.84	.84
Values Incongruency				
Coefficient alpha	.86	.85	.88	.85
Alternative forms alphas	.70 .75	.70 .73	.72 .79	.68 .74
Correlation between forms	.82	.81	.84	.82
Mood Enhancement				
Coefficient alpha	.73	.68	.75	.74
Alternative forms alphas	.39 .68	.33 .57	.36 .72	.54 .73
Correlation between forms	.61	.57	.64	.54

levels of internal consistency and criterion validity. We used item combinations performing best against the test criteria outlined below to construct factor scales. This procedure was designed to produce item clusters that hang together, providing reliable measures of program attitude dimensions that at the same time predict advertising response. For the details of the technical aspects of the item analysis, see the Appendix.

Our search for tangible evidence of the content validity of the program attitude measures was provided by factor and item analysis results:

1. Factor analysis confirms the existence of the key program attitude dimensions as evidenced by their separate contributions to the explained item variance and by the exclusivity of factor loadings, primarily in the cases of Factors 1 and 2.
2. Item analysis and reliability coefficients confirm that the subsets of items have high internal consistency and reliably measure the same elements of the construct. As Table 5.2 indicates, further evidence reveals that this high internal consistency is maintained across experimental treatments.
3. Correlations of the program attitude measures with commercial measures, or measures of program content reaction used in previous studies, demonstrate the

TABLE 5.3 Results of Bivariate Correlations of the Three Program-Attitude Scales With Alternate Measures by Viewing Condition

	Program Involvement		Values Incongruency		Mood Enhancement	
	ASI Favorites Measure	0-10 Liking Scale	ASI Favorites Measure	0-10 Liking Scale	ASI Favorites Measure	0-10 Liking Scale
Total Sample	.70	.79	−.27	−.38	.52	.61
Artificial (no distractions)	.70	.80	−.26	−.38	.49	.64
Hand-held commercial rating devices	.75	.82	−.26	−.41	.57	.65
Simulated natural (distractions present)	.67	.75	−.29	−.37	.50	.53

convergence of the dominant first program attitude scale and, to a more modest extent, the third scale, with other measures, both at the full sample level and across treatments (Table 5.3). (We included IPSOS-ASI's 5-point favorites program reaction measure and the 0 to 10 liking scale, discussed earlier, in the original questionnaire for just such comparative purposes.)

These results provide strong support for the content validity of the program attitude measures used in this study, particularly the dominant Program Involvement scale. The failure of the Values Incongruency scale to demonstrate strong, consistent convergence with other measures is insufficient to invalidate its role in program attitude or content involvement measurement for at least two reasons. First, the values scale assesses attitudinal reaction on a different and more specialized level than does the more general program involvement scale or, for that matter, previously used summary measures. Second, unlike these other measures, it does not relate strongly to the dependent advertising response measures.

> This study provides preliminary empirical support to a Mood Enhancement effect by the strong and exclusive loading of two key items on this factor.

The absence of strong correlation with ad response measures, however, only indicates that this dimension, as measured, may not be an influential element of program attitudes as they affect advertising response. It does not mean that the dimension fails to measure some element of program attitudes. Furthermore, it may be that this preliminary analysis incompletely assessed the general personal values component of program attitudes, as mentioned earlier. This is almost certainly the case with the third program attitude scale. There is, however, strong intuitive as well as theoretical support for a significant Mood Enhancement dimension to program involvement. This study provides preliminary empirical support to that effect by the strong and exclusive loading of two key items on this factor, both measuring different aspects of humor: "This was one of the funniest shows I've ever seen," and "Programs like this put me in good spirits and make me laugh." Further item development, perhaps in a somewhat different direction, however, is needed before this dimension can be adequately revealed and validated.

Returning to the dominant Program Involvement scale, additional analyses show preliminary evidence of construct validity:

1. Correlations between this scale and previously used summary program attitude measures, as indicated in Table 5.3, are extremely strong.

2. This scale clearly discriminates between differentially treated respondents as indicated by difference-of-means tests performed on this variable between viewing conditions. These tests reveal a strong ability to discriminate between the simulated natural and each of the other viewing conditions. (We will return to this topic and its importance in Chapter 9.)

In the case of the Values Incongruency scale, however, there are impediments to straightforward testing for construct validity. In the first place, we do not find—nor should we expect to find—convergence of this scale with other, previously employed program attitude measures. That this is a dimension of program content reaction is largely confirmed by factor- and content validity-analysis results. It is, however, a more specific, negative, and less dominant aspect of program attitudes and is not at all comparable to other summary evaluative attitude measures. A more useful indicator of its validity is provided by its distinctiveness, demonstrated by consistently negative correlation with the entertainment value scale and the summary attitude measures. The possibility remains, however, that further item development is needed to fully reveal the role of this dimension in explaining the conformation of program attitudes and their effect on advertising response.

The final Mood Enhancement scale demonstrates some level of convergent validity, but at a lower and less consistent level than the first scale. Discriminate validity is generally lacking. Of the four items associated with this factor, only two exhibit strong and exclusive factor loadings; the remaining two do not exhibit exclusivity: "One of those uplifting programs that helps people forget their problems," and "Part of the fun in watching a show like this is imagining oneself in the same situations." This suggests that we may have tapped into a potentially valid dimension of program attitudes but that the attitude item inventory in this exploratory study has incompletely revealed it.

6

The Hidden Power of Television Programming Revealed

As this chapter will demonstrate, television program involvement has a significant positive effect on commonly employed measures of advertising effectiveness, particularly under simulated natural viewing conditions.

The higher the level of viewer involvement in the program, the greater the measured advertising effectiveness. A variety of multivariate analyses support this conclusion, including repeated attempts to make the relationship disappear by introducing control factors. Time and again, however, the apparent causal linkage between involvement and advertising effects was evident.

Along the road to making this discovery, we found that the single most important determinant of advertising response scores is the environment in which the viewer is exposed to the programming and the advertising. An artificial, forced-exposure setting—one typical of commercial copy testing methodologies—produces inflated scores that are relatively unrelated to program involvement and that, as we will see, suffer from their ability to discriminate. The scores are so high they fail to reveal differences between tested advertising executions. We will discuss this in more detail in Chapter 8.

> The link between program involvement and advertising effectiveness is clearly positive, and we now know why the literature of the past four decades was inconclusive.

The appearance of the program involvement-advertising effects relationship in the simulated natural condition and its failure to appear under artificial forced-exposure conditions appears to have settled the industry's standing debate. For almost 40 years, researchers and theorists have argued whether the link between involvement is positive, negative, or nonexistent. We believe we have solved this mystery, putting the debate to rest. The link between program involvement and advertising effectiveness is clearly positive and just as clearly we now know why the literature of the past four decades was inconclusive.

The methodological foundations for the positive and negative perspectives were dramatically different. Large-scale, natural environment studies with recall as the predominant criterion measure supported the former, whereas small-scale, highly artificial forced-exposure laboratory studies using a variety of response measures characterized the latter. The present study, in which we attempted to control for methodological differences, mitigated the possibility of spurious findings and improved prospects for the truth.

PROGRAM INVOLVEMENT'S RELATIONSHIP TO ADVERTISING RESPONSE

The results presented in Chapter 5 confirmed our first hypothesis. They revealed the existence of multiple reliable and valid measures of television program attitudes, the most important of which we have labeled Program Involvement. Television Program Involvement is a 10-item factor with an aggregate level (split sample) reliability of .98 and an alpha reliability of .92. It is based on items measuring attitude such as, "Parts of this program touched my feelings," "I was really involved in this program," and "This program really made me concentrate."

What we do not yet know, however, is whether this new Program Involvement factor, as hypothesized and suggested by the preliminary analyses, is positively related to advertising response and, if so, for what dimensions and under what circumstances. To test the hypotheses associated with these questions, therefore, we used a multivariate analysis of variance model (MANOVA), described in Chapter 4.

We will cite additional technical details concerning particulars of the MANOVA model as they become relevant. We should reiterate one point, however, to explain why we chose to use MANOVA instead of univariate analysis of variance on each criterion separately.

TABLE 6.1 Advertising Response Variable Intercorrelations

	Behavioral Intentions Change	Copy-Point Credibility	Purchase Interest	Aided Message Recall	Proven Recall
Behavioral intentions change	1.0	.26	*.41*	.16	.06
Copy-point credibility		1.0	*.31*	.72	*.44*
Purchase interest			1.0	.16	.09
Aided message recall				1.0	*.63*
Proven recall					1.0

NOTE: Italicized correlations are so high that they would have distorted traditional univariate tests. Hence, the need for MANOVA.

In the earlier discussion of analysis methods, we suggested that two fundamental reasons led us to the choice of this model. The first is based on statistical grounds. Whenever one expects intercorrelations between the component measures of a composite dependent construct (here, advertising effectiveness), univariate test results are not strictly correct. They are incapable of considering or "adjusting for" the potential impact of these intercorrelations on the overall construct and, hence, on the results. Several correlations that appear in Table 6.1 suggest the justification for MANOVA. Note, for example, the strong correlations between the various recall measures and between themselves and the response vector. Copy-point credibility is slightly tainted, as well.

The second reason is a qualitative extension of the first. The concept advertising effectiveness includes an interrelated range of elements: recall, persuasion, and a number of additional response variables. By examining the effects of the independent variables on this integrated concept, at the same time looking at the singular contributions of each specific component individually, we can determine whether the overall construct, advertising effectiveness, is significantly affected by all independent variables or factors. Subsequently, we can determine the extent to which each individual component contributed to the overall multivariate, or construct-level, results.

ARTIFICIAL VIEWING CONDITIONS INFLATE ADVERTISING RESPONSE SCORES

Our second hypothesis is that viewing conditions affect advertising response measures (ranging from recall to persuasion). The more artificial the

TABLE 6.2 Mean Scores on Five Advertising Response Criteria by Viewing Conditions

Criterion	Viewing Condition[a]	
	Artificial Forced-Exposure Conditions-Combined	Simulated Natural Environment Conditions
Behavioral intentions change[b]	12.9	11.1**
Copy-point credibility[c]	43.6	33.8*
Purchase interest[d]	15.0	15.6**
Aided message recall[e]	69.2	45.5***
Unaided (proven) recall[f]	71.3	41.6***

NOTE: Viewing conditions presented for the first of three two-way models only as discussed in this chapter.
a. Represents the average pre-post change across the four test commercials on a 10-point constant sum scale.
b. Because the scores for the two artificial forced-exposure cells were not significantly different from one another, they are averaged here for analysis.
c. Represents the average percentage of "true" copy points made in the four test commercials that were believed.
d. Represents the average purchase interest score for the four test commercials on a 5-point purchase interest scale.
e. Represents the average percentage of copy points recalled (with prompting) for the four test commercials.
f. Represents the average percentage of unaided proven recall for the four test commercials. Proven recall means clear recall of some visual or audio element of the commercial.
$*.05 \leq p > .01; **.01 \leq p \geq .001; ***p < .001.$

viewing environment, we hypothesized, the more inflated the scores. The data clearly support this hypothesis. Table 6.2 presents the mean scores on the five advertising effectiveness criteria across the two viewing conditions. The mean values in the table represent weighted, marginal means for each response criterion, at each level of the program exposure environment variable for the full sample. The weights are the sums of the individual means, divided by the number of respondents in each cell.

As is readily apparent, the mean response scores are often substantially different between viewing conditions. More specifically, mean response scores for each criterion increase as we move from conditions representative of the freely motivated, in-home viewing environment (the right column) to the highly artificial "theater test" conditions (left column).

> When people are forced to pay attention in an artificial environment, their measures of advertising response are higher than in a "real world" viewing situation.

In other words, the more artificial and unnatural the environment, the higher the response scores. When people are forced to pay attention, their recall scores and other measures of advertising response, not surprisingly, are higher than in a "real world" viewing situation. This increase is most dramatic in the case of commercial recall. Artificially exposed respondents recalled, on average, 69.2% of the copy points made in test commercials with prompting, where respondents in more naturalistic conditions identified only 45.5%. Furthermore, the unaided proven recall level was 71.3%, on average, among those respondents artificially exposed to the advertising across the four test commercials, versus 41.6% among the naturally exposed respondents.

A similar effect is evidenced in the case of higher order response measures, as Table 6.2 makes clear. Under artificial forced-exposure conditions, the mean change in pre-post exposure behavioral intentions toward the four test brands was 12.9%, 16% higher than the positive change in intentions observed among those exposed under simulated natural conditions.

The results of univariate tests of the significance of differences in advertising response between exposure conditions reveal then, as expected, that the main effect of viewing conditions on advertising response is significant for every measure. Thus, Hypothesis 2 is confirmed: Advertising response varies significantly with the opportunity to process focal stimuli as influenced by the differing environmental conditions surrounding television exposure. Furthermore, the direction of these differences underscores the importance of choice of exposure conditions to the collection of representative test scores in all advertising testing.

PROGRAM INVOLVEMENT IS POSITIVELY RELATED TO ADVERTISING RESPONSE

To test our third hypothesis (which states that the more positive the program attitudes—or the more interesting and involving the viewing experience—the more effective the advertising the program carries will be), we examined the relationship between involvement and advertising response separately across the five response criteria (see Table 6.3).

This analysis reveals the hidden power of television programming. For each of the five measures of advertising response, scores rise as the level of program involvement goes from low to high. Among people whose responses place them in the lowest program involvement level, for example, behavioral change (measured on the 10-point constant sum scale) is 9.5%. Among those whose involvement scores are average, behavioral change rises to 12.5%; among people high

TABLE 6.3 The Effects of Program Involvement on Advertising Response

	Advertising Response Criteria								
	Behavioral Intentions Change		Copy-Point Credibility		Purchase Interest		Aided Message Recall		Unaided Proven Recall	
Program Involvement	Mean[a]	Effect[b]	Mean	Effect	Mean	Effect	Mean	Effect	Mean	Effect
Low (unfavorable)	9.5	-2.61***	35.5	-0.42***	14.2	-0.92	56.6	-0.31**	58.6	-1.30
Moderate	12.5	0.26	40.7	0.05	14.7	-0.46	60.7	-0.10	63.0	0.89
High (favorable)	14.6	2.35***	44.6	0.39***	16.4	1.38**	66.7	0.41***	64.2	0.39
Overall Mean	12.2		40.3		15.1		61.3		61.9	

a. Mean scores here and elsewhere represent the mean (average) scores on each advertising response criterion for the three levels of Program Involvement. In this table, total sample data are reported.

b. Effect coefficients represent the differences in means for each advertising response criterion at a given level of Program Involvement compared to the overall (total sample) mean.

$**.01 \leq p \leq .001; ***p < .001.$

in program involvement, behavioral change jumps to 14.6%. All of these univariate effects are significant at the ($p < .05$) level.

The mean values in Table 6.3 represent the weighted means for each response criterion, at each level of program involvement, for the full sample, without regard to exposure condition or viewing environment. These values include, therefore, all those in the experimental sample demonstrating low, moderate, or high levels of program involvement, regardless of exposure condition.

> The more people are involved in a television program, the greater will be the effectiveness of advertising carried by the program.

Thus, Hypothesis 3 is clearly confirmed: As program involvement rises, so does advertising response. Stated differently, the more people are involved in a television program, the greater will be the effectiveness of advertising carried by the program.

PROGRAM INVOLVEMENT EFFECTS
VARY BY VIEWING CONDITION

Although the data analyzed thus far offer strong support for the positive effects hypothesis earlier chapters discussed, one question remains: Can it be that viewing condition (forced-exposure versus simulated natural) explains in part why the literature of the past four decades has told, in effect, different stories? Is it possible, for example, as Hypothesis 4 suggests, that program involvement and advertising response are most strongly and positively linked under natural or simulated natural conditions, whereas there is no relationship (or perhaps even a negative one) under highly artificial forced-exposure viewing conditions?

Not surprisingly, when we tested the interactive effects of program involvement and viewing condition on all five measures of advertising response, some interesting interactions did, in fact, emerge. The significance of these interactions has several important implications, which we will treat in greater detail subsequently. Here are the findings thus far.

TABLE 6.4 Univariate F-Test Results for the Program Involvement Model

Criterion	Viewing Conditions	Program Involvement	Interaction
Behavioral intentions change	2.65[a]	5.47**	0.78
Copy-point credibility	11.8***	6.32**	2.40*
Purchase interest	4.52**	2.53[b]	0.74
Aided message recall	69.7***	5.27**	5.65***
Unaided (proven) recall	77.8***	0.35	2.85**

a. Achieves marginal significance at the .07 level.
b. Achieves marginal significance at the .08 level.
*.05 $\leq p$ > .01; **.01 $\leq p \geq$ .001; ***p < .001.

First, the results confirm the importance of the next stage in the analysis—a comparative examination of program-attitude effects within the two contrasting viewing environments most frequently used in advertising and copy research— and for the examination of program-environment effects.

Second, the results demonstrate the critical importance of the choice of test environment in investigations of program-environment effects.

Third, we show quite clearly that, as noted earlier, researchers commit a fundamental error when they directly compare the results obtained from artificial laboratory designs with those obtained from on-air testing, as though the differences in exposure environments were inconsequential to the results.

Table 6.4 tells us that, for three of the five advertising response measures, viewing conditions and program involvement interact. That is to say, program involvement has a significantly different effect on advertising response among people in one exposure condition than in another.

These univariate analyses and multivariate discriminate function analyses reveal that there are interactions between viewing conditions and program involvement. But what are they, and how do they relate to advertising response? To solve these puzzles, we need to explore the effects of program involvement on advertising response within the different exposure conditions.

PROGRAM EFFECTS WITHIN THE FORCED EXPOSURE ENVIRONMENT

Tables 6.5 and 6.6 present the results of multivariate testing for the effects of program involvement within the artificial, forced exposure treatment and the simulated natural environment condition.

These two approaches represent the two polar testing environments in which most previous program environment research has been carried out, hence, their relevance for the comparative examination of program-involvement effects here. As we said in Chapter 3, the intervening "modest distraction" treatment is, like the "no distractions" condition, fundamentally artificial and, because it does not exhibit effects sufficiently (or statistically) different from the latter viewing condition to warrant separate consideration, we do not include it in this analysis.

Test results (Table 6.5) show that program involvement fails to produce a significant multivariate effect on advertising response within the artificial forced-exposure viewing environment. This is substantiated by results of univariate testing. Canonical discriminate analysis results also fail to reveal the presence of a significant dimension underlying the advertising response effects of program attitudes in the artificial forced-exposure viewing environment. Taken together, they indicate that under typical artificial testing conditions, program attitudes or content-involvement have virtually no impact on communications effectiveness. This is a conclusion that at least one researcher hinted at (Kennedy, 1971); it was openly suggested by Twyman (1974).

> The only circumstances under which the negative-effects hypothesis finds even directional support are in the artificial, forced-exposure environment.

Although the mean scores in Table 6.7 show a tendency for the negative hypothesis to be supported for two measures of recall (aided message recall and unaided proven recall), these effects fail to achieve statistical significance. Nevertheless, it is intriguing to note that the only circumstances under which the negative-effects hypothesis finds even directional support are in the artificial, forced-exposure environment—the very place where the negative-effects hypothesis was observed in the academic literature.

PROGRAM EFFECTS WITHIN THE SIMULATED NATURAL ENVIRONMENT

One obtains a very different perspective after analyzing the relationship between program involvement and advertising effects within the simulated

TABLE 6.5 The Effects of Program Involvement on Advertising Exposure Within Artificial and Simulated Natural Viewing Conditions

A. Multivariate Significance Tests

Test Statistic	Artificial Forced-Exposure Environment		Simulated Natural Exposure Environment	
		Approximate F		Approximate F
Pillai-Bartlett	.098	1.65	.169	2.47**
Wilks' Lambda	.904	1.54	.835	2.56**

B. Univariate Significance Tests

Univariate Criterion	Artificial Forced-Exposure Environment	Simulated Natural Exposure Environment
Behavioral intentions change	0.83	4.42**
Copy-point credibility	1.23	7.28**
Purchase interest	0.60	3.09**
Aided message recall	2.23	7.59**
Unaided (proven) recall	2.34	2.60

C. Canonical Discriminant Analysis Results

	Artificial Forced-Exposure Environment		Simulated Natural Exposure Environment	
	Root 1	Root 2	Root 1	Root 2
Significance	(ns)	(ns)	**	(ns)
Cancorr.	.273	.153	.381	.153
Cancorr. Squared	7.5%	2.0%	14.5%	2.4%

D. Criterion-Canonical Variate Correlations

	Artificial Forced-Exposure Environment	Simulated Natural Exposure Environment
	Root 1	Root 1
Behavioral intentions change	.19	−.61
Copy-point credibility	.15	−.79
Purchase interest	.08	−.51
Aided message recall	−.61	−.80
Unaided (proven) recall	−.61	−.37

NOTE: (ns) = not significant.
*$.05 \leq p > .01$; **$.01 \leq p \geq .001$; ***$p < .001$.

TABLE 6.6 The Effects of Program Involvement on Advertising Exposure Within Treatment Means and Effects for Program Involvement

Criterion Variable	Involvement Level	Artificial Forced-Exposure Environment		Simulated Natural Exposure Environment	
		Mean	Effect	Mean	Effect
Behavioral	Low	12.9	−1.30	6.4	−4.72*
intentions	Moderate	13.6	−0.63	12.6	1.46
change	High	16.2	1.93	14.4	3.26*
Overall mean		14.2		11.1	
Copy-point	Low	42.4	−.157	24.1	−.97***
credibility	Moderate	42.4	−.156	36.6	.270
	High	47.1	.313	40.8	.70*
Overall mean		44.0		33.8	
Purchase	Low	16.0	−0.51	13.2	−2.27*
interest	Moderate	15.8	−0.71	15.7	0.070
	High	17.8	1.22	17.9	2.30*
Overall mean		16.5		15.6	
Aided message	Low	71.9	.335	34.1	−1.14**
recall	Moderate	64.4	−.422*	48.4	0.290
	High	69.5	.087	53.9	0.850*
Overall mean		68.6		45.5	
Unaided	Low	75.0	5.14*	34.8	−6.80*
(proven)	Moderate	67.0	−2.87	47.3	5.70
recall	High	67.6	2.27	42.8	1.20
Overall mean		69.9		41.6	

*$.05 \leq p > .01$; **$.01 \leq p \geq .001$; ***$p < .001$.

natural environment condition. Here, we see a positive relationship for four of the five measures of advertising effectiveness, even stronger relationships than we observed when we analyzed the total sample, as reported in Table 6.3. These results suggest the hidden power of television programming, which, if tapped, could significantly improve media effectiveness and efficiency.

The effect of program involvement on advertising response achieves a high level of multivariate significance and, with the exception of proven audio/visual recall, demonstrates significant univariate effects on each of the individual ad response criteria. Canonical discriminate analysis results substantiate the univariate results: All criteria are found to be useful and significant in discriminating between program-attitude levels except for unaided proven recall (Table 6.5).

TABLE 6.7 Mean Values on Potential Covariates Within Levels of Program
Involvement: Simulated Natural Environment Only

Covariate[a]	Program Involvement			Treatment Mean (n = 140)
	Low (n = 56)	Moderate (n = 46)	High (n = 38)	
Respondent age	4.09	3.85	3.82	3.94
Respondent income	4.18	4.48	3.58	4.11
Respondent education	3.30	2.89	2.55	2.96
Product usage	6.85	6.93	10.83	7.96
Television attitudes	9.25	9.65	9.28	9.39

a. Numbers in the first three columns represent the mean value of each potential covariate at each level of
the program involvement factor. Individual covariate means across the levels of the factor appear in the far
right column. Inspection of these means indicates whether or not their magnitude is relatively similar across
the factor. This, in turn, suggests whether factor effects are genuine and whether variation in the dependent
variable is due to the effects of the factor, and not, to any significant extent, to the influence of uncontrolled,
extraneous variation in other variables. If the individual means of the potential covariates within each level
of the factor as well as their own respective means are of similar size, it is probable that these variables are
inconsequential to the relationship of primary importance. The first potential covariate, Age, for example,
demonstrates very little variation across the levels of program involvement hence, does not "move," or
covary with the effects of involvement on ad effectiveness. The impact of the factor on ad effectiveness is
not shared in any way with the effects of respondent age.

   The Product Usage variable, on the other hand, may bear some scrutiny. It may suggest that test brand
usage covaries with high levels of program involvement in producing the effect of high involvement on
advertising effectiveness.

   In each of these cases, low involvement is accompanied by a statistically
significant negative effect on response and high involvement by a statistically significant positive effect. Even in the case of unaided proven recall—
where the highest level of advertising response occurred in people moderately
involved—it is noteworthy to observe in Table 6.6 that among people with low
involvement, unaided proven recall reached its low water mark of 34.8%, rising
to 42.8% percent (a 23% difference) among people high in involvement.
Therefore, it can be said that under more natural viewing conditions, as involvement levels increase, advertising effectiveness improves significantly.

   The canonical correlation associated with the significant root or dimension
underlying these results explains about 15% of the advertising response variability between attitude levels. This represents a substantially larger amount than
was observed across all viewing conditions. In terms of practical significance,
this is potentially equivalent to a 15% improvement in the efficiency of a $50
million television schedule, representing $7.5 million in savings. It is apparent,
therefore, that program involvement has a significantly greater impact on
television advertising effectiveness under viewing conditions mirroring the
natural program environment.

Table 6.6 depicts the response functions associated with the effects of program involvement on each of the advertising effectiveness criteria. These functions graphically demonstrate that although the absolute level of mean response is usually higher in the artificial forced-exposure condition, it is considerably less responsive to increases in the level of program involvement than in the simulated natural exposure environment.

This is most evident for behavioral intentions, where mean change rises from 6.4% among viewers with low involvement to 14.4% among those highly involved, a 125% increase as involvement levels rise under simulated natural viewing conditions. In comparison, under artificial forced-viewing conditions, behavioral intentions change rises from 12.9% among viewers with low involvement to 16.2% among those highly involved, a 26% increase.

In the case of copy-point credibility, the mean change among viewers with low involvement rises from 24.1% to 40.8%, a 69% increase under simulated natural viewing conditions. In comparison, copy-point credibility rises from 42.4% among viewers with low involvement to 47.1% among those highly involved, an 11% increase, under artificial forced viewing conditions.

With the purchase interest measure, the mean change among viewers with low involvement rises from 13.2% to 17.9%, a 36% increase under simulated natural viewing conditions. Under artificial-forced viewing conditions, purchase interest rises from 16.0% among viewers with low involvement to 17.8% among those highly involved, an 11 percent increase. Also, reported consideration of test brands for future purchase following program/commercial exposure was 36% higher among those in the simulated natural environment condition with the highest involvement scores than among those with low levels of program involvement.

With the aided message recall measure under simulated natural viewing conditions, the mean change rises from 34.1% among viewers with low program involvement to 53.9 among those with high involvement, a 58% increase. Under artificial-forced viewing conditions, aided message recall actually drops from 71.9% among viewers with low involvement to 64.4% among viewers with moderate involvement, then rises to 69.5% among viewers with high involvement.

What we have seen is that among simulated natural environment respondents, the relationship between low and high involvement viewers is convex, moving from low to high levels of program involvement although at a diminishing rate. This convex pattern is apparent, to a varying degree, with most of the functions describing the relationships between program involvement and advertising response in the simulated natural exposure environment.

In this, we can see that, in the simulated natural environment, communications effectiveness is particularly responsive to increases in program involvement from the lower to middle level of the program involvement scale. This may well reflect the difference between a low involvement, detached state of viewing and the commencement of a state of involvement in the program material, represented in its effects on advertising response.

This area, in fact, shows the most difference in the nature of response between the contrasting artificial forced-exposure and simulated natural environments. Moving from low to moderate program involvement levels in the artificial forced-exposure environment, advertising response either decreases or remains unchanged for all criteria (with the exception of behavioral intentions change).

The response function associated with aided recall in the simulated natural environment shows a similar relationship to that observed for the credibility criterion. The mean proportion of message claims recalled with prompting increases almost 60% as attitudes toward the program move from the lowest to the highest level. In the case of proven audiovisual recall, however, unaided message playback increases 36% from low to moderate program involvement levels, but then decreases, seemingly supporting a no-effects or even negative-effects position.

Furthermore, as program involvement scores move from low to moderate, the direction of recall effects is negative for the artificial forced-exposure environment and positive for the simulated natural environment. The changes in the direction of mean response, moving from the moderate to the high involvement levels in each environment, although discrepant with the patterns expected, are of little or no statistical significance. In each case, the observed effects of high program involvement must be attributed to chance and the signs of the nonsignificant effects are at least consistent with the directions expected from previous research.

PROGRAMMING'S HIDDEN EFFECTS: A SUMMARY OF THE EVIDENCE

When measured under traditional artificial forced-exposure laboratory conditions, advertising receptivity or effectiveness is not significantly affected, in general, by differences in viewer levels of involvement with programs. The single exception occurs with the aided message recall criterion, in which case we found that when program involvement increases from a low to moderate level, it produces a significant negative effect on the ability to recall message claims with prompting. The effect of program involvement on unaided proven message recall may be said to approach significance ($p < .10$).

Thus, advertising response in the artificial forced-exposure environment is either invariant to program involvement at lower levels or changes to an extremely modest extent (with the partial exception of recall). Any increase in response on the advertising effectiveness criteria occurs moving from moderate to high program involvement levels. These increases are not substantial, however, averaging only 11% across the five criterion measures. It is nevertheless interesting that even though these increases in mean response at the high involvement level are not statistically significant and are frequently numerically lower than mean response at low involvement levels, some response build does occur, moving from moderate to high program attitudes, for each of the five criteria, even in this artificial forced-exposure viewing environment.

> Under simulated-natural test conditions, the greatest increases in mean response occur as involvement increases from low to moderate levels.

Response patterns under the more naturalistic viewing conditions are, or should be, of greater practical interest, however, and Tables 6.5 and 6.6 indicate that they differ substantially from those observed within the artificial forced-exposure testing environment. Under simulated-natural test conditions, the greatest increases in mean response occur as involvement increases from low to moderate levels, although response continues to build—monotonically in the case of purchase interest—throughout the range of the factor. In general, response patterns conform to the familiar "diminishing returns" function, with response increasing, but at a slower rate, as program involvement levels increase.

It may be, therefore, that as involvement in a program increases under natural viewing conditions, so too does the effectiveness of advertising the program carries but also at a diminishing rate. Beyond some point of highly favorable reaction to program content, or intense program involvement, however, it may be that advertising plateaus, or even declines somewhat, in effectiveness. This is, of course, highly speculative, yet seems worth future investigation.

This comparative analysis within the two testing environments sheds light on the probable sources of dispute in the literature over the nature and direction of program effects on commercial performance. Although researchers have presented evidence supporting many individual findings that have contributed toward resolution of the debate, two fundamental conclusions are evident from this study:

1. *Under artificial forced-exposure test conditions,* only in the case of unaided message recall—a key criterion in most forced-exposure studies—was support provided for the negative-effects hypothesis. Otherwise, the relationships between the advertising effectiveness criteria and program involvement were shown to be nonsignificant—findings uniquely associated with artificial forced-exposure test conditions. Even so, however, some response build occurs for most effectiveness measures moving from the moderate to high position on the multidimensional program-attitude measure, seemingly attesting to the power of program involvement effects.

This, as you will recall from our earlier discussion, is the only response variable that does not display a statistically significant positive relationship between program involvement and advertising response. There is no significant evidence of the negative-effects hypothesis, even in the artificial forced-exposure environment condition, which most closely mirrors that of academic studies, which initially suggested this hypothesis. Although there is small evidence for the negative-effects position in the case of one advertising response criterion—unaided proven recall—in the artificial forced-exposure condition, even here the results fail to achieve statistical significance at the $p < .05$ level.

2. *In the simulated-natural test condition,* in clear contrast, response effects are positive and significant for four of the five effectiveness criteria (the exception is unaided proven recall). The program involvement measure, moreover, explains a substantial proportion of the variation in commercial response scores. Furthermore, as this environment more closely conforms to the actual in-home conditions under which exposure typically occurs, one can expect the results to be more representative of relationships obtained in the real world.

Using the multidimensional program attitude measure under naturalistic testing conditions, therefore, clearly shows promise from an applied standpoint. It remains to be demonstrated, however, whether this measure is superior in explanatory significance to standard industry unidimensional measures and whether it "captures" something other than simple viewer attention.

We will present analyses pertinent to the first of these issues (Hypothesis 5) in the balance of this chapter. We address those pertaining to the second issue in later chapters.

ARE THE EFFECTS
OF PROGRAM INVOLVEMENT
REAL OR SPURIOUS?

From this point forward, however, our interest centers around the results we obtained within the simulated natural environment. We conduct all the remaining analyses in this chapter exclusively within this treatment condition. This decision proceeds from our previous comparative environment analyses, which strongly suggest that results obtained under artificial exposure conditions are inherently misleading and do not represent advertising response scores that would result from those obtained under natural, in-home viewing conditions—and by implication from those obtained in more appropriate simulated-natural testing conditions.

The findings reported here concerning the strength of our program involvement measure in predicting advertising response are in fact "real" and not the product of uncontrolled variation in extraneous variables (i.e., spurious). For example, it is possible that respondents in our three level-of-involvement groups might differ in terms of important variables such as demographics, product usage patterns, and attitudes toward television.

Conceivably, it could be differences in these variables that account for the differences in advertising response rather than involvement itself. But this proved not to be the case. A detailed set of covariate analyses were undertaken— and reported in the Appendix—revealing that the effects of program involvement observed in this chapter hold even after other so-called control factors are taken into account.

As Chapter 4 mentioned, we assigned respondents to experimental cells to provide for a constant level of demographic variability within each cell. It is possible, however, that other uncontrolled sources of variation may be contributing to the observed relationships between program attitudes and advertising response. For example, program involvement may vary with extraneous factors such as test-brand product-category usage behavior or with attitudes toward television, variables correlated with advertising response. If so, the observed relationships between program involvement and response may be spurious due to the intervening influence of these potential covariates.

To determine, therefore, whether observed effects are uncontaminated by sample cell differences in demographic characteristics, product usage behavior, or attitudes toward television, we reanalyzed the data using multivariate analysis of covariance (MANCOVA) to control the influence of these factors. We selected five variables as covariates in this analysis (which, as noted, was limited to respondents in the simulated natural environment condition).

Demographic Characteristics:

1. Respondent age
2. Education
3. Family income

Product Usage:

4. Average frequency of purchase across the four product categories represented in the four test commercials

Attitudes Toward Television:

5. Prior to exposure, respondents completed a multi-item attitude inventory designed to assess their attitudes toward television viewing.

Subsequent factor analysis of this item inventory revealed two minor, and one dominant factor. Scores on this latter factor scale, representing the benefits or value derived from television viewing, were selected as the final covariate.

Prior to conducting MANCOVA, we computed mean response scores on each potential covariate within each level of program involvement (Table 6.7).

The goal was to determine whether, by simple inspection, there was reason to believe that covariate mean scores differed substantially with level of program involvement. Substantial differences in the magnitude of mean scores for a given covariate across the levels of the involvement factor could indicate that the variation in advertising effectiveness scores, attributed solely to involvement levels, might reflect some degree of covariation with an extraneous variable. Results demonstrate that although evidence of what might be considered significant covariation appears to be lacking, some question remains in the case of at least one variable (product usage).

The results of the within-cell multiple regression of the advertising response criteria on the set of five covariates appear at the top of Table 6.8.

Asterisks referring to significance levels in the right-hand columns indicate retained significance. These results, together with the univariate test results to be found in the lower portion of the table, show that the set of covariates does not significantly affect advertising response, either at the multivariate or univari-

TABLE 6.8 Analysis of Covariance Test Results: Simulated Natural Environment

A. Multivariate Tests

Test statistic	MANOVA Within-Cells Regression	Program Involvement Effects Adjusted for Five Covariates
Pillai-Bartlett	0.264	0.134
Approximate F	1.470	1.85*
Wilks's lambda	0.760	0.868
Approximate F	1.460	1.88*

B. Univariate Tests

Univariate Criterion	Within-Cells F Tests R^2	F	Program Involvement Adjusted for Five Covariates
Behavioral intentions change	.063	1.78	4.52*
Copy-point credibility	.073	2.08	4.86**
Purchase interest	.052	1.44	2.82
Aided message recall	.076	2.17	5.26**
Unaided (proven) recall	.052	1.44	2.20

*$.05 \leq p > .01$; **$.01 \leq p \geq .001$.

ate levels, within the categories of the program involvement factor. Yet, the effects of the covariate set do approach statistical significance in the case of the credibility criterion and the aided recall criterion. There is no straightforward interpretation of this near significance, however, as none of the beta coefficients associated with the individual covariates achieves even marginal significance on either criterion.

Although the intervening influence of the covariates is, therefore, nonsignificant, removing their effects nevertheless alters the relationships between program involvement and advertising response to a minor extent. As seen in a comparison of the covariance-adjusted significance test results appearing to the right in Table 6.8 with the unadjusted results in Table 6.5, the effect is a slight reduction in the original strength of the relationships.

Statistical significance is retained, however, at the multivariate and univariate levels, with the exception of the originally marginally significant purchase interest criterion. In this case, covariance adjustment results in a reduction in the proportion of variance explained by program involvement by a slight 5%, which is, however, sufficient to render the relationship nonsignificant at the $p < .05$ level (the adjusted significance level is $p < .07$).

With the behavioral intentions change criterion, on the other hand, covariance adjustment does not appreciably alter the relationship, despite the fact that only in this criterion did any of the five individual covariate beta coefficients achieve significance at the ($p < .05$) level. Here, we observed that the income covariate alone exerted a marginally significant intervening influence that, when removed, resulted in a slight improvement in the strength of the relationship between program involvement and the criterion.

> Holding demographics, attitude, and product usage constant, the relationship between program involvement and advertising effectiveness remains positive.

Thus, although removing the combined effects of the five covariates results in a slight overall weakening of the originally observed relationship between program involvement and advertising response, none of the covariates can be identified as an individually important source of extraneous variation. The cumulative effect of the slight influence exerted by each of the five covariates individually does result in a relationship of slightly diminished strength, but even this cumulative effect fails to achieve statistical significance. We can therefore conclude that efforts to maintain a constant level of demographic, attitude, and product usage variability across experimental cells were, on the whole, successful and that the observed relationship between program involvement and advertising effectiveness remains positive and significant and substantially unaltered by uncontrolled factors.

INVOLVEMENT SCALE PREDICTS
ADVERTISING EFFECTIVENESS

Our final primary hypothesis, Hypothesis 5, states that several reasons, theoretical as well as practical, exist that allow us to assert that program content reaction or involvement has several dimensions, and that involvement, as measured by our multidimensional scale, has far greater explanatory significance, in terms of the advertising effectiveness criteria, than the traditional unidimensional measurement scales.

Hypothesis 1 has already satisfied the first condition. Analyses pertaining to the second condition demonstrate that Hypothesis 5 is confirmed as well. The multidimensional involvement measure used in this research has a significantly higher degree of explanatory significance on the advertising response criteria than any other unidimensional measure used in parallel testing. But, to reiterate our rationale and present the empirical bases on which confirmation of Hypothesis 5 is grounded:

First, we cited strong independent evidence (Laurent & Kapferer, 1985) attesting to the multidimensional nature of the involvement construct in numerous application situations; and, as we showed in Chapters 3 and 4, we found this to be particularly evident in communications research.

Second, as we also observed earlier, if multiple concurrent determinants underlie specific program preferences, the antecedent attitudes and involving elements associated with the programs will be multidimensional as well.

Third, although a unidimensional summary-affect measure such as a multi-point program-liking scale may explain a significant amount of variance in advertising response criteria, it reveals little of the program characteristics or specifics of viewer reaction underlying program involvement. In other words, program elements and viewer reactions to them, as they relate to the different dimensions of commercial response, remain unknown. Such information could be extremely valuable to the media planner while contributing to our knowledge of how television advertising works.

> The multidimensional program involvement measure has a higher degree of explanatory power than single question measures.

Given comparable levels of explanatory significance on the commercial effectiveness criteria, these arguments alone appear sufficient to encourage further development and application of the multidimensional measurement approach. In addition, however, comparative analyses of the measurement approaches demonstrate that the multidimensional program involvement measure has a higher degree of explanatory significance on the effectiveness criteria than either a traditional program-liking scale or the IPSOS-ASI, Inc., 5-point Favorites measure. (The 11-point program-liking scale, in this instance, gauges liking by response to the question, "For the episode of (the program that you just watched, say *Baywatch*), please give your personal rating based on a scale from 0 to 10." The IPSOS-ASI measure asks: "Do you consider the program _____ to be (1) your favorite, (2) one of your favorites, (3) good, (4) fair, or (5) poor?")

Furthermore, we found this greater explanatory significance to be uncontaminated by the influence of extraneous factors such as product usage and attitudes toward television to a far greater extent than either one of the other two summary-affect measures.

COMPARATIVE ANALYSIS OF ALTERNATIVE PROGRAM INVOLVEMENT MEASURES

We performed the same MANOVA analysis used on the program involvement measure separately on the IPSOS-ASI Favorites measure and on the liking scale, again within the simulated-natural test environment. Results of these analyses, which appear in Table 6.9, demonstrate that neither of the alternative summary-affect measures achieves multivariate significance on the advertising effectiveness construct. Nevertheless, we examined univariate test results on the individual response criteria with some interesting findings.

Whereas the relationship between program content reaction and higher-order commercial response (persuasion and purchase intent) is nonsignificant for both unidimensional measures, this is not the case with commercial recall. The relationship between aided recall and program reaction achieves positive statistical significance in the case of both the IPSOS-ASI, and the 0-to-10 liking measures. We also found a significant positive relationship between program liking and the unaided proven message recall criterion. These results offer strong substantiation for the findings of previous on-air studies concluding significant positive program environment effects, the vast majority of which limited advertising effectiveness measurement to commercial recall.

Finally, we used MANCOVA to adjust the relationships between each of the summary-affect measures and the commercial response criteria for the same five potential covariates for which we controlled the program involvement commercial response relationships (Table 6.8). Results demonstrate significant covariate effects within the levels of both of the traditional summary-affect measures on the response criteria. As a comparison of the original and covariance-adjusted univariate effects shows, controlling for the influence of extraneous factors substantially weakens originally significant relationships for both unidimensional measures. For the IPSOS-ASI measure, significance is retained only in

TABLE 6.9 MANOVA and MANCOVA Test Results: ASI Favorites and Liking-Scale Measures for Simulated Natural Environment

A. Multivariate Test Results

	Original MANOVA		MANCOVA Within-Cells Regression		Multivariate Effects Adjusted for Five Covariates	
	Favorites Scale	*Liking Scale*	*Favorites Scale*	*Liking Scale*	*Favorites Scale*	*Liking Scale*
Pillai-Bartlett test	0.146	0.094	0.297	0.30	0.104	0.081
Approximate F value	1.45	1.33	1.74*	1.68*	0.98	1.09

B. Univariate Test Results

	Favorites Scale				*Liking Scale*			
	Within-Cells		*Covariance*			*Within-Cells*	*Covariance*	
Criterion	*Unadjusted F*	R^2	*F-Tests F*	*Adjusted F*	*Unadjusted F*	R^2	*F-Tests F*	*Adjusted F*
Behavior intentions change	0.12	.078	2.35*	0.14	1.49	.073	2.07	0.18
Copy-point credibility	3.09*	.094	2.87*	1.47	4.52*	.090	2.60*	1.72
Purchase interest	0.84	.062	1.83	0.78	1.71	.067	1.91	0.94
Aided message recall	4.93**	.091	2.78*	3.29*	4.73**	.087	2.52*	3.06
Unaided (proven) recall	2.36	.044	1.28	1.29	4.28*	.050	1.38	0.84

*.05 ≤ p > .01; **.01 ≤ p ≥ .001; ***p < .001.

the case of aided recall, and at a reduced level. In the case of the program-liking scale, none of the significant effects on three criteria prior to covariance adjustment were retained. A comparison of similar test results on the involvement measure reveals, on the other hand—and in clear contrast to the IPSOS-ASI results—that the originally significant multivariate relationship is retained after covariance adjustment.

Whereas covariance adjustments at the univariate level effect minor reductions in the strength of some originally observed relationships, at no time do the within-program involvement levels regressions of the individual criteria on the covariates achieve statistical significance, as can be seen by comparing Tables 6.9 and 6.10. Finally, in comparing, this time, the covariance-adjusted squared canonical correlations between each of the measures and the criterion set, we found that only in the case of the program involvement measure, again, is statistical significance achieved and retained. The multidimensional program involvement scale explains 70% and 50% more of the variation in advertising effectiveness than the program-liking and Favorites measures, respectively.

Computing simple bivariate correlation coefficients between each of the advertising response criteria and the alternative program content reaction measures (Table 6.10) reveals the superiority of the multidimensional measure. These combined results provide a strong argument for the superior predictive validity of the multidimensional program involvement measure on each of the response criteria.

> Both unidimensional measures of program attitudes lack the sensitivity associated with the multidimensional program involvement measurement approach.

The results associated with the testing of Hypothesis 5 are neither surprising nor unexpected. Both unidimensional measures of program attitudes clearly lack the sensitivity associated with the multidimensional program involvement measurement approach, and this is reflected by their inability to capture the full range of program content reaction and its effects on advertising response. The more obvious difficulty lies in their failure to adequately measure true program content reaction in terms of the range and hierarchy of its component elements as they affect commercial responses. Furthermore, the relationships between the

TABLE 6.10 Bivariate Correlation Coefficients: Advertising Response Criteria by Alternate Attitude Measures

Advertising Response Criterion	ASI Favorites Measure	11-Point Liking Scale	Involvement Scale
Behavioral intentions change (pre-post)	.06	.06	.23**
Copy-point credibility	.18*	.24**	.32***
Purchase interest	.12	.13	.21**
Aided message recall	.22**	.26**	.33***
Unaided (proven) recall	.10	.18*	.20**

*.05 ≤ p > .01; **.01 ≤ p ≥ .001; ***p < .001.

summary-affect approach to program attitudes measurement and commercial response are found to be potentially subject to uncontrolled sources of variation to a far greater extent than are the same relationships when the program involvement approach measures them.

Table 6.9 makes this evident by comparing the effects of covariate adjustment of the program involvement scale on advertising effectiveness in Table 6.10 with the same tests and comparisons for rival measures shown in Table 6.9.

Finally, program content reaction, measured in traditional, unidimensional fashion, fails to reveal the full impact on advertising effectiveness or its true explanatory significance. We have obtained persuasive evidence on theoretical as well as practical grounds for the multidimensional measurement approach's superiority. This provides, in turn, a strong incentive for further development and refinement of a multidimensional program involvement profile measure, to be used as a valuable diagnostic as well as predictive tool.

People, Products, and Campaigns Most Sensitive to Programming Effects

The previous chapter confirmed the direct relationship between program involvement and advertising response. This chapter extends these findings by examining whether the positive effects of program involvement on advertising response differ for different types of people, for different product usage patterns, for new and established advertising campaigns, and for fact-based versus image advertising.

For example, do we find the involvement-advertising response relationship only among younger consumers and not among those who are middle-aged? Or, does the relationship hold only in the case of, say, new products or particular types of advertising executions?

This knowledge is not trivial. The chances of an efficient effective media buy—even an entire campaign—are greatly improved if advertisers and media buyers

> Understand that people usually select, rate, and decide to view and continue to watch a particular program primarily on the basis of program involvement
>
> Realize that the more involved viewers are with the program material, the greater their receptivity to and exposure to embedded commercial material and hence advertising effectiveness
>
> Know how a particular demographic group, user group, or type of campaign interacts with program involvement and advertising effectiveness.

This chapter's goal is, therefore, simple. We examine, in four loosely connected sections, (a) demographic factors, (b) attitudes toward television and television-viewing behavior, (c) a variety of product- and brand-usage data, and (d) different types of products and advertising campaigns, using the MANOVA analytic routine. Our objective is to determine whether the positive relationship we have seen between program involvement and advertising response holds up among consumers with different demographics, television-viewing habits, and product usage patterns, or whether the results are constrained to only certain types of people in certain circumstances.

These analyses use data only from the simulated-natural exposure treatment group—the environment within which we found program effects to be the most reliable and valid—and, therefore, the test environment that produces the results in which advertisers should be most interested.

We've discovered that the effects are consistent. Although the numbers suggest that the effects of television programming on advertising response appear to be greater in some circumstances than in others, these differences fail to produce signs of a statistically significant interaction. What we see, for example, is seemingly stronger effects among younger consumers, people who watch the most television, and those who have positive attitudes toward television. The effects seem to be stronger for new and fact-based advertising campaigns.

These results, probably owing to the small sample size, are not of sufficient magnitude to yield a reliable statistically significant outcome. Thus, we can conclude that almost everywhere we look, the positive relationship between program involvement and advertising response, which we first reported in Chapter 5 in our total sample results and then saw magnified in the simulated natural viewing environment, is supported.

> In almost every relationship and analysis we examined, the higher the program-involvement level, the greater the effectiveness of advertising in the program.

We have shown in all but a few analyses that overall advertising effectiveness does differ according to viewer program involvement level across the levels of the control variables. In the clear majority of cases, as viewer involvement in programming varies across the control factor categories, advertising effectiveness is affected with differing intensity levels. In most cases we examined, the higher the program involvement level, the greater the effectiveness of advertising in the program.

ARE THE EFFECTS OF PROGRAM INVOLVEMENT ON AD RESPONSE UNIFORM ACROSS ALL SITUATIONS?

The analyses and comments are concerned with one issue: The presence and significance of viewer involvement levels as they influence (or fail to influence) relationships—some considered known and charted, others less familiar—between explanatory variables and advertising effectiveness. We have arranged these into four broad categories; some of continuing interest to researchers and media planners due to their routine, ongoing application, and others that explore relationships a bit farther afield. The categories and analyses within them are:

1. *Demographics.* Our goal is to investigate the sensitivity of advertising effectiveness to differences in program involvement among people who vary in age, education, and socioeconomic status.

2. *Television attitudes and viewing behavior.* Our purpose is to explore whether program involvement effects are different among people who vary in their attitudes toward television and viewing behavior. These two measures include:

a. Self-reports of the amount of time spent viewing television on an average weekday night. To minimize any contextual effects bias in the questionnaire, we collected and averaged two identical measures, one at the beginning and one at the end of the interview.

b. A 14-item Attitudes Toward Television battery placed in the pre-exposure questionnaire. The most parsimonious factor-analytic solution for these items resulted in two factors: one, decidedly positive toward the roles of TV and exemplified by a *strongly agree* response to "Watching TV is one of the best ways to relax and escape from everyday problems for awhile." The other factor was decidedly negative with *strongly agree* responses to such items as "Watching TV makes people mentally lazy."

3. *Product and brand-user status and usage rate.* Our purpose here was to examine the effects of product involvement among people differentially involved in the category and with the brand. The variables include:

a. Product-category user status: We categorized respondents as heavy or light users of each test brand category based on their mean self-reported use of all brands in the category.

b. Brand usage rate: The mean level of test-brand usage.

c. Usage rate, durables: The mean usage of two test brands falling into the household durable goods classification.

d. Usage rate, packaged goods: The mean usage of two test brands falling into the personal packaged goods classification.

This category comprises an organized variety of analyses performed first on the test-brand data alone, then with the clutter-brand data alone, and finally with combinations of the two, depending on the availability of the necessary data.

For analyses that involve test brands alone, all criteria are available. When we combine test and clutter brands in an analysis, only two criteria are available for testing, purchase interest (a higher order response measure) and a recall measure. Despite limitations on the number of criteria available for testing, however, those available are, at the very least, enough to provide useful insights into potentially important relationships.

4. *Different types of products and advertising campaigns.* We examine whether the positive effects of program involvement on advertising response are the same or different for different types of products and advertising campaigns. Toward this end, we asked two different questions:

a. Does the effectiveness of advertising for new brands (two represented) differ depending on respondent program involvement levels? Similarly, does advertising effectiveness for established brands (two represented) vary significantly depending on viewer involvement level?

b. Does overall advertising effectiveness for four image-related ads vary significantly with program involvement levels? Similarly, does advertising effectiveness for four factual commercials vary significantly according to program involvement level?

Again, the goal behind these analyses is to determine through analysis of variance models, which, if any, demographic, usage, and product-campaign factors appear more sensitive than others to the effects of viewer involvement on advertising response.

Having confirmed the positive-effects hypothesis, such information in a micromarketing environment should be helpful to media buyers. For example, assume a designated target to be 25 to 35 years old, moderate socioeconomic status, and a heavy user in the product category. Also, assume that people in this target group happen to be far more involved with certain programs that never carry a marketer's ads because the numbers had placed those target viewers' eyes predominantly on less costly (in terms of CPM) programs.

Given the large amount of data we collected and analyzed in our effort to determine the nature of program involvement effects, full factorial summary tables presented for each variable would be overwhelming and unnecessary. Instead, we give the standardized averaged response across criterion measures for each of three levels of the program involvement factor within the particular factor. For perspective, the first analysis presents a full table.

Stated differently, these abbreviated results come from the usual multivariate and univariate analyses, but with the independent factor means summed and averaged across the dependent variables instead of the more familiar approach where one examines the factors' cell means and effects in conjunction with each criterion measure individually. The analytical test results and cell information remain unaffected. But what may be lost by eliminating data is gained by the focus and clarity of summary means, because they indicate at a glance the comprehensive or overall nature of the relationships involved. More details of this analysis are in the Appendix.

PROGRAM INVOLVEMENT/ADVERTISING
EFFECTIVENESS AND DEMOGRAPHICS

This section addresses the question of whether the program involvement/advertising effectiveness relationship is the same among all demographic groups.

Age is the most consistently used demographic variable for segmentation and media decision-making purposes for many advertised products. Table 7.1 presents the averaged effects, across all response criteria, of program involvement on advertising effectiveness by age. For analytic purposes, as well as to preserve, as closely as possible, age categories in the traditional target (women, 18 to 49) we have placed respondents into three categories, young (18 to 29), mid-boomers (30 to 35), and older boomers (36 to 49).

TABLE 7.1 Effects of Program Involvement on Overall Advertising Effectiveness, Controlling for Respondent Age

	Respondent Age								
	Young (18-29) (N = 55)			Mid-Boomers (30-35) (N = 34)			Older Boomers (36-49) (N = 51)		
Program	Low	Average	High	Low	Average	High	Low	Average	High
Involvement	(N = 19)	(N = 22)	(N = 14)	(N = 14)	(N = 9)	(N = 11)	(N = 23)	(N = 15)	(N = 13)
Overall advertising response	−.32	.21	.42	−.12	.27	.28	−.28	.11	.20

Given the appearance of clear differences in mean response, with relatively strong monotonic build in overall response, moving from the low to high program involvement levels among the young and older groups, and relatively flat response at the middle level, one might anticipate a significant multivariate interaction between age and involvement on overall advertising effectiveness.

This is not the case, however, and MANOVA analyses failed to find any statistically significant interactions between program involvement and advertising response within the categories of age. Once again, this suggests that the positive relationship between involvement and advertising response is similar, in this case, for all three age groups. Although the data in Table 7.1 suggest that the program involvement/advertising response connection is stronger among younger consumers than older, these observed differences are not statistically significant.

> The positive relationship between program involvement and advertising response is similar for the different levels of education.

Education. Although the overall advertising response levels across the five criteria in Table 7.2 suggest differences between groups—the high school-educated consumer seems more sensitive to the effects of programming than the college-educated viewer—MANOVA analysis found no statistically significant interaction between program involvement and advertising response within the

TABLE 7.2 The Effects of Program Involvement on Overall Advertising Effectiveness, Controlling for the Effects of Educational Attainment Level

	Respondent Educational Level					
	Low (Some High School/ High School Graduate) (N = 63)			Middle to High[a] (Some College/ Postgraduate) (N = 77)		
Program Involvement	Low (N = 20)	Average (N = 21)	High (N = 22)	Low (N = 36)	Average (N = 25)	High (N = 16)
Overall advertising response	−.26	.18	.50	−.25	.19	.05

a. The middle (some college) and high (college graduate/post graduate) groups were combined in this table because of the existence of cells with as few as three cases.

education categories. In other words, the positive relationship between program involvement and advertising response is similar for the different levels of education.

Socioeconomic status is one of the variables most frequently used to select market segments and to make media decisions. As W. L. Warner originally conceived this variable in 1941, it was a weighted composite of occupation (weight: 4), source of income (weight: 3), house type (weight: 3), and dwelling area (weight: 2). In 1958, A. B. Hollingshead developed a weighted three-variable scale consisting of residence, occupation, and education (Runyon & Stewart, 1987).

There are two reasons for mentioning this background material. First, marketing and advertising researchers have adopted socioeconomic status because it often successfully differentiates between people in terms of their buying behavior or advertising response patterns or both. Second, although experience has shown that both weighted and unweighted composites have been successful in discriminatory tasks, the unweighted combination of occupation, education, and income produced the cleanest results in the present research.

Table 7.3 demonstrates the relationship between program involvement and advertising response within the levels of socioeconomic status, the latter variable comprising occupation, educational attainment, and income (summed, standardized, and divided into three groups at the individual level). In this case, we present the complete data for all five measures of advertising response and an overall average level of advertising response.

TABLE 7.3 Effects of Program Involvement on Overall Advertising Effectiveness, Controlling for Respondent Socioeconomic Status

Program Involvement	Respondent Socioeconomic Status								
	Low (N = 55)			Middle (N = 44)			High (N = 45)		
	Low	Average	High	Low	Average	High	Low	Average	High
Advertising response									
Behavioral intentions change	−.49	−.04	.33	−.19	.50	.95	−.20	−.08	−.64
Copy-point credibility	−.57	−.48	.72	−.19	.15	.16	−.19	.09	−.15
Purchase interest	−.27	−.11	.46	−.16	.25	.45	−.11	.09	−.12
Aided message recall	−.51	.59	.67	−.34	.09	.33	−.11	.05	−.16
Unaided proven recall	−.63	.28	.27	−.29	.40	−.14	.27	.07	−.09
Overall advertising response	−.50	.24	.49	−.23	.28	.35	−.07	.04	−.23

As with the two previous demographic variables, age and education, MANOVA finds no statistically significant interaction between television program involvement and socioeconomic status. Seemingly consistent patterns that we see in the data in Table 7.3, and the fact that the probability of this interaction occurring by chance is only 15%, leads us to say more about what we've observed.

Note that among respondents who have been categorized as low or middle in socioeconomic status, advertising response scores post impressive gains as their program involvement level increases for four of the five dependent variables. (These effects are significant at the $p = .01$ level.)

As an illustration, examine the first variable in Table 7.3, behavioral intentions change. Among people low and moderate in socioeconomic status, low involvement yields very low (actually negative) scores, whereas among respondents high in program involvement, the scores are strongly positive. The exception to this rule is unaided proven recall, which as we saw in Chapter 6, does not appear to be linked with differing levels of program involvement.

One of this examination's more interesting findings is, therefore, that for the low and middle socioeconomic groups, impressive rises in advertising response accompany involvement in programming. The overall (average) advertising response scores further substantiate this. Thus, we can say that for those categorized as low and middle in socioeconomic status, the relationship between program involvement and advertising response is positive and even a bit stronger than we observed in Chapter 6.

Among women categorized as high in socioeconomic status, on the other hand, there appears to be no relationship between program involvement and advertising effectiveness. The response pattern of this variable may, however, result from the relatively small number of respondents in the high socioeconomic status category, which contributes to highly volatile, that is, unstable data.

THE EFFECTIVENESS RELATIONSHIP
AND TELEVISION VIEWING BEHAVIOR

This section addresses the question of whether the program involvement/advertising effectiveness relationship is the same across respondent viewing behaviors and attitudes toward television.

The analyses and discussions here involve variables that shed important insights on the television-viewing characteristics of American women, as well as their attitudes toward television viewing, as these factors influence the positive program involvement-advertising effectiveness relationship. They are (a) the amount of time spent viewing television on an average weekday night, based on an average of two self-report measures included in the questionnaire; and (b) the factor analytic solution to an item inventory designed to probe respondent views about contemporary television and the value of watching TV.

Time spent viewing television. Here again, there is no statistically significant interaction between weeknight viewing and program involvement, although the data in Table 7.4 seem to suggest a more powerful relationship among people who are heavy weeknight viewers.

In contrast, among low to average viewers of weeknight television, advertising effects rise as we go from low to average involvement, but then fall back again, suggesting a possible inverted U-shaped relationship.

Attitudes toward television. The next two tables resulted from a factor analysis of 14 items that reflect contemporary perspectives on the role of TV in peoples' lives. Two major factors emerged from the analysis: one with a core structure of five items, reflecting a clearly positive state of mind toward television; the other with a core structure of four strongly loading items, reflecting a clearly negative posture toward television. In both, we summed and standardized respondent scores at the individual level and sorted them into three categories.

TABLE 7.4 The Effects of Program Involvement on Overall Advertising
Effectiveness, Controlling for Average Weeknight Television Viewing

| | Average Weeknight Viewing | | | | | |
| | Low to Average[a] (0 to 2.5 hours) (N = 67) | | | High (2.5 ≥ 5 hours) (N = 76) | | |
Program Involvement	Low (N = 30)	Average (N = 25)	High (N = 9)	Low (N = 26)	Average (N = 21)	High (N = 29)
Overall advertising response	−.30	.20	.11	−.19	.29	.45

a. The low and average groups were combined in this table because of the existence of cells with as few as two cases.

Looking at the positive TV attitudes variable, Table 7.5, we see overall response across the effectiveness criteria increase substantially, moving from low to high program involvement for every level. We found the relationship between positive attitude and program involvement, although it further substantiates the positive effect of program involvement on advertising effectiveness, statistically similar across the different TV attitude levels.

The overall results for the effects of program involvement on advertising response within the levels of negative attitudes toward TV viewing (Table 7.6) are similar. In general, as we move from low involvement to high involvement, advertising response scores rise dramatically. In each case, these effects are significant ($p < .01$ level), and there is no significant interaction of involvement with attitudes. These effects appear to be most pronounced among people whose negative attitudes appear to be about average. Note that among this group overall, advertising response scores go from −.34 among low involvement viewers to .66 among high involvement viewers.

> Even those claiming negative attitudes toward television viewing, program content, or both appear to become involved in programming and influenced as a result.

Thus, the positive-effects hypothesis once again asserts itself. Even among those claiming to have negative attitudes toward television viewing, program

TABLE 7.5 The Effects of Program Involvement on Overall Advertising Effectiveness, Controlling for Positive Attitudes Toward Television

	Positive TV Attitudes								
	Low (N = 43)			Average (N = 47)			High (N = 50)		
Program Involvement	Low (N = 19)	Average (N = 10)	High (N = 14)	Low (N = 18)	Average (N = 17)	High (N = 12)	Low (N = 19)	Average (N = 19)	High (N = 12)
Overall advertising response	−.30	−.01	.21	−.51	.18	.25	.03	.30	.46

content, or both, such feelings do not appear to prevent them from becoming involved in programming and influenced as a result of this involvement. And as this involvement increases, so too does the advertising's effectiveness. Thus, the overall results appear to support, once more, the hidden power of television programming. Viewers expressing negative attitudes toward television appear to be just as susceptible to involvement in programming as others.

Given what at first appeared to be an irregular and unexpectedly positive relationship between program involvement and advertising response among those with self-reported negative attitudes, it would appear, in this context, that what respondents report in one situation and what they experience in another are at odds.

To place these findings in a clearer perspective, it is useful to recognize that people in all socioeconomic strata watch TV. But within each stratum are those who appear to feel some form of guilt or other negative sentiments about watching television, whereas others are ambivalent about viewing. For example,

TABLE 7.6 The Effects of Program Involvement on Overall Advertising Effectiveness, Controlling for Negative Attitudes Toward Television

	Negative TV Attitudes								
	Low (N = 53)			Average (N = 36)			High (N = 51)		
Program Involvement	Low (N = 19)	Average (N = 18)	High (N = 16)	Low (N = 15)	Average (N = 13)	High (N = 8)	Low (N = 22)	Average (N = 15)	High (N = 14)
Overall advertising response	−.24	.25	.18	−.34	.18	.66	−.20	.11	.24

42% of all Americans now say they watch too much TV, up from 31% of all Americans in the late 1970s. But there is no denying that the often socially desirable position, particularly among educated Americans, is to denigrate television. It would appear inevitable, therefore, for some social desirability bias to insinuate itself into these findings.

The feelings of many people who express negative attitudes toward television viewing are apparently not forceful enough to stop them from watching. And, as Table 7.6 shows, simply because people say they regard TV unfavorably does not prevent them from becoming involved in programming.

The results of the analysis demonstrate, therefore, that the overall positive relationship between program involvement and advertising effectiveness exists, regardless of the fact and degree of a viewer's negative TV attitudes. But it would be a mistake to ignore the fact that an individual may give many reasons for a negative attitude toward TV. Some are undoubtedly sincere; they disapprove of some programming themselves or they wish to limit children's viewing.

DO PROGRAMMING INVOLVEMENT EFFECTS VARY BY PRODUCT CATEGORY AND PURCHASING PATTERNS?

Beginning in the late 1970s, and continuing to the present, one of the most pressing problems facing marketers is the effective management of the fragmented remnants of former mass markets that their niche-related branding and positioning strategies have created. In many categories, marketers must now attempt to stitch together markets that appear to be hopelessly fragmented by race, age, lifestyle, and other factors into new versions of "mini-mass" markets. At the same time, this means abandoning time-honored means of targeting and media-market matching, and even ways to determine the efficiency of communications strategies.

The relatively recent explosion of choices that marketers provide has become, in many respects, their nemesis as brands have found it difficult to hold onto their core identity. Much of this was (and still remains) the fault of marketers' short-term orientation, beginning in the 1980s and applied with a vengeance in the early 1990s. This orientation pursued a policy of short-term, promotional sales gains at the cost of long-term brand identity and equity building. At the time, one industry spokesperson stated that many unenlightened brand marketers have made it simple for consumers to "trade down and tune out" venerable brand names by switching dollars from image-building and retention to trade and consumer promotions and by producing "cookie-cutter" advertising (Liesse, 1991). As a result, new breeds of shoppers emerged: the "brand experimental," or the "brand irrelevant" consumer ("The Party's Over," 1992).

For these shoppers, at least, brand proliferation had all but obscured brand differences in many categories. In 1975, the average American supermarket carried 9,000 items; today, that figure has risen above 30,000. In 1994, consumer product firms launched a record 20,076 new products into U.S. supermarkets and drugstores—a 14.3% increase over 1993 ("It's Official," 1995).

If product and brand proliferation and the psychological effects of "hyperchoice" in the marketplace (Settle & Alreck, 1988) have forced brands into parity, even commodity status, and in other cases behind store brands (Kanner, 1995; Mogelonsky, 1995); and if the advertising positioning strategies of competing brands in the same category are more similar than different, it would not be surprising to find that the effect of program involvement on advertising response failed to differ between product and brand-usage preference, or even between different types of advertising campaigns.

Product category user status. Table 7.7 presents the overall results for the relationship between program involvement within the two usage categories averaged across the five advertising effectiveness criteria. For each of the four product categories represented by a test brand, (in addition to several other product categories not used in the analysis), we questioned respondents about their frequency of purchase. We divided the category-usage data for which test brands existed into light versus heavy users for each. We averaged overall response across the five criterion measures for each program involvement level within the two groups. For simplicity of presentation, the analysis of category data was accomplished by taking the overall means for each of the four test-represented categories and averaging these figures for each level of involvement and usage.

> The relationship between program involvement and advertising effectiveness is similar between light and heavy users of the test-brand product categories.

TABLE 7.7   Effects of Program Involvement on Overall Advertising Effectiveness, Controlling for Respondent Product-Category User Status

	Respondent User Status						
	Light Users (N = 41)				Heavy Users (N = 99)		
Program Involvement	Low	Average	High		Low	Average	High
Overall advertising response	−.37	.15	.40		−.10	.19	.24

We find the relationship between program involvement and advertising effectiveness to be similar among light and heavy users of the product categories represented by test brands. For both light and heavy users, the familiar, strong, monotonic increase in overall advertising response occurs moving from low to high program involvement.

Test-brand usage. Table 7.8 presents the overall averaged response scores for the effects of program involvement across the consumption levels of the study's four test brands. To compute test-brand usage, we summed and averaged individual respondents' self-reported, pre-exposure test-brand usage for each product category across the four brands. We then sorted these averaged scores into low, average, and high test-brand usage categories. Then, as in all tables thus far (with the exception of Table 7.7), response was recorded at low, average, and high levels of program involvement within three brand usage levels for each advertising effectiveness criterion.

Tests of statistical significance failed to confirm that respondents' going-in brand-usage behavior was mediated to any significant extent by program involvement. Overall results clearly demonstrate once again that advertising effectiveness increases as program involvement increases within each level of test brand usage.

Even among those who were the heaviest users of the advertised brands, increases in program involvement brought about a 250% increase in program advertising response.

Household versus personal packaged goods. In the remaining analyses using test-brand data and the full advertising response battery, we split the four core test campaigns into two separately analyzed subsets of campaigns representing opposite products or campaign goals. Our objective is to determine whether

TABLE 7.8 Effects of Program Involvement on Overall Advertising Effectiveness, Controlling for Respondent Brand Usage

| | | Low (N = 42) | | | Test-Brand Usage Average (N = 26) | | | High (N = 72) | |
Program Involvement	Low	Average	High	Low	Average	High	Low	Average	High
Overall advertising response	−.31	.18	.20	−.06	−.06	.16	−.30	.28	.45

different types of products and their advertising campaigns exhibit greater response sensitivity to the effects of program involvement.

To this end, we recoded data based on mean response for the four ads to represent mean response for two ads to enable direct analysis of the effects of program involvement on advertising effectiveness for:

1. two household durables
2. two goods for personal consumption

and subsequently,

3. two campaigns for new brands
4. two campaigns for established brands

In none of the analyses do the same two brands appear together a second time. Table 7.9 shows the results of the first of these analyses.

At the multivariate level, MANOVA results show that the effects of program involvement on advertising response is statistically similar for household dur-

TABLE 7.9 Effects of Program Involvement on Overall Advertising Effectiveness for Household Durables, Personal Nondurables

| | Household Durables | | | Personal Nondurables | | |
Program Involvement	Low (N = 56)	Average (N = 46)	High (N = 38)	Low (N = 56)	Average (N = 46)	High (N = 38)
Overall advertising response	−.05	.25	.22	−.07	.22	.41

ables and personal nondurables. We see, however, that the effects of program involvement appear to be even greater for the nondurable package goods products. As program involvement moves to the average or moderate level, we see once again the expected jump in advertising response. At the highest involvement level, however, the mean response remains at about the same level.

The MANOVA results for the analysis of the effects of program involvement on advertising response for the two personal nondurable packaged goods test-brand campaigns shows even stronger effects. This relationship is statistically significant at the $(p < .01)$ level. The columns to the right demonstrate the strong monotonic relationship between program involvement and overall mean advertising effectiveness, moving from low to high involvement.

> Increases in program involvement bring about strong increases in advertising effectiveness, and differences in advertising response between involvement levels are highly, and statistically, significant.

Not only do increases in program involvement bring about strong increases in advertising effectiveness, but the differences in advertising response between the involvement levels are highly and statistically significant. These results seem to be in keeping with Korgaonkar and Bellenger's (1985) findings of the effectiveness of nondurable packaged goods campaigns over those of durables—particularly routinely purchased household durables.

DO PROGRAMMING INVOLVEMENT EFFECTS VARY FOR DIFFERENT PRODUCTS AND ADVERTISING CAMPAIGNS?

New versus established brand campaigns. Table 7.10 presents the results of MANOVA analyses of the effects of program involvement on the effectiveness of advertising for two new test brands and two established test brands. The new brands are line extensions of well-known existing products, each with different names and offering different benefits that distinguish them from their parents.

TABLE 7.10 Effects of Program Involvement on Overall Advertising Effectiveness for New and Established Brand Campaigns

	Type of Campaign					
	Two New Brands			Two Established Brands		
Program Involvement	Low (N = 56)	Average (N = 46)	High (N = 38)	Low (N = 56)	Average (N = 46)	High (N = 38)
Overall advertising response	−.27	.20	.36	−.14	.10	.15

The two established brands, in contrast, represent product categories that are different from those characterized by the new brands.

Table 7.10 demonstrates again the expected monotonic response increase for both the new and established brand campaigns, reflecting the positive effect of program involvement on advertising response. Yet, whereas this relationship is highly significant in the case of new campaigns, with a multivariate significance level of $p < .002$, it fails to achieve significance in the case of established campaigns ($p < .14$).

This latter relationship, liberally interpreted, may be said to approach statistical significance, however. This statistical test means that the finding could have occurred by chance only about 14% of the time. This is akin to calling the outcome of future coin tosses as, "I'm going to toss this coin three times and you're going to see three heads." Because it is unlikely that one could do this through chance alone, it suggests that something else is going on. Perhaps the coin is biased or the tosser is clairvoyant. In any event, although this outcome does not meet our typical standard for scientific confidence, it is nevertheless interesting and in the same positive direction as our other findings.

> This discovery, that new product advertising may be more sensitive to program involvement effects than established product advertising, is not a total surprise.

This discovery, that new product advertising may be more sensitive to program involvement effects than established product advertising, is not a total surprise. Several previous investigations have examined the differences in consumer response to new versus established campaigns. They found significant differences between new and mature brands in terms of their advertising effectiveness as well as their response to differences in media weight and timing.

Results on the individual criteria in the present analysis concur with these findings and provide additional insight into new versus mature brand advertising effects. For the established brands, both copy-point credibility and aided recall were significant at the univariate level, exhibiting strong increases in mean response as involvement moved from the lowest to highest levels. The most pronounced gains in advertising response for the new brands, moving from low to high involvement, were found on the purchase interest and behavioral intentions change (persuasion) measures, although the impact of program involvement on the effectiveness of new brand advertising response was statistically significant across all response criteria.

It seems natural that advertising for established brands, even though it involved a new execution, exhibited its strongest impact on the credibility and recall measures. By and large, consumers are familiar with the brands, recall key copy points and, in effect, demonstrate that the advertising has reinforced awareness of the brand and reaffirmed their beliefs associated with it—the traditional goal of established brand advertising. Therefore, finding that purchase interest, behavior intention change, and aided recall are related to new campaigns for new brands is hardly surprising.

With new product and line extension advertising, a new benefit presumably heightens viewer interest. Such advertising will be particularly effective if viewers perceive this benefit as desirable but lacking in their current brand. Thus, with new products, significant effects on purchase interest and behavioral intentions change (as well as the statistically significant changes in unaided proven and aided recall scores) suggest that viewers find a benefit offered in one or both new brand campaigns desirable and missing from their current brand.

Although one should not presume too much consumer cognitive processing on advertising for a low-involvement packaged good, it is well established that new-brand advertising does better in arousing consumer interest or attention than advertising for mature brands. The reason seems to be that differentiation itself, in the guise of newness, is the key to enhanced receptivity. It is equally possible that the presumably differentiating element, because it is new, is enough to cause enhanced viewer processing of the advertising (Stewart & Furse, 1984/1985).

TABLE 7.11 Effects of Program Involvement on Overall Advertising Effectiveness for Factual and Brand Image Advertising Campaigns

Program Involvement	Four Factual Campaigns			Four Image Campaigns		
	Low (N = 56)	Average (N = 46)	High (N = 38)	Low (N = 56)	Average (N = 46)	High (N = 38)
Advertising response						
Aided message recall	−.27	.12	.26	−.20	.11	.32
Purchase interest	−.16	.01	.22	.05	.11	−.08
Overall advertising response	−.22	.07	.24	−.08	.11	.12

Factual and image-related advertising. We used all eight commercials (four test-brand and four clutter ads) in these analyses of the comparative effectiveness of factual and image-based campaigns. Four commercials qualify as purely image-related ads; the others are clearly factually oriented executions. As with previous analyses, we examine the same type of relationships, but this time using a limited advertising response battery consisting of two measures, the only two that were collected in the same way for both test and clutter ads in this analysis. These are purchase interest and aided copy-point recall. Because the analysis is restricted to two dependent variables, we present the mean results of program environment on each of the advertising effectiveness measures, as well as the familiar overall mean results.

Table 7.11 presents the results of the analyses for the eight campaigns and reduced response battery. Looking at the overall results, it is immediately apparent that the effects of program involvement on the advertising response measures are modest for image campaigns (right columns), but appear substantially stronger overall for the factual campaigns. These findings are demonstrated by the results of the MANOVA analysis in Table 7.11 and are largely due to the significant effect of program involvement on both dependent variables for the factual campaigns and only for aided message recall for the image campaigns. An additional but weaker contribution to an overall stronger monotonic function, displayed in the results for the factual campaigns, is provided by the marginally significant ($p < .08$) effect of program involvement on the purchase interest measure.

8

New Insights Into Advertising Test Methods

Advertising testing, often called copy testing, is usually undertaken to evaluate one or more copy strategies or executions (or both) in rough or "near finished" form prior to running a finished commercial in the real world. This is commonly referred to as pretesting in distinction from posttesting, which is undertaken after a commercial has been "finished," and sometimes after it has actually run in the marketplace.

Views of advertising pretesting may be divided into three camps: those who are highly skeptical of its value (or for various reasons never had any use for it), those who continue to search for more robust and "predictive" methods in what often appears to be an indifferent agency environment, and those who prefer one copy-testing methodology over others and employ it on a regular basis. This chapter presents a new perspective on copy testing in light of our discoveries concerning the respective roles of the exposure environment and program involvement on ad response scores.

> The simulated-natural testing environment may offer greater potential for far more valid, reliable, discriminating, and ulti-mately more predictive testing.

What we have learned is that the simulated-natural testing environment overcomes many of the known problems and limitations associated with the most frequently used methods—the artificial, forced exposure test and on-air test. The simulated-natural testing environment, defined according to the remedial features that we will suggest in this chapter, may offer greater potential for far more valid, reliable, discriminating and ultimately, more predictive testing of commercials than methods previously employed.

True, the simulated-natural treatment condition of this study was, in effect, created in a laboratory setting. Yet, testing requires some controls; accordingly, we made the location, the study's purpose, and nature of stimulus presentation (program/advertising) as unobtrusive as possible. The respondents knew they were being tested. But for what exactly? The information we gave in the instructions and, indeed, the experiment itself could not have given away the purpose of the study other than that it had something to do with television.

For example, we obtained measures of behavioral intentions, pre- and posttest, for two product categories for which no corresponding commercials were shown. It is comforting to note that for these categories, the pre- and posttesting scores were virtually identical.

As this chapter will show, advertising response scores in the simulated-natural exposure condition were lower (in absolute terms) than in the artificial forced-exposure condition. Unobtrusive observation of respondents in the simulated-natural environment condition demonstrated why the response scores were lower and seemingly more realistic than those in the artificial forced-exposure environments: Some respondents had apparently ignored their location and were behaving quite like people watching TV at home (moving about, intermittently thumbing through magazines, making coffee and snacks, chatting, and generally engaging in behaviors mirroring the in-home television environment).

We also learned that advertising response scores vary considerably depending on whether viewers are more or less involved in the program. Indeed, we discovered that the rank order for eight commercials tested varied considerably across the two viewing environments.

This suggests that the exposure environment employed in a given copy test and the specific program environment in which the test commercials are embedded may interact with one another to generate the commercial effectiveness scores management sees. One exposure environment may suggest a strongly performing commercial whereas another environment may suggest the same commercial is weak. We suggest the simulated natural viewing environment and high program involvement measures are most likely to give advertisers the information they need to make the best decisions.

THE PROBLEMS WITH
TELEVISION COPY RESEARCH

Virtually all traditional commercial testing systems *may* be riddled with faults, faults that challenge their reliability and validity. As Ted Dunn remarked to the Advertising Research Foundation all the way back in 1984, "It's been said by various detractors of television copy research, stick a television commercial in front of a respondent, ask him a few questions, and you have a television copy research study."

Alvin Achenbaum, speaking at a conference of the American Marketing Association (1985) over a decade ago, was more strident:

> Copy tests are, in my opinion, no better than market tests in their performance. To take the most prevalent technique used today, so-called recall measurements are irrelevant, they are not in fact related to consumer purchase proclivities or purchasing behavior, yet marketers continue to use and rely on that measuring stick. . . . But copy tests lack for more than a relevant measurement device. The fact is they fail on almost every aspect of good research design—from the small samples they use to the unrealistic stimuli involved, to name only two. (cited in Jensen, 1994, p. R3)

Advertisers and marketing researchers have known for years that advertising copy-test scores vary depending on the environment in which exposure takes place.

Advertisers and marketing researchers have known for years that advertising copy test scores vary depending on the testing environment in which exposure takes place. We discussed the general nature of this phenomenon in Chapters 2 and 3 and empirically confirmed it in Chapter 6. As we discussed, the two primary and traditional modes of exposure are the artificial, forced-exposure test environment and the natural test environment. The latter may be considered, on the one hand, the true in-home environment, as in day-after recall (DAR) or telephone/personal interview coincidentals, or on the other hand, the simulated natural environment—with the proper methodology calling for extensive efforts to mirror the in-home viewing environment. This includes unobtrusively controlling for the many possible extraneous factors, or covariates, which have the frequent habit of rendering actual in-home test scores unreliable.

Clear reasons also exist for the typically significant differences in commercial test-score levels that, as we mentioned, result from forced artificial versus simulated natural exposure environments. The clearest reason, of course, is that respondents in an artificial environment are required to give their undivided attention to the visual stimuli. Frequently, these stimuli are themselves highly artificial and would appear to encourage high scores. The McCollum/Spielman approach, which often airs the same commercial twice in an hour of theater-like testing, is an example. When there is nothing else to view but the stimuli, it is natural that respondents will pay more attention, be more conscious that they are in a test, remember more of the commercial, and perhaps even engage in helpful acquiescence bias—particularly for humorous ads.

This may be why recall scores in the current research were, on average, 60% higher in the forced-artificial environment than they were in the simulated natural environment, and 36% higher across all measures. This suggests a reason why an advertising agency or an advertiser might avoid natural-environment advertising testing and use artificial forced-exposure approaches instead: The scores are higher. These higher scores are largely spurious, of course, and directly attributable to the testing methodology, but many people in the advertising business use copy testing only as a point of policy (and grudgingly, at that) and cannot get management's approval to air an advertisement without a "good" score. Frequently, forced-artificial environment testing will give them that score, whereas natural environment testing will not.

Many commercial researchers firmly believe in the quality of an advertisement being tested—perhaps seeing a slow but steady response build and longer term impact. If they are able to get the initial scores that management will approve only through forced-artificial testing, they do it. Agency management, for its part, may know or appreciate little of the value of the copy-testing process or may know the client does not, and that only a "high-scoring" commercial is satisfactory.

Prior to formally testing Hypothesis 7 (simulating the physical details of the natural program environment and adhering to methodological details will yield lower advertising response scores but with greater face validity and ability to discriminate between commercials tested than traditional forced-exposure testing), a short review of our methods and relevant findings is appropriate. Initially, and close to the focus of this chapter, we showed that efforts taken to simulate the physical details of a more natural program environment will yield lower advertising response scores, but they will be more face-valid and able to discriminate among executions with greater sensitivity. With regard to the reliability of the two copy-testing environments, Chapters 4 to 6 demonstrate that it is found in far greater quantities in the simulated natural environment. We are revisiting the issue here only to point out that a comparison of reliability between the polar testing modes (and the claimed superiority by advocates of forced-exposure testing) is ultimately an exercise in futility.

> The key issue lies with the testing system's ability to discriminate clearly between executions—whether roughs or full productions.

However, given the difficulty (and walls of artificiality) that advertising researchers and copy-testing advocates have confronted in demonstrating testing-system reliability, conventional wisdom says that reliability is welcomed if it can be demonstrated, but the key issue lies with the system's ability to discriminate clearly between executions—whether roughs or full productions. This extends to individual executions as well, to determine good versus not-so-good, with the requisite diagnostics. Given these two points, we intend to demonstrate that the simulated natural environment testing methodology produces greater discrimination in scores among ads than does the forced-artificial environment.

COPY-TEST EXPOSURE ENVIRONMENTS AND ADVERTISING RESPONSE

As we said in Chapter 4, we assigned a random selection of 470 female heads of households (primary purchasers of the test products) to one of four different hour-length prime-time programs, episodes of which had not been previously aired. Two of these programs were hypothesized to be high in involvement potential, the other two to be low. To ensure that results were representative of women in and out of the workforce, we also randomly assigned respondents by day-part, maintaining constant demographic variability within each of the resulting 12 cells (three day-parts by four programs). This design ensured about 40 respondents per day-part, per program, with constant demographic variability—an adequate representation of working women while controlling for any viewing-time effects on the results.

Furthermore, for our purpose here, we randomly assigned respondents to the traditional, artificial forced-exposure environment and to the simulated natural environment. Those assigned to the forced-exposure viewing environment were led in groups of 12 to 15 into an undecorated room with folding chairs arranged in a semicircle in front of a video monitor. They were instructed to turn their attention to the monitor *only* and refrain from conversing with one another. In the simulated natural viewing condition, small groups were brought into a room that simulated, as closely as possible, a typical comfortable living room. These respondents could watch, read, eat, converse, write a letter, or do as they wished; they were told so.

Following the program, respondents completed the postexposure questionnaires containing all key measures of advertising response for the eight embedded ads and program involvement.

The new program involvement measure, discussed in detail in Chapter 5, resulted in 30 items tapping into the cognitive, emotionally based, behavioral, and mood-affecting dimensions along which research in advertising, communications, psychology, and other disciplines has measured the motivations behind program selection and the range of peoples' reactions to program material.

We factor-analyzed responses to this 30-item program involvement inventory into three dimensions. The most important and significant factor, Entertainment Value, captured a far more complete range of program-content reaction than measures previously used. Following a thorough item analysis, this factor revealed a measure of high internal consistency and reliability. Once again, we measured advertising response along five dimensions:

1. Unaided brand name and main point (proven recall)
2. Aided copy-point recall
3. Copy-point credibility for each message recalled

4. Purchase interest, using the industry's usual 5-point rating scale
5. Pre-post exposure change in brand purchase intentions, using a constant-sum scale

> The relationship between involvement and advertising response does indeed vary significantly depending on exposure environment.

In Chapter 6, we confirmed the core hypothesis—the one that posited a significant interaction between program involvement and the exposure environment. The relationship between involvement and advertising response does indeed vary significantly depending on exposure environment. The chapter also showed that the differences in commercial effectiveness scores were substantial, comparing the artificial forced-exposure results with the simulated natural environment results. Given all that has been written concerning the shortcomings of, and inaccuracies generated by, the forced-artificial exposure environment, it was appropriate to test our sixth hypothesis.

This hypothesis states that response scores may be higher in the forced-exposure environment, but this only reflects the inherent artificiality of that form of testing environment. The resulting scores will lack the sensitivity to discriminate with acceptable accuracy among copy executions, in contrast with the same test when performed under simulated natural conditions. In other words, because of the more natural environment in which exposure takes place, the simulated-natural test condition will yield lower, more realistic, face-valid advertising response scores than the forced-exposure test condition where respondents exhibit (and are urged to do so) an artificially high level of attention to the only stimuli available, whether they are interested or not.

In considering these results, it is not unrealistic to attribute greater discrimination in advertising response scores among those in the simulated natural environment to the more natural environment in which exposure actually takes place. This is an important assertion from the copy-testing perspective because the ability of respondents to discriminate between test ads along the various response criteria used is one of the most fundamental steps toward separating effective from ineffective commercials.

CONFIRMATION OF HYPOTHESIS 7
AND IMPLICATIONS FOR HYPOTHESIS 6

Although the findings associated with Hypothesis 6 have potential implications in areas ranging from media buying decisions to program concept testing procedures, our concern here is with their meaning and potential importance from an advertising testing approach (i.e., copy research). This testing function is critical because it can determine the outcome of the decision regarding which particular execution, copy theme, and image will represent the advertiser's product and its positioning to the target audience. This is all the more important in today's fragmented markets where the audience is potentially more specific and particular with regard to the advertisement, its content, and delivery. As we have seen, however, there is evidence that continued widespread reliance on advertising testing conducted under artificial forced-exposure testing conditions may produce misleading results.

Under the traditional forced-exposure conditions, the negative effects of viewing involvement failed to obtain statistical significance.

When we examined the MANOVA results for the artificial forced-exposure conditions, we found no significant change in advertising response scores for any of the five variables as the level of viewer involvement in the program moved from low to moderate to high. In other words, using the newly developed multidimensional measure of program involvement against a full range of advertising response measures, it appeared that under the traditional forced-exposure conditions (typically employed by proponents of the negative-effects hypothesis), these negative effects of viewing involvement on advertising response failed to obtain statistical significance, even at a marginal level. Instead, only weak, directional agreement in the case of two advertising response measures supported this hypothesis. The results were dramatically different when we examined the data from the simulated natural viewing environment.

Table 8.1 presents the mean advertising response scores for the commercials included in the study. In the first column are the mean scores for the forced-exposure environment; the second column lists the scores from the simulated

TABLE 8.1 Mean Advertising Response for Eight[a] Television Commercials by Viewing Environment

Criterion	Artificial Forced-Exposure	Simulated Natural Environment	Index[b]
Behavioral intentions change	14.2	11.1**	1.28
Copy-point credibility	44.0	33.8**	1.30
Purchase interest[c]	42.5	38.7*	1.10
Aided message recall	74.8	44.2***	1.69
Unaided proven recall[d]	28.5	12.6***	2.26
Average	40.8	27.1	1.53

a. Mean response data common both to the four test commercials and four clutter commercials are available for the aided recall, unaided proven recall, and purchase interest criterion variables. In the case of the behavioral intentions change and copy-point credibility criteria, data is available for the test commercials only.

b. Our index is the ratio of the forced-exposure score to the simulated-natural score. The index shows that, on average, artificial forced-exposure scores are 53% higher than simulated-natural scores.

c. Data for the purchase interest criterion were available for each of the eight commercials but involved a different response format for the clutter commercials; hence, a composite variable was used.

d. To report mean response for all eight commercials, in the same way, the unaided proven recall measure was computed differently than it was in Chapter 6. The variable used in this chapter essentially reflects proven name registration only for the eight commercials.

$*.05 \leq p > .01$; $**.01 \leq p \geq .001$; $***p < .001$.

natural environment. Recall from Chapter 4 that each respondent saw the same eight commercials. For four of them, data on all five criterion measures are available; for the other four clutter ads, incomplete data are available. To maximize the amount of data with which to examine our hypothesis, we have augmented the test commercial data with data from the clutter commercials on those criterion variables for which data are available in both exposure environments.

As the table's notes indicate, the operational definitions for three measures common to the eight commercials (purchase interest, aided message recall, and unaided brand recall) required modification to accommodate the additional data. This had the effect of changing the absolute elevation of the scores compared to data presented earlier in Chapter 6. For all five criteria, the difference in response scores between the two exposure conditions are significant at the $p < .05$ level and in the expected direction. Overall, the forced-exposure scores are 53% higher than the average simulated natural environment scores across the five advertising response criteria.

These differences in mean response levels between the two exposure conditions offer strong evidence, once again, of the artificiality of the forced-exposure

TABLE 8.2 Coefficients of Variation for Eight[a] Commercials by Viewing
Environment

Criterion	Artificial Forced-Exposure	Simulated Natural Environment
Behavioral intentions change	0.94	1.28*
Copy-point credibility	0.40	0.68*
Purchase interest	1.10	1.20
Aided message recall	0.31	0.90**
Unaided proven recall	1.43	2.34**
Average	0.84	1.28

a. Data in this table directly reflect, for each criterion measure, the commercials and data available in Table 8.1.
*$.05 \leq p > .01$; **$.01 \leq p \geq .001$.

method and its results. Copy test scores in this environment systematically, significantly, and deceptively (albeit unintentionally) overstate viewers' advertising responses.

SIMULATED NATURAL TESTING: BETTER ABILITY TO DISCRIMINATE

To further examine the comparative levels of response discrimination in the two test environments, we next calculated coefficients of variation for each measure in each environment (keeping in mind that each respondent saw the same eight commercials). Taking the data in common for each commercial, we calculated a coefficient of variation for each measure of advertising response. This statistic is the standard deviation of a set of scores divided by the mean of the scores. Because the mean scores for the forced-exposure environment are higher than those for the simulated natural environment, the coefficient of variation adjusts for this artificially inflated difference. This, in turn, allows further comparison between groups, supported by a measure of relative variability between them.

Table 8.2 demonstrates that variation, and ultimately ability to discriminate, is noticeably greater among the eight commercials in the simulated natural environment than under traditional, forced-exposure conditions. The single exception, once again, is the purchase interest measure. Although it is in the expected direction, variation is not great enough to reveal a clearly significant difference. Taken together, however, these results offer strong evidence that one may obtain higher levels of discrimination and sensitivity by copy testing in simulated natural environments.

Although we could cite all of the above as sufficient for the confirmation of Hypothesis 7, an additional step in the analysis can strengthen the conclusion or render it trivial. One of the primary questions in the minds of interested advertisers and advertising researchers is whether they would reach the same conclusions about advertising effectiveness under the two exposure conditions. Unfortunately, there are no data to examine regarding different executions for the same brand, product, or company. What we can examine, however, are scores for the same eight commercials in terms of criteria common to all. Using MANOVA's mean response vector, we rank-ordered the performance of the eight commercials under both conditions. Table 8.3 shows the ranks to be similar although clearly not identical. The Spearman rank-order correlation coefficient between the two viewing environments, for example, is a respectable, but not outstanding 0.73.

(The Spearman rank-order correlation coefficient, rho, is used to determine whether two different rankings on the same cases—in this application, commercials—are similar or different. Rho does not require data with the same arithmetic scale distances between them, as points on a ruler. Rather, rho requires only nominal or ordinal rank-ordered data to calculate a correlation coefficient between two sets of rank-ordered data. The values of rho range from −1 to +1, as in other correlation coefficients, and describe the direction by sign and degree of general strength of the relationship between the two ranks.)

> There is a more than reasonable possibility that the two exposure environments might lead to different conclusions about a particular piece of copy.

Yet, there are differences between the two. One does not reach the same conclusions under the two viewing conditions. Hence, there is a more than reasonable possibility that the two exposure environments might lead to different conclusions about a particular piece of copy.

TABLE 8.3 Rank Order of Commercial Performance Across Measures of Advertising Response[a]

Commercial	By Viewing Environment		By Program Involvement	
	Forced-Exposure	Simulated Natural	Low Involvement	High Involvement
H	5	2	3	1
G	3	4	6	2
D	1	1	1	3
A	4	3	2	4
E	2	5	5	5
F	8	8	8	6
B	6	7	7	7
C	7	6	4	8
		rho = .73		rho = .43

a. Rank orders reflect only those criteria in common for all eight commercials.

The remaining two columns of Table 8.3 provide more disturbing evidence, however. Here the eight commercials have been rank-ordered in terms of the same mean advertising response vector and low versus high involvement programs. It is readily apparent that the ranks are quite different. This suggests that the exposure environment employed in a given copy test and the specific program environment in which the test commercials are embedded may interact with one another to generate the commercial effectiveness scores management sees. One program or exposure environment (or both) may suggest a strongly performing commercial whereas another combination may suggest that the same commercial performs weakly.

In this, we can see the work from the early 1970s on the unreliability of on-air recall scores casting a long shadow. As we noted, that work indicated that the single best predictor of advertising recall scores was viewer attitudes toward the program in which a commercial was shown (Clancy & Kweskin, 1971). The results of these analyses, therefore, provide clear confirmation of Hypothesis 7, which says that the simulated natural environment would produce more discriminating scores. In this chapter, we found not only more discriminating scores, but the very troubling discovery that the rank order of the eight commercials tested was different under different viewing conditions.

The New Standard
for Media Buying:
Cost Per Thousands Involved

Marketers expect media planners and buyers to maximize the size of the target audience reached with commercial material while minimizing the costs. The yardstick the industry uses to measure efficiency most frequently has been the cost per thousand reached by the message or campaign (CPM).

The CPM has long been an acceptable decision aid for advertisers and media people as a quick way to compare the relative cost efficiencies of alternative program buys. A.C. Nielsen, the syndicated media audience-measurement service, is the largest company providing the numbers that go into the television CPM formula. Nielsen's methods provide the most commonly used measures of people's television viewing practices and program selections. Based on a variety of procedures and samples, Nielsen provides advertisers with estimates of the number of viewers tuned to and watching a particular program. Advertisers use these estimates to calculate cost efficiencies related to a media buy or ad campaign. The greater the number of households or viewers in Nielsen's sample apparently watching a given program, the larger the estimate of the number of total viewers in the parent population having been exposed (the denominator of the CPM) and the higher the program's rating. The higher the program's rating, the higher the cost of commercial time within the program (the numerator of the cost-efficiency ratio).

Audience data provided by Nielsen and other services allows advertisers to calculate CPMs for virtually any combination of demographic, product usage, and in some cases, the psychographic characteristics of target groups. Audience data are no longer limited to imprecise "Households Viewing," but also include specific "Persons Viewing" in distinct demographic groups.

Yet, although the improvements have value, Nielsen has accomplished little in terms of successfully adjusting the numbers themselves for known or suspected inaccuracies in the audience estimates. As Bogart (1986a) pointed out in his discussion of the shortcomings of conventional CPMs, these cost-efficiency calculations still treat all target ad impressions alike, regardless of whether they are based on (a) total audience, (b) total exposure opportunity, (c) total target exposure opportunity, or (d) actual target exposure. Clearly, the CPMs will differ in each case. The Nielsen numbers (from the samples) include distracted viewers, rapid channel-changers (Nielsen's program ratings are based on an average minute, and commercial time is counted in the ratings), those missing from the room, and those tired of pushing the people meter buttons or recording every program change in their diaries (Beville, 1988; Bogart, 1986b; Clancy & Shulman, 1995; Edmondson, 1997; King, 1994; Lloyd, 1987; Lodish, 1986; Milavsky, 1992; Raymondo, 1997; Rubens, 1989). The advertiser, however, still pays for these viewers.

If program involvement enhances advertising effectiveness, then costs per thousand people *involved* (CPMI) should replace costs per thousand exposed.

If program involvement enhances advertising effectiveness and if involvement means more than simple viewership or attention, then cost per thousand people *involved* (CPMI) should replace the CPM as the tool of choice for media selection decisions. With rare exceptions, syndicated TV audience data fail to distinguish between exposure opportunities and actual exposure in deriving audience size counts. Also, with rare exceptions, the syndicated TV audience data fail to distinguish between involved and attentive exposure and restless, fleeting exposure. We have shown that the more involving the program—the more opportunities for personal connections it creates for the viewer by fostering involvement—the greater the level of advertising processing. When good, highly involving programming is followed by good, highly involving advertising, the associated CPMI's—the cost per thousand people actually involved in the programming—could define a new benchmark of advertising efficiency.

This idea, although in different terms, is to be found throughout the literature describing the shortcomings of the conventional CPM for generating cost-efficiency figures. At the same time, a parallel notion runs through the literature—the idea that involvement in programs, or the overall program environment effect, is a key arbiter of viewer availability, receptivity, and response to commercial messages (Beville, 1988; Bogart, 1986a, 1986b; Grunert, 1996; Krugman, 1967, 1983; Lloyd, 1987; Lodish, 1986; Murry et al., 1992; Stipp & Schiavone, 1996).

Lodish (1986), for example, states,

> The precisely wrong approach to evaluating media plans is to just count the potential exposures [at, he implies, any level of audience specificity]. Many media buyers prefer to judge the effectiveness of their media planning and buying by how low their cost per thousand audience . . . is above alternative media schedules. In almost every case this is a precisely wrong methodology. . . . The environment in which an ad appears may have a significant effect on the . . . viewer. (p. 127)

This media (or vehicle) environment effect may be caused by viewer attitudes toward the vehicle, the mood it provokes, or the viewer's degree of involvement.

> Research has documented that some programs minimize inattentive, restless, and distracted viewing behavior, increasing the likelihood of exposure to the commercials.

Research has documented, however, that some programs—those that involve, engage, or have an impact on the viewer—minimize inattentive, restless, and distracted viewing behavior and frequent channel-switching. Such programs also increase the likelihood of exposure to the commercials they carry (Clancy & Shulman, 1991, 1995; Leach, 1981; Rust, 1987).

The implications for improved cost-efficiency calculations and the value of the CPMI concept are implicit in the comments of Leo Bogart, who was involved with the issue from its inception. Bogart (1986b) has stated,

> Useful though the concept of cost per thousand may be, it can lead to errors of judgment when caused to consider communication as something that exists out of context with the media environment. [Further] . . . the user of CPM may be well

aware that he can communicate only as well as permitted by the character of the vehicle and the setting it offers him. (pp. 320-321)

AGENCY MEDIA DEPARTMENTS: VICTIMS OF CIRCUMSTANCE OR INERTIA?

In 1984, Michael Naples, president of the Advertising Research Foundation, wrote of the growing frustration many advertisers and advertising researchers felt about the continued usage of the impotent CPM and the unwillingness of many media departments and firms to develop a more sophisticated methodology to assess the efficiencies—with hints toward the effectiveness—of their media buys. Naples said that to most media people, audience numbers, program ratings, demographics, and a bit of additional data gathered by the syndicated services

is all there is. . . . [and] if not all there is, then certainly all that is used in media planning and buying. . . . The fact is that in most media planning today, ratings of one sort or another have become the surrogate for what advertisers want but do not yet have. What is needed is a commercial exposure and effectiveness measure that can be integrated into the buying process just as gross rating points have been. (p. 39)

> Measuring and applying CPMIs is a simple, reliable, and valid adjustment procedure—as simple as the positive relationship between audience involvement and advertising response.

We believe that audience measurement incorporating CPMIs may best answer the industry's needs. Measuring and applying CPMIs is a simple, reliable, and valid adjustment procedure—as simple as the positive relationship between audience involvement and advertising response. At the same time, many in the industry believe that advertising agency media departments still buy most television time using the same simplistic criteria they used in the 1950s. They take audience counts at more or less face value and, in doing so, take rating points the same way. They may haggle over unit costs a bit, but ultimately cost per insertion is divided by the audience counts, regardless of untested, unverified, and unadjusted figures.

This is what agency critics are saying about all but the largest firms: They are behind the times on most counts; research and media are basically concerned only with "demographics, GRPs, and the syndicated numbers"; the walls between the functional areas remain standing. But agency media and research departments should not take all the blame. Although many advertisers have actively supported the search for more and better quality programming—environments where they dramatically improve the chances of involved exposure to their advertising—a greater number are interested solely in the number of eyeballs they reach. Given this fixation by advertisers, it's no wonder that most agencies have been forced to stand "behind the numbers" (Ross, 1997).

But at the 1994 American Association of Advertising Agencies annual conference, Procter & Gamble's former chairman Edwin L. Artzt expressed his surprise that agencies "are a bit reactionary" and "aren't anxious to encourage changes," to meet new media-related developments (Goldman, 1994). At the 1995 AAAA meeting, Sprint's chairman and Chief Executive Officer, William T. Esrey, repeated Artzt's point. He pointed out that clients will be holding agencies "more closely accountable for results than ever before," suggesting that the reason was not so much a demand for greater value from advertising dollars, but because "we know the technology is there [for measuring audiences' and advertising's effectiveness] more precisely than you have done in the past." Esrey spoke of outmoded "attitudes born of the mass-marketing era," and agencies "mired in the past," knowing only "profiles of consumer demographics" (Goldman, 1995b). This was a short step from simply restating the complaint that media departments rely on safety in the traditional numbers, the CPMs they deliver, and by which they make their decisions.

Our purpose in pointing out agency culpability is to underscore the need for (a) better predictive measurement capabilities, (b) more creative media planning, and (c) a more accurate and effective method to calculate cost-efficiency ratios.

ADVERTISING EFFECTIVENESS REQUIRES INVOLVING PROGRAMMING

Achieving a more-than-acceptable level of advertising effectiveness requires involving programming that maintains audience attention and involvement. As Krugman (1983) stated, the most likely formula for advertising effectiveness is to link involving programming with involving advertising. With increasing television alternatives and the propensity for viewers to zap commercials, compelling programming may not be enough to sustain viewer involvement into commercial breaks. There must also be high-quality, targeted, and engaging advertising, and there appears to be a general consensus among advertisers that the agencies are not accomplishing that portion of the task very well.

There is consistent and harsh criticism for what may be deemed good advertising—the kind of advertising that may surprise, shock, or delight you; advertising that wins awards for its effects but leaves the viewer without a clue as to benefits promised or even the sponsor. But there is an ever-increasing demand for effective advertising. Artzt, Esrey, Bogart, and others were directing their criticism at agencies and their ability to turn out more effective advertising as much as at the media departments for their antiquated approach.

Betsy Frank, then senior vice president, Saatchi & Saatchi Advertising, New York, has suggested the need for "programs that can actually increase usage levels in their time periods—programs so compelling they don't just cannibalize the other networks, they actually attract new viewers who weren't even watching television that hour before" (Motavalli, 1989, p. 158). Many of her clients need the beneficial characteristics of broadcast network television "because it carries their commercial messages to the appropriate breadth of viewers." Here is where the notion of program excellence and more conventional interpretations of the program environment can be seen to converge.

As Engel, Warshaw, and Kinnear (1983) pointed out, the notion of CPM can be easily abused. The CPM assumes that costs are the dominant consideration in media selection, whereas any one of a myriad of other considerations could be of primary importance. Engel et al. provides an example: selectivity in reaching target markets. The authors confirm what we already know about the ratio's denominator: It could be total circulation, readership, viewership (and, of course, several levels of each),

> none of which is modified to ascertain the number of prospects reached. A CPM of $2.83 could easily become a CPM of $20 because of inefficient coverage of the target market. . . . Thus, formulas of this kind should be used only when the denominator is refined to generate cost per thousand prospects reached. (pp. 292-293)

The CPMI seeks to provide a similar refinement but with a simple adjustment procedure that eliminates the difficulties frequently encountered in arriving at specific figures such as CPMR (cost per thousand reached), in a timely fashion.

Echoing Engel et al. (1983), Bogart (1986b) writes, "As a measure of efficiency, cost per thousand is only as good as the data it is based on, which may or may not be accurate" (p. 320). Cost per thousand is the "common coin of the advertising realm," but its convenience and general acceptance should not be confused with true value.

THE CONCEPT OF COST
PER THOUSANDS INVOLVED

In 1989, Bogart returned to the widely recognized flaws in the numbers and the need to consider the program environment in media buying decisions. He stated that ingenious attempts were being made to improve the quality of syndicated audience counts and the ratings they depend on; however, "there will surely be a desire on the part of advertisers to know more about audiences than the revised ratings will tell them" (p. 89). Referring to a small-scale study conducted in Springfield, Massachusetts, Bogart provides yet another example of the shortcomings in audience measurement approaches reviewed in earlier chapters. Involving 100 households and stop-motion video cameras, the study found that "no one was in the room 15 percent of the time the television was on, and when in the room, they only looked at the TV three-fifths of the time" (p. 89).

Although this study demonstrated yet again the difference between syndicated audience counts and viewership, it also reminds us of the questionable meaning of traditional audience statistics and leads Bogart to assert that "the program environment will have to be routinely considered in all future ad scheduling" (p. 89). Researchers, he maintains, have largely ignored the importance of the editorial context on viewing behavior and, hence, the receptivity to commercial material. More forcefully, he states that the surrounding program content is not a neutral backdrop, however: "There is abundant evidence that mood and mind-set carry over from moment to moment in the [total] audience experience."

It is common knowledge that less involving programs are far more prone to zapping, grazing, surfing, or VCR playback zipping than are more compelling programs.

It is not by chance that the importance of program involvement or the program environment on advertising response has been rekindled by practitioners and scholars (Baumgartner et al., 1997; Bogart, 1986a, 1986b, 1989; Clancy, 1990; Clancy & Shulman, 1995; Goldman, 1994, 1995b; Jensen, 1994; Lloyd & Clancy, 1991; Murry et al., 1992; Stipp & Schiavone, 1996). We now recognize that involvement enhances response effects in a variety of circumstances and areas of inquiry. In programming, of course, viewer involvement leads to positive advertising effectiveness. Within the industry, it is common knowledge that less involving programs are far more prone to zapping, grazing, surfing, or VCR playback zipping than are more compelling programs. It is hardly surprising that advertising effectiveness and advertising cost-efficiency are closely related to the concept of program involvement or attitudes.

Research documenting the distracted, restless nature of contemporary television viewing fills agency and advertiser files. Research has also documented that some programming—programming that involves, engages, or in some manner connects with the viewer—minimizes viewer restlessness, propensity to engage in distracted viewing, and frequent channel-changing. At the same time, such programs increase the likelihood of exposure to the commercials they carry. These findings provide clear evidence of both a statistically and practically significant positive impact on a full range of advertising effectiveness measures for involved viewers versus the uninvolved (Clancy & Lloyd, 1988; Lloyd, 1987; Lloyd & Clancy, 1991; Ross, 1996; Stipp & Schiavone, 1996).

The implications of these findings for improved cost-efficiency calculations and media planning and buying procedures are direct: In evaluating the cost efficiency of a media buy, costs per thousand based on virtually any form of syndicated audience counts should be adjusted to reflect the size of the far more valuable proportion of the audience: the program-involved viewers within the total audience, who are more likely to be exposed to, receptive to, and, perhaps, influenced by, the commercials.

> If media involvement is a significant determinant of advertising response, knowledge of target media involvement levels could aid a campaign's success.

The obvious question for media planners, however, is how can they determine which programs are likely to involve their targets? And how can that information be factored directly into media buying decisions in a valid, systematic way? Answering first from the conceptual level, the answer is quite clear: If program involvement enhances advertising effectiveness, and if involvement means more than simply exposure or viewership, then CPMI should replace CPM as the tool of choice for media decisions. Media vehicles differ considerably in terms of their capacity to generate involvement, even holding constant audience size, composition, and rating. Clearly, if media involvement is a significant determinant of advertising response, knowledge of this phenomenon should be a primary target for further investigation—knowledge of target media involvement levels could aid an advertising campaign's success.

COST PER THOUSAND INVOLVED: TESTS OF VIABILITY

Given the industry's reluctance to incorporate so-called qualitative program data into its efficiency ratios, the first questions media planners would ask include:

1. Do individual programs differ in their ability to involve viewers, and do members of the same program viewing audience differ significantly in their level of involvement toward the program?
2. Just how closely related are CPM and CPMI for the same programs?
3. Would media planners and buyers make the same media buys if the decision were based on the proposed CPMIs rather than CPMs?

If the program environment effect operated only in some aggregate fashion across several programs and viewing audiences, the findings reported in previous analyses and summarized in the last section of this chapter could be considered of largely theoretical interest alone.

If individual programs clearly differ in terms of their ability to engender different involvement levels among viewers, however, that gives strong support to the notion of placing buys—regardless of ratings—in programs that tend to be higher on both target involvement and CPMIs.

The individual level of analysis confirmed our hypothesis that the more interesting and involving the viewing experience, the more effective the advertising it carries will be. To illustrate, let us remind the reader that in Chapter 4, we pointed out that this research was based on four different prime-time, hour-long television programs, two of which were designated as above average

TABLE 9.1 Significant Differences Among Programs in Their Ability to Involve Viewers

Individual Viewer Involvement Level	Hypothesized Program Involvement Level	
	High	Low
Low	18.2%	80.7%
Moderate	36.3%	16.1%
High	45.5%	3.2%

in involvement and two below average. The designations were based on a proprietary television program viewing study undertaken among a cross-section of more than 1,000 adult Americans.

Taking data from the simulated natural test environment and a supposedly high-involvement program and a low-involvement program, we sorted consumers into three different levels, low, moderate, and high involvement. We discovered that indeed program content varies radically in terms of the involvement level of individual viewers. Note that among people who were exposed to the hypothesized high involvement program, 45.5% of viewers were highly involved. This contrasts to the 3.2% of people exposed to the hypothesized low involvement program. (See Table 9.1.)

This clearly shows the differential power of prime-time programming in involving consumers. Involvement clearly differs both between and within individual programs. Given that programs differ in involvement, and, as we saw in Chapter 5, involvement is linked to enhanced advertising effectiveness, then programs that are more involving should be worth more.

Subsequent analyses substantially extend these findings; they provide support to the old—but to some still radical—notion of placing buys in programs that have smaller audiences and ratings but that attract and hold a particular target audience. They also provide support to the notion of CPMIs.

But how closely related are CPMs and CPMIs, for the same set of programs? The results of a quartile analysis of 40 different television programs provides an initial answer. The analysis directly compares, quartile by quartile, the coincidence of the same programs, the efficiencies of which were computed both by CPM and by CPMI. As Table 9.2 demonstrates, the results are correlated, but by no means redundant.

TABLE 9.2 Cost per Thousand (CPM) Versus Cost per Thousand Involved
(CPMI) Quartile Analysis

| | *CPM* | | | |
CPMI	Top 25%	Second 25%	Third 25%	Bottom 25%
Top 25%	60%	40%	0%	0%
Second	20%	40%	20%	20%
Third	20%	10%	40%	30%
Bottom	0%	10%	40%	50%

NOTE: Both approaches are related, but they are not the same. Note that only 6 out of 10 programs ranked by the CPM method as in the top 25% are also ranked in the top quartile by the CPMI method.

> A media planner who selected the best set of programs using
> CPMs would not select the same programs as a planner using
> CPMIs.

The table shows that 6 of the 10 programs in the top quartile are the same for both CPM and CPMI, but four are different. Five out of 10 programs in the bottom quartile for CPMs are also in the bottom quartile for CPMIs. Thus, a media planner who selected the best set of programs using CPMs would not select exactly the same programs as a planner using CPMIs. That the programs selected using the two approaches are not the same, however, tells us virtually nothing about media efficiency. It could very well be that both perform similarly in terms of some criterion of advertising effectiveness per dollar spent.

To investigate this possibility we closely examined the programs selected by each method that were found to be in the top quartile (i.e., the top 10 programs based on CPMs and the top 10 based on the CPMI approach). As just noted, 6 of these programs overlapped. To measure the overall advertising effectiveness of each, we rank-ordered each program by its CPM and CPMI. We computed CPM the conventional way: We divided the unit cost for a 30-second insertion in each show by the published syndicated audience counts (females, age 18 years and older) for the show. We derived the CPMI by multiplying the same syndicated audience counts (females, 18 and older) for each program by the involvement-adjusted index values. In other words, the same unit costs appear in the CPMI numerator as in the CPM numerator, but we divided the former by the involvement-adjusted audience counts, a function of the involvement factor scale (to be explained below). We contend that this adjustment, based as it is on the proven ad effectiveness-building of viewer involvement, leads to more accurate audience figures and cost-efficiency ratios. Its primary significance is a far more realistic measure of the commercial-carrying value of a given program for a given audience.

Finally, we calculated each program's predicted advertising effectiveness score, then averaged and indexed these scores. This and subsequent exploratory analyses are based on the regression of individual respondent multidimensional program involvement scores on the MANOVA advertising response vector. Basically, to the extent that programs differ in terms of their involvement scores (which they do), and involvement scores are positively related to advertising effectiveness scores (which they are), then different programs can be characterized by different predicted advertising effectiveness scores. Based on independent research and other data, we were able to estimate advertising effectiveness scores for 40 different prime-time and news/current events programs.

Once we computed the predicted advertising effectiveness score for each of the 40 programs, we took the mean score and derived an index value for each program by dividing the raw effectiveness score for each program by the overall mean. The index value for each program can be interpreted, therefore, as the program's predicted effectiveness value, or stated differently, the program's involvement-adjusted, commercial-carrying value.

> The predicted mean advertising effectiveness index for programs in the top quartile according to CPMI is a full 23% higher than it is according to CPM.

Table 9.3, columns 3 and 5, shows these results. Comparing these columns demonstrates that the predicted mean advertising effectiveness index for programs in the top quartile according to CPMI is a full 23% higher than it is according to CPM. In short, programs appearing in the key top quartile, as calculated by CPMI, produce a significant boost in effectiveness.

TABLE 9.3 Ad Effectiveness Indices for Programs in the Top Quartile According to Cost per Thousand (CPM) and Cost per Thousand Involved (CPMI) Criteria

Top Quartile Program	CPM Cost	CPM Index	CPMI Cost	CPMI Index
1	$10.92	.96	$8.17	1.67
2	12.07	1.08	9.29	1.39
3	12.43	.67	9.80	1.53
4	12.78	1.08	11.18	1.08
5	12.91	1.39	11.60	1.47
6	13.19	.99	11.81	1.40
7	13.51	.67	11.84	1.08
8	13.67	1.67	11.99	.96
9	14.08	.90	12.12	1.30
10	14.52	1.16	12.52	1.16
Mean	x = $13.01	x = 1.06	x = $11.03	x = 1.30

+23%

+ 18%

Media buyers also need to know, however, whether there are any meaningful differences in CPM for programs selected on the basis of the conventional or proposed approaches. For Table 9.3, we also computed and averaged conventional CPM as well as CPMI for programs in the top quartile, as determined by the two approaches. Calculated according to traditional CPM, the average cost equals $13.01. When calculated by CPMI, however, the average cost is $11.03, an 18% savings.

The potential merit of the CPMI approach to cost-efficiency calculations is shown by higher levels of predicted effectiveness as well as lower costs. A further extension of the analysis is appropriate, however, to (a) demonstrate to the media planner the superiority in overall cost-efficiency by using CPMI rather than CPM, and (b) to satisfy requirements implicit in Hypothesis 7, that media planners would indeed make different decisions using CPMI.

Another look at the data in Table 9.3 provides even stronger support for the argument that a CPMI-based approach to media selection leads to improved, more efficient media buys than the traditional CPM approach. Dividing the CPMI advertising effectiveness index mean of 1.30 by its comparable mean CPMI cost of $11.03 (and multiplying by 100) provides an 11.8 estimated advertising efficiency value. The same calculations on the top 10 programs selected by the traditional CPM approach yield a comparable value of 8.1. The resulting efficiency ratios show a 46% improvement based on CPMI—a cost-efficiency improvement difficult to ignore.

These analyses support our hypothesis that if program involvement enhances advertising effectiveness and if involvement means more than simply viewership, then the greater the viewer's involvement in a program, the stronger the effects of the advertising shown in that program.

CPMI is different from CPM, and CPMI should replace CPM as the tool of choice for media selection decisions. We base this conclusion on painstaking efforts to operationalize and ensure the reliability and validity of the variables employed, on strict attention to methodological details, and on thorough data analyses.

As a result of this discovery, it would appear that the contentions earlier researchers and writers made to this effect are correct—program involvement or attitude does indeed vary significantly by program, and media decisions should take this into account.

All this suggests that CPMI and CPM may be very different and that media decisions would be different and more efficient if based on CPMI rather than the traditional CPM. Because the concept of CPMI appears to offer what advertisers want and need, media planners, in turn, should begin to take viewer involvement into account in a more systematic and sophisticated fashion.

10

The Hidden Effects of Print Media Environment

The previous chapters have demonstrated that there is hidden power in television programming. Some programs are more involving than others, and the higher level of involvement, the greater the effectiveness of television advertising, audience size, composition, and costs held constant. This begs the question: Does the same mysterious phenomenon hold true for print?

Advertising space salespeople have been selling the idea of editorial involvement as long as special-interest magazines have existed. It does not take much research to realize that golfers who read *Golf* magazine are interested in golf clubs; skiers who read *Skiing* want to know about the new parabolic skis; auto buffs who read *Car & Driver* are fascinated by cars and accessories. Women read *Vogue* and *Harper's Bazaar* as often for the ads as for the articles.

These are the easy cases. Unlike much television content, which is designed to entertain, distract, or divert, much of the editorial content in *Tennis, Better Homes & Gardens, Guns & Ammo,* and *Quiltmaker* is designed to educate, inform, and teach about tennis, homemaking, shooting, and quilts. The editorial content reinforces the advertising.

AUTHORS' NOTE: This chapter is co-authored by Steve Tipps, senior vice president, Copernicus: The Strategic Marketing Investment Group. Tipps designed and directed the original research, which was sponsored by *The New York Times.*

> Are people who are involved in the articles more involved with the advertising than people who have a low involvement in the articles?

But what about the more difficult cases, where the connection between the publication's editorial content and the advertising is not as obvious—or does not exist? What about general-interest print vehicles—magazines and newspapers such as *Newsweek, People, The New York Times, The Wall Street Journal,* and others, where there is not a clear relationship between editorial and advertising? Are people who are involved in the articles more or less involved with the advertising than people who have a low involvement in the articles? We hypothesized that print vehicles act much like television, that people who have high involvement in the news and feature articles also have high involvement in the advertising.

HOW THE PRINT MEDIA
STUDY WAS DESIGNED

To extend the findings of our original study, we conducted a follow-up study that measured involvement in print media. This 1997 study was undertaken among a regional cross-section of 926 regular readers of selected print vehicles. The hour and a half interview included a media habits and usage survey, coupled with a simulated natural laboratory experiment, which extended the methodological rigor of the previous study. The media usage survey provided detailed profiles of users of specific media, based on demographics, category usage, category involvement, media usage, and media involvement. The experiment was designed to measure the relative impact that image-based and response-based advertising had on consumer response for both national and local advertisers as measured across three broad media categories: three national newspapers, two local newspapers, and two magazines.

> Respondents were exposed to national and local ads, image and response ads, and airline, technology, department store, and fashion ads, identical in both media.

The experiment used test advertisements from 14 companies. We had seven local and seven national advertisers, and we made a further distinction between image and response ads in each of four categories. Among national advertisers we used image ads from two airlines, response ads from two airlines; image ads from two computer companies, and response ads from two technology companies. Among local advertisers, we used image ads from two department stores, response ads from two department stores; image ads from two retailers, and response ads from two fashion marketers. In other words, respondents were exposed to national and local ads, image and response ads, and airline, technology, department store, and fashion ads. The test ads were identical in both the newspapers and the magazines.

The simulated natural laboratory experiment captured consumer attitudes and likely purchasing behavior for test and control brands before and after exposure to a test advertisement. We looked at the variables in several ways, which included pre-to-post changes in these values by examining the pre-post shift in test-brand ratings. In these analyses, we look at the post-only ratings for some of them, and one behavioral shift as we did in the study of television involvement. The measures included related recall of the advertisements, overall rating of advertised brands and their competitors, rating of the same set of brands on "good value for the money," and purchase intent (1 year) for all brands studied.

The 926 respondents were exposed to different combinations of media and advertisements. (They were not exposed to department store or fashion clothing advertisements in national newspapers because the papers do not carry that advertising. Similarly, they were not exposed to airline, department store, or fashion response advertisements in the magazines because the publications do not carry such ads.) We attempted to balance each cell demographically, although this was not always possible.

We screened all respondents to establish that they used at least two of four test-product categories and that they were regular readers (at least half the issues) of at least one of the test publications. We showed them the test advertising in one of the publications that they read regularly. We included this restriction because advertisers and publishers are most interested in the advertising responses of their most faithful readers, those who receive most of the impressions and those the advertisers are targeting. Consequently, this study does not have low-involved media users in the same sense that the television study has; these are all regular readers. Therefore, in this analysis of print media, we do not see three levels of involvement but two: moderate and high.

MEASURES USED IN THE PRINT STUDY

The measures of advertising effectiveness used in the print study were similar to those used for the TV experiment. We evaluated response to the test advertisements in terms of proven advertising recall, attitudes toward the brand, perceptions of good value, (post-test ad) purchase interest, and the pre-post change in behavioral intentions.

In developing a measure of involvement with publications, we drew on the items used to evaluate involvement with TV programs, including those related to publication quality (e.g. "Is a higher quality publication than others," "Is a leading publication in this metropolitan area"), an emotional connection (e.g. "Touched my feelings," "Identify with people written about in articles"), part of respondent life (e.g. "Contains information important to me," "One of the most important parts of day/week"), and uniqueness ("Different than any other publication I could read"). Based on tests of convergent and predictive validity, four items were finally selected to represent the involvement construct: "Is a higher quality publication than others," "Is very thought-provoking," "I identify with people I read about in the publication," and "Many of the articles really touched my feelings." These were summed to form a single involvement scale. Then, on the basis of their involvement scores, respondents were classified into one of two groups: moderately involved and highly involved.

Because we had adopted the print involvement items from the TV research, we sought corroboration for the new involvement scale from other measures of general media usage that could provide a more robust profile of our two involvement groups. We looked at various measures of media usage, media use environment, commitment, and attitude. For media usage, we measured the percentage of issues read, the percentage of respondents who subscribe to the vehicle, and the minutes they spend reading each vehicle. For media use environment, we measured the presence of other people, noise level, frequency of interruptions, and attention to the ads. For commitment, we asked for agreement with various statements such as: "There are many ways to get information, and they are all fine;" "I use a variety of sources and don't rely on any vehicle any more than other sources;" "I use a variety of sources and this vehicle is my favorite source;" and "If I could have only one source of information, it would be this vehicle." To measure attitudes toward the media vehicle, we asked respondents their reaction if the vehicle were no longer available (i.e., "Would not be able to replace it" to "Would easily replace it with one other source") and their feelings if the vehicle were no longer available (i.e., from "Very distressed" to "Happy to see it go").

> Highly involved respondents were more likely to say that if they could only have one source of information, it would be the test publication.

Our results (see Table 10.1) showed that the readers we classified as highly involved were, indeed, much more committed to and reliant on their publications. Although they spent only marginally more time reading their magazine or newspaper, and read it in similar surroundings (in terms of number of people in the room and level of distractions), the time they spent clearly had greater personal impact. It was quality time. Highly involved respondents were more likely to say that if they could only have one source of information, it would be the test publication; that the test publication was irreplaceable, and that they would be very distressed if it were no longer available.

To test our hypothesis that people who have a high involvement in a print media vehicle will be more positively affected by advertising in that media, we examined the relationship between involvement and advertising response separately across the five response criteria (see Table 10.2).

This analysis begins to reveal the hidden power of print editorial. For all but one of the five measures of advertising response (unaided proven recall), scores rise as the level of print involvement goes from moderate to high. It is intriguing to note that this one exception is for the very same variable that, in our television study, failed to show a significant relationship with advertising response as reported in Chapters 6 and 7. Table 10.2, however, is the data analyzed without MANCOVA and before we had tested for the influence of covariates.

TABLE 10.1 Test Publication Readership Habits and Attitudes According to Respondent Involvement With Publication

	F Sig	Mean (919)	Moderate (531)	High (388)	Scale
Subscribe to test publication	0.9483	.43	.43	.43	percentage yes
Typical amount of time spent reading publication	0.1171	40.96	39.96	42.33	minutes
Other people in room while reading publication	0.0651	1.34	1.32	1.37	1 = Alone, 2 = Other in room
Amount of background noise	0.9125	1.64	1.65	1.64	1 = A lot to 3 = Little/none
Amount of interruptions	0.2219	1.93	1.91	1.96	1 = Frequently to 3 = Hardly ever
*Percentage of ads seen/read	0.0165	2.74	2.68	2.83	1 = Most all to 4 = Hardly anyone
*Reaction if publication was no longer available	0.0000	2.26	2.37	2.12	1 = Would not be able to replace it to 4 = Would easily replace it
*Feeling if publication was no longer available	0.0000	2.09	2.21	1.93	1 = Very distressed to 4 = Happy to see it go
*Extent to which rely on publication for news/entertainment	0.0000	2.34	2.20	2.54	4 = If I could only have one source of information it would be test publication to 1 = There are many ways to get information and they are all fine
*Publication liking	0.0000	4.16	4.05	4.30	5 = Excellent to 1 = Poor

*$p < .05$.

TABLE 10.2 The Effects of Publication Involvement on Advertising Response

Publication Involvement	Behavioral Intentions Change (1)		Purchase Interest (2)		Favorable Brand Attitudes (3)		Perceptions of Good Value (4)		Proven Recall (5)	
	Mean	Effect	Mean	Effect	Mean	Effect	Mean	Effect	Mean	Effect
Moderate	1.11	-0.61	37.21	-1.37	59.54	-1.66	58.61	-1.16	11.65	-0.08
High	2.59	0.87	40.49	1.91	63.56	2.35	61.41	1.64	11.84	0.11
Overall mean	1.72		38.58		61.21		59.77		11.73	
F statistic	3.91		6.45		9.64		4.24		0.02	
Significance level of F	0.057		0.011		0.002		0.040		0.900	

NOTE: Scale (1), 1 = *Definitely will not purchase* to 5 = *Definitely will purchase*, indexed 0 to 100. Post-pre change score = –100 to +100. Scale (2), 1 = *Definitely will not purchase* to 5 = *Definitely will purchase*, indexed 0 to 100. Scale (3), 1 = *Does not describe* to 5 = *Describes completely*; indexed 0 to 100, averaged across three items in measure. Scale (4), 1 = *Does not describe* to 5 = *Describes completely*, indexed 0 to 100. Scale (5), 0 = *No proven recall*, 100 = *Proven recall*.

TABLE 10.3 Advertising Response Variable Intercorrelations

	Behavioral Intentions Change	Purchase Interest	Favorable Brand Attitudes	Perceptions of Good Values	Proven Recall
Behavioral intentions change	1.00				
Purchase interest	.38	1.00			
Favorable brand attitudes	.084	.47	1.00		
Perceptions of good value	.12	.38	.54	1.00	
Proven recall	.04	.03	−.01	−.01	1.00

NOTE: Italicized correlations are so high that they would have distorted traditional univariate tests. Hence, the need for MANOVA.

THE NEED FOR MULTIVARIATE ANALYSIS OF COVARIANCE

In earlier discussions of analysis methods, we suggested that two fundamental reasons led us to the choice of this model. The first is based on statistical grounds. Whenever one expects intercorrelations between the component measures of a composite dependent construct (here, advertising effectiveness), univariate test results are not strictly correct. They are incapable of considering or adjusting for the potential impact of these intercorrelations on the overall construct and, hence, on the results. Also, multiple measures of a construct result in a stronger construct because you eliminate the idiosyncratic bias that any single item might have. Several correlations that appear in Table 10.3, therefore, suggest the justification for MANCOVA. Note, for example, the strong correlations between purchase interest, favorable brand attitudes, and perceptions of good value.

The second argument in favor of MANCOVA stems from the fact that the project used actual, in-market advertisements and unedited media. As such, it was not possible to control for several factors in the experimental design of the study such as previous exposure(s) to the test ad, previous familiarity and involvement with the test brand, or additional (i.e., different) advertising for the test brand. To account for the effect that these factors might have had on the response to the test ads, covariance analysis—the COVA part of MANCOVA—was needed. That is, we adjusted the advertising response measures by setting other factors (the covariates) on an equal basis across the two test cells, that is, the moderate and high involvement groups. Once these factors have been accounted for, and the advertising response measures have been adjusted, any differences that remain between the cells can be attributed to the different levels of respondents' involvement with their publications. To be used in this analysis as in the television study, a covariate had to satisfy two conditions:

1. It had to have a significant relationship with the advertising response measure in question, for example, be significantly correlated (positive or negative).
2. It had to be differentially distributed across the test media cells, for example, its average could not be the same in each media cell.

We drew potential covariates from four conceptual areas: previous involvement with the test ad, product usage and affinity, advertising clutter in the test media (because we did not edit the media to strip out other advertising), and respondent demographics. Measures in each of these areas were found to be correlated with at least one of the advertising response measures. We then computed mean scores for these potential covariates within each level of involvement to determine if the two groups differed in terms of these measures (Table 10.4).

We found a significant difference ($p < .05$) for seven covariates: age, years of education, household income, marital status, sex, have seen/read test issue before, and how much read. This indicated that it was necessary to use covariance analysis to set the two involvement cells equal in terms of these variables. If we did not do this, the advertising response scores in the two cells would be driven not only by involvement, but by the covariates as well, and we would be unable to accurately test our hypothesis.

UNCOVERING THE HIDDEN POWER
OF PRINT EDITORIAL

Table 10.5 shows the MANCOVA test results. The second column indicates that, after adjusting the scores of all five advertising response measures according to the differences between the two involvement cells on the covariates, there is still a significant ($p = .011$) difference in overall advertising response. We have found significant support for our hypothesis. Not only have we demonstrated that print involvement is significantly related to print advertising effectiveness, but we have shown a strength of relationship similar to that of television program involvement.

TABLE 10.4 Covariates Tested for Use in MANOVA Analyses

Potential Covariate	Included in Model	Notes of Scale
Demographics		
Age of respondent	Yes	Years
Years of education	Yes	Years
Household income		$000s
Employment status		Percentage full-time
Marital status (1)		Percentage married
Marital status (2)		Percentage single
Presence of child < 19 years		Percentage yes
Presence of child < 7		Percentage yes
Presence of child 7 to 12		Percentage yes
Presence of child 13 to 18	Yes	Percentage yes
Presence of child 19+	Yes	Percentage yes
Gender		Percentage male
Race		Percentage white
Media Usage		
Seen/read test issue previously		Percentage yes
How much read		1= *read none* to 5 = *read all*
Seen test ad previously		Percentage yes
Number of times saw test ad		0 = *0* to 4 = *4+ times*
Time since saw test ad		1 = *1 day* to 6 = *6+ months ago*
Frequency see test brand ads	Yes	1 = *every day* to 6 = *never*
Category Usage		
Familiarity with test brand		1 = *never heard of it* to 4 = *extremely familiar*
Past purchasing of test brand	Yes	Percentage ever purchased
Test brand is most often purchased	Yes	Percentage yes
Category spending	Yes	Category spending standardized within each test product category
Category shopping frequency	Yes	Number of past year category purchases/ shopping trips standardized within each test product category

More important, perhaps, we have seen these effects for print, despite the fact that we restricted the print study to only two levels of print involvement—moderate and high. This is not an insignificant issue because the television analysis reveals the biggest effects to be between those low in involvement and the two other groups. Thus, print involvement does prove to be a powerful performer despite the constraints imposed on it by our methodology.

TABLE 10.5 Analysis of Covariance Test Results—Univariate Tests: Publication Involvement Adjusted for Covariates

Publication Involvement	Behavioral Intentions Change (1)		Purchase Interest (2)		Favorable Brand Attitudes (3)		Perceptions of Good Value (4)		Proven Recall (5)	
	Mean	Effect	Mean	Effect	Mean	Effect	Mean	Effect	Mean	Effect
Moderate	0.92	−0.80	37.29	−1.29	60.49	−0.72	58.71	−1.06	11.73	0.00
High	2.88	1.16	40.48	1.90	62.30	1.09	61.22	1.45	11.72	−0.01
Overall mean	1.72		38.58		61.21		59.77		11.73	
F statistic	3.12		8.18		13.10		3.71		0.00	
Significance level of F	0.047		0.004		0.000		0.044		0.995	
Multiple R^2	.036		.351		.191		.118		.025	

> Scores rise as the level of involvement goes from low to high for all but one of the five measures of advertising response.

Next, we turn to the scores on the individual advertising measures, to understand the nature and direction of the involvement-ad effectiveness relationship. This analysis clearly reveals the power of magazine and newspaper editorial environment. The values in Table 10.5 represent the covariance-adjusted means for each advertising response measure, at each level of publication involvement. Scores rise as the level of involvement goes from low to high for all but one of the five measures of advertising response.

Among people whose responses place them in the moderate publication involvement level, for example, purchase interest (measured on a 0 to 100 probability scale) is 37.29. Among people high in publication involvement, purchase interest increases by three points, or 9%, to 40.48. Similar relationships are seen in terms of favorable brand attitudes, good value, and pre-to-post behavioral intentions change. The only advertising measure in which moderate and high involvement respondents were not different was proven recall: Respondents in the two cells recalled the test ads with equal frequency.

We should remind our readers once again that unaided proven recall was the only variable in our previously reported television analysis that failed to show a significant relationship to viewer involvement. Whether it is something in the measurement of proven recall or some unknown theoretical construct or cognitive process that attenuates the connection between involvement and recall must remain a mystery at this time.

These findings provide strong support for our hypothesis. In multivariate and univariate tests, we see print advertising response significantly and positively influenced by reader involvement.

> The more people are involved in a magazine or newspaper, the greater will be the effect of the advertising carried by the publication.

Thus our hypothesis is generally confirmed: As involvement in a publication rises, so do all but one measure of advertising response. Stated differently, the more people are involved in a magazine or newspaper, the greater will be the effect of the advertising—in terms of behavioral intentions change, purchase interest, favorable brand attitudes, and perceptions of good value—carried by the publication.

We can feel confident about making this general claim because the data were generated across 14 test ads, four test-product categories, three publication types, and 926 respondents. Our findings were not the result of an idiosyncratic ad or product or publication that would make generalizations suspect.

The findings are also significant for the print media because the publications we tested were not special interest magazines and newspapers. One would expect to find eager readers of *Car & Driver, Sail,* and *Ski* magazines to be strongly affected by advertisements for cars, boats, and skis. That's half the reason why they read the magazine in the first place. But it is not intuitively apparent that involved readers of general interest magazines and newspapers would also be more favorably influenced by the advertising in these publications than readers who are less involved. This study clearly suggests that once again intuition often does not lead us to the correct conclusion.

11

Uncover the Hidden Power of Television Programming and Print Editorial

There is no question that the advertiser's world has grown more difficult over the last 10 years or so. Consumers are exposed to a blizzard of television commercials and print advertisements every day, ads that, on average, are significantly less effective than they were two decades ago. Among the reasons for this declining performance, as we discussed in Chapter 1, are media fragmentation, increased advertising clutter, consumer zapping and zipping, weak advertising executions, and inadequate media budgets.

One answer to these difficulties is, of course, to spend more money. Buy more time on more programs and hope to catch more viewers as they reach for the remote. Spending more money, however, is not an option for most advertisers. Another answer is better advertisements, advertising that is interesting, engaging, and informative, advertising that actually sells the product's points of difference. Spend the same amount of money on advertising that has a real effect on sales. That answer is, unfortunately, beyond the scope of this book. A third answer—the one this book addresses—is to unleash the hidden power of television and print. Spend less money to greater effect by placing the advertising in those programs and publications that involve the target viewers and readers.

A 30-YEAR-OLD MYSTERY SOLVED

As we pointed out in Chapter 2, marketing and advertising researchers have engaged in intellectual warfare over the impact of the television program environment on advertising effectiveness for over 30 years. All agreed

189

that the program environment significantly affects viewer receptivity to, and therefore the effectiveness of, television advertising, but they did not know whether the television viewing environment helps or hinders advertising effectiveness. Does a program in which the viewer is involved suck the life out of the commercials or does it actually help the commercials?

> If programming affects advertising performance significantly, the way in which advertisers count audiences must move beyond traditional media buying methods.

If programming affects advertising performance significantly, the way in which advertisers and marketers define and count program audiences (CPM, ratings, demographics, and the like) must move beyond the traditional methods they use to buy media. Moreover, if viewers of specific programs watch with varying levels of program involvement, and if this involvement directly affects their responses to the commercials, failing to recognize the importance of program involvement could lead advertisers to make substantial errors in where they run their spots.

Industry studies over the years have concluded both positive and negative effects. One of the earliest was Donald Smith's in 1956, using a sample of over 800 females in Tuscaloosa, Alabama. Based on data from diaries kept by sample respondents regarding their in-home television viewing behavior, and on periodic follow-up interviews, Smith found clear evidence of a positive relationship between enhanced viewer attention levels and liking for programs and an increased ability to recall advertising those programs carried.

Four years later, Horace Schwerin's work in 1960 lent support to the negative-effects hypothesis. Schwerin exposed respondents in a theater test environment to commercials embedded in one of three television programs: a quiz show, a musical, and a courtroom drama. Following exposure, respondents rated their reactions to the program content on a three-level scale—relaxed, concentrated, or tense. Schwerin concluded that recall of a given commercial was lower when the viewers rated themselves as tense than when they rated themselves as relaxed.

Since that time, researchers have conducted a variety of studies, some concluding a positive effect, some finding a negative effect. Our study of the literature, however, showed anomalies in all the studies. Virtually all published research concluding positive effects apparently employed natural environment and on-air designs, although the measurement of advertising effectiveness was confined, in most studies, to recall. Those concluding negative effects tended to use highly controlled, artificial forced-exposure designs but usually a somewhat greater range of response measures. Those concluding positive effects tended to use representative samples of viewers; those concluding negative effects tended to use convenience samples. Those concluding positive effects tended to use natural on-air stimuli; those concluding negative effects tended to use 30-minute program videotapes with ads embedded or as carried by the vehicle.

Because we were interested in solving this 30-year-old mystery, we designed a research project that would address all the anomalies, and along the way we discovered many other things.

HOW WE CONDUCTED OUR STUDIES

Our study of television and print involvement involved reasonably large samples of the general public in a time-consuming laboratory experiment. The television sample consisted of nearly 500 women, ages 18 to 49, representing a demographically heterogeneous cross-section of the female residents of a large Midwestern metropolitan area. The print sample consisted of more than 900 regular readers of six publications. These samples create significant improvements to internal validity and findings that can be generalized, compared with the samples many previous investigations used.

Our studies employed multiple-treatment experimental designs, including a unique, simulated natural exposure environment. In the television study, our design made it possible to make direct comparisons between results obtained under artificial and natural viewing conditions. And in contrast to most uncontrolled on-air, natural environment testing, this study's measurement of a wide range of respondent personal attitudes, product usage patterns, and TV viewing characteristics allowed detailed testing of findings within cells for any significant effects of these potential covariates.

> Rather than measure advertising response with a single judgmental scale, we measured television and print attitudes and involvement on numerous dimensions.

Rather than measure program or print content effects on advertising response with a single judgmental dimension/measure such as tense versus relaxed or sophisticated versus business-oriented, we measured television and print attitudes and involvement on numerous dimensions. We also made considerable efforts to establish the reliability and construct validity of the unique media involvement measures we employed.

In the study of television advertising, which represents the majority of chapters in this book, respondents were exposed to one of four different full-length episodes of popular network programs (the program plus commercial time). Actual commercials not previously aired in the test area were embedded in the programs at natural program breaks, and realistic program fade-in and fade-out occurred at the beginning and end of the program and at commercial breaks during the program. In addition, we took steps to simulate an in-home setting in the natural environment condition. These were intended to produce greater response variability while significantly enhancing our ability to generalize the findings.

We measured commercial response using a range of standard industry approaches from recall to persuasion. Restricting advertising response to single dimensions (such as recall) can be expected to provide a misleading impression of actual commercial performance and may limit the conclusions that one can draw concerning the relationship between program environment and advertising effectiveness. In the same manner, we explored the effects of print media involvement on print media advertising effectiveness, using a multidimensional array of advertising response measures.

Finally, following the primary analysis, we used covariance analysis in both studies to determine whether observed effects reflect the impact of the independent variable alone (i.e., media involvement), uncontaminated by respondent differences, demographics, product usage patterns, and other variables. Although some prior investigations have controlled for the potential influence of respondent differences, many others have simply stopped at reporting observed effects without going on to establish the integrity of these effects.

WHAT WE DISCOVERED FROM OUR RESEARCH

We established the existence of multiple reliable and valid measures of television program attitudes, the most important of which we have labeled involvement, a 10-item factor based on such statements as "Parts of this program touched my feelings," "I was really involved in this program," and "This program really made me concentrate."

We found that viewing conditions affect advertising response measures (ranging from recall to persuasion). The more artificial the viewing environment, the more inflated and sensitive the scores. When people are forced to pay attention, their recall scores and other measures of advertising response are higher and less discriminating than in a "real world" viewing situation. Worse, we discovered that even the rank order of performance of a commercial depends on viewing condition. Stated differently, if you change the viewing environment, you might select a different winner in a pretesting shoot-out.

We found that for each of the five measures of advertising response, scores rise as the level of program involvement goes from low to high. Among people whose responses place them in the lowest program involvement level, for example, behavioral change is 9.5%. Among those whose involvement scores are average, it rises to 12.5%; and among people high in program involvement, behavioral change jumps to 14.6%. The more people are involved in a television program, the greater will be the effectiveness of advertising carried by the program.

Our study of print advertising found similar effects. For all but one of the five measures of advertising response (proven recall), scores rise as the level of print involvement rises. (This study measured only moderate and high involvement because it had a constrained involvement sample; every one of the respondents was a regular reader of the publication.)

> Our study of television advertising clearly found that viewing condition explains in part why the literature of the past three decades has told different stories.

Our study of television advertising clearly found that viewing condition explains in part why the literature of the past three decades has told different stories. Program involvement and advertising response are most strongly and positively linked under natural or simulated natural conditions, whereas there is no relationship (or even a negative one) under highly artificial viewing conditions. Our results confirm the critical importance of the choice of test environment in investigations of program environment effects. Researchers commit a fundamental error when they directly compare the results obtained from artificial laboratory designs with those obtained from on-air testing, as though the differences in exposure environments were inconsequential to the results.

Under simulated natural viewing conditions, a significant positive effect of television program involvement was revealed for four of five measures of advertising effectiveness. The higher the level of involvement, the greater the measured advertising effectiveness. A variety of multivariate analyses support this conclusion, including repeated attempts to make the relationship disappear by introducing control factors. Time and again, however, the apparent causal linkage between involvement and advertising effects was evident.

Along the road to making this discovery, we discovered that an important determinant of advertising response scores is the environment in which the programming and advertising is presented. A highly artificial, forced-exposure setting—one typical of commercial copy-testing methodologies—produces inflated scores that are relatively unrelated to program involvement and that suffer from their ability to discriminate. The scores are so high they fail to reveal differences between tested advertising executions.

PROBLEMS WITH INDUSTRY
IMPLEMENTATION OF CPMI

As we have discussed, data supplied by the syndicated television rating services often fails to reflect accurate program audience counts and, as a result, accurate program ratings. Inaccurate counts prevent the computation of accurate cost-efficiency information. At the same time, many external factors are difficult or virtually impossible to control, exacerbating this problem. Everything from viewer commercial avoidance tactics and restless viewing patterns to the obsolete planning and buying methods of many agency media departments contributes to a situation where published program audience counts often have little in common with actual advertising viewership. As a result there are

1. Misleading data regarding actual audience exposure
2. Questionable estimates of audience members reached
3. Misleading ratings and unit costs
4. Inaccurate cost-efficiency calculations for individual program buys as well as for entire campaigns

and—for our purposes, the most important consideration of all—

5. No consistent way in the industry to take the previously hidden and mysterious effects of television program and print involvement into account.

Toward the end of yielding more effective advertising, we have proposed the construct of cost per thousand people involved (CPMI). We believe that the CPMI is a viable replacement for the traditional cost per thousand (CPM). Program involvement (and, it would appear, print involvement) enhances advertising effectiveness. It provides a great deal more than simple exposure or viewership figures. And it leads to different, more sensitive and accurate data for the evaluation of individual programs' cost-efficiencies.

It would be misleading, however, to suggest that we have addressed all the issues associated with implementing this alternative approach. The most fundamental obstruction, however, continues to elude resolution: the hesitation of media planners and many advertisers to introduce so-called qualitative media data into the planning and buying functions on a routine basis. Many reasons for defending the status quo are offered: "Such integration would be too complex," or "The approaches have not been proven valid," and more.

Over the years, the senior author of this book has developed several marketing science models that major companies have used to improve marketing and media decision making. One model, called Discovery,^{sm} is the next generation of the Litmus^{sm} model, which was described in detail in *Simulated Test Marketing* (Clancy, Shulman, & Wolf, 1994). Discovery, like Litmus before it, includes estimates of involvement for many different media vehicles to forecast the awareness of a new product that will be generated by exposure to television, print, radio, website, and billboard advertising, as well as public relations on a month-by-month basis following new product launch. Another model, the Copernican Media Optimizer,^{sm} is the next generation of a media optimization approach described in Chapter 4 of *The Marketing Revolution* (Clancy & Shulman, 1991). It too employs estimates of the differential involvement (i.e., impact) of up to 60 different television, print, radio, and alternative media vehicles to identify and describe a financially optimal target and media schedule for a new or established product or service. Common to both models is the general skepticism of agency and client media executives about the use of involvement scores.

> Every agency media planner carries an implicit set of assumptions in his or her head about the differential effectiveness of different media.

The fact is however that every agency media planner carries an implicit set of assumptions in his or her head about the differential effectiveness of different media—audience size, composition, and cost held constant. Agency planners are quick to claim, for example, that a 15-second commercial is worth about two thirds of a 30-second commercial, and that a full-page ad for an airline in *The Wall Street Journal* is worth perhaps 55% of a 30-second spot on *ER*. They rarely make explicit these implicit assumptions that go into media buying, and as a consequence, there is as much variability within an agency as between agencies in terms of these considerations. One example will suffice.

We did a new-product forecast using Discovery and projected failure (indeed, most new product forecasts suggest failure). Our model traced the problem to a low-level of awareness, a result in large part of ineffective advertising (copy-test scores indexed below 1.0) and relatively weak media vehicles (they indexed well below 1.0 in involvement). The agency went crazy, complaining not about the copy-test scores, over which we had no control (they had collaborated with the client on selecting the advertising testing firm), but about the media impact numbers we had provided and employed in our model.

The agency demanded to know what involvement/effectiveness number we had used for each media vehicle in the model. We said we would be happy to share this information if they would make explicit their implicit assumptions about the differing effectiveness of different media vehicles. They said they didn't have such numbers. We responded, "Yes, you do. They're in your heads, and you just need to put them down on a piece of paper." (Copernicus's numbers are based in part on a survey we do among a national cross-section of agency media executives in which we take them through an exercise designed to estimate the effectiveness of advertising for the same brand with the same campaign in different media vehicles.)

The agency finally agreed, and after taking a survey among their media planners, came back with a consensus estimate. As in the children's game of I'll-show-you-mine-if-you'll-show-me-yours, we shared numbers, and happily, ours were similar to the agency's. This gave the agency some confidence that we knew what we were doing. Where the numbers were different, the client and agency opted to use our numbers because they had an empirical basis, grounded in more than the judgments of a single agency.

A conclusion we have drawn from this and other experiences like it is that marketers, advertising agencies, and media executives are not rushing to embrace the formal measurement of media involvement, even though they implicitly employ such assumptions in the form of judgments, intuition, and the like every day.

> Unfortunately, advertising is a ratings-driven industry that encourages media people to stick with the conventional and familiar safety-in-numbers mentality.

Unfortunately, advertising is, as Bogart (1986b), Beville (1988), and others state, a ratings-driven industry where the current television landscape encourages media people to stick with the conventional and familiar safety-in-numbers mentality. Beville summarized this when he wrote,

> There are several complexities to the concept of qualitative ratings that are not found in conventional audience size measurements. Quantitative measurement is relatively simple and clear: The numbers—whether household demographics ratings or share of audience projections, national or local—are developed by syndicated services using standardized and readily understood terms. (p. 131)

When told that *Seinfeld,* on Thursday at 9 p.m. during one week, achieved a share of 29.5 nationally, 22.6 in Philadelphia, and 31.8 in San Francisco, the meaning is clear (and even more so when trends of all available weekly shares are followed).

Yet, even 10 years ago, there was evidence of an interest in the qualitative approach. David Poltrack, senior vice president at CBS, wrote in 1989 that only quantitative dimensions can yield a degree of precision and certainty, whereas qualitative avenues are "far less amenable to definition and scientific study" (p. 25). He then went on to say, "I would argue that this preoccupation [with the numbers and ratings] has led to industry practices that have significantly inhibited the development of sound media planning and buying practices."

Point by point, Poltrack (1989) reveals the biases and methodological shortcomings and inconsistencies behind syndicated audience counts and ratings, and he notes, significantly, that television options, including national network, national spot, national cable, national syndication, local television, and local cable, are all measured using different methodologies. Obviously, the often wide variations in the methods used to measure audiences for these different venues leads to hideous problems from the media's and advertiser's perspective, when they attempt to compare one media option with another, not to mention comparing cost-efficiencies of one versus another.

Poltrack (1989) enumerates the factors that exacerbate the problems with contemporary measurement approaches—variable cooperation rates among metered households, collection and reportage of incomplete data, and other sources of viewer response bias. As a result of these limitations in current measurement, he said, "I believe our preoccupation with the quantification of media audiences has been the cause of the evolution of the media planning and buying process into its present mechanical commodity-like form" (p. 25).

The industry's preoccupation with CPM, says Poltrack, has led to "evaluation of different media vehicles on the basis of their relative CPMs against some narrow age-based target. This approach ignores the relevance of any demographic parameter other than age" and makes the absurd assumption that "each 18-year-old is equal in value to each 49-year-old and that everyone over 50 has no value whatsoever" (p. 25). When the advertiser selects media based on CPM, and the audience measurement method varies from medium to medium, this "renders such comparisons invalid" (p. 25). Finally, "the qualitative variations both within each medium and between media will often outweigh variations resulting from this less than ideal framework" (p. 25).

Poltrack says of his research regarding qualitative data,

> As we continue to gather and analyze these data, we are becoming more and more convinced that the difference between a successful television program and an unsuccessful program and the difference between a successful advertising campaign and an unsuccessful campaign can be found in the qualitative realm; how and what form of communication takes place with the viewer, rather than in the quantitative realm. We believe that we can enhance our programming product [and, hence, the viewer's receptivity to quality advertising] by tapping these qualitative insights.

MORE BENEFITS TO BE DERIVED
FROM IMPLEMENTING CPMI

Agency and advertiser reluctance to adopt an entirely new system, particularly an unfamiliar qualitative system is understandable. Comfortable and familiar processes and procedures die hard. Two points must be made, however, concerning the alleged complexities posed by the CPMI concept.

First, as we have demonstrated, the approach offers potentially significant increases in the effectiveness and efficiency of program buys while remaining dependent on familiar, conventional syndicated audience data. Involvement scores for programs have not been conceived or intended to replace syndicated data, but as a refinement to existing data and inherent methodological problems. Computing and using involvement scores can be augmentative, possessing far higher levels of sensitivity, reliability, and validity, as well as far greater flexibility in use.

Second, the CPMI is designed to provide media planners not with a new audience measurement system, but rather with a simple and much-needed improvement to the media buying process itself. As advertisers continue to recognize the importance of the program environment on the effectiveness of their increasingly costly commercial buys, agencies can anticipate stronger demand for an approach that will aid in delivering cost efficiencies and target-level effectiveness.

Concurrently, one would expect a decreasing level of satisfaction with the use of simple, unidimensional scales of program liking or, worse, attention scores to guide media decisions. We have addressed the former's limitations, but a cautionary note is in order regarding the apparently widespread and erroneous belief that simple measures of program attention are readily acceptable substitutes for involvement measures.

> Exploratory analyses found that attention and involvement are related to each other and that both are related to advertising effectiveness to varying extent.

Exploratory analyses we conducted found attention and involvement to be related and that both are related to advertising effectiveness to varying extents. Using multivariate analysis of covariance, however, the relationship of attention to advertising response deteriorated to nonsignificance, controlling for the effects of program involvement. Yet, when the analysis was repeated in reverse by controlling for the effects of attention, the relationship between program environment and advertising response remained strong and increased slightly. This issue requires more analysis with a greater number of commercials before anyone can reach firm conclusions.

Another fundamental issue is prediction. If one accepts the positive-effects hypothesis and the conclusions we present, the obvious question is, how does the prediction approach outlined earlier aid in selecting the best environment for commercial placement? Due, in part, to the multitude forms of measured (as well as unmeasured) television, this question may deserve more detailed and specific treatment. The methodology, however, remains straightforward. For currently aired programming, a simplified version of this methodology, using a simulated natural exposure condition, the involvement item battery or equivalent, multiple ad response measures, and administration over several episodes in suitable market(s) would provide all the raw material necessary to generate prediction scores and index values. The resulting norms should be viable for a considerable period of time (while administering measurement waves on a smaller scale, to provide early warning of potential disturbances).

Predicting preseason programming response, pilots, and even one-time program specials such as mini-series can be accomplished, ironically, in much the same way the networks currently test them. The critical difference, however, would be substituting the key methodological elements employed in the current program environment effects study, while abandoning approaches that include meandering focus group research, small nonprobabilistic accidental samples, artificial test environments, and relatively barren unidimensional liking scores.

IMPLICATIONS FOR ADVERTISING
COPY-TESTING METHODS

One of the more significant findings to emerge from this research was the discovery that the effects of program involvement on advertising response were systematically related to the environment in which exposure to programs and advertising took place. As we've noted, studies employing artificial forced-exposure testing environments invariably concluded that there was a negative effect from increasing program involvement on advertising effectiveness. Studies employing a natural on-air testing methodology invariably concluded that as involvement in programming increased, so too did the effectiveness of the advertising carried. This finding was replicated in our own work, which attempted to simulate the natural in-home viewing environment.

From the applied perspective, the implications are substantial. Due to the artificiality of the forced-exposure test environment, there is always the question of whether the measurements reflect respondents' true reactions to the commercials, reactions biased by the artificial nature of the test environment, or an interaction between the two. True, in the artificial testing environment, researchers can control the influence of extraneous factors, thus helping to minimize some sources of potential bias. This benefit is outweighed, however, by the environment's artificiality, which produces unrealistically high respondent attention levels and commercial copy-test scores.

> This research confirmed that advertising response scores are lower but more realistic under simulated natural viewing conditions with typical distractions available.

On the other hand, in the simulated natural viewing environment, exposure occurs in a test environment closely simulating the natural in-home viewing environment, while ensuring unobtrusive controls over most potential contaminants of advertising response scores. This research confirmed that advertising response scores are lower but more realistic under simulated natural viewing conditions with typical distractions and alternatives to viewing available.

The simulated natural viewing conditions also provide the advertising researcher with a greater opportunity to accurately assess response discrimination between copy executions than is possible in the typical artificial testing environment. Within the artificial environment, respondents are not encouraged to communicate among themselves—in fact, they are enjoined from it—and are not expected to divert their attention from the visual stimuli. Because the program and commercials are the only stimuli available, it is natural that most advertising response scores are higher than in the freely motivated, simulated natural viewing environment.

Equally important, freely motivated, selective viewing under the simulated natural environment may be the ideal copy-testing environment. Because true validity is elusive in copy testing, accurate discrimination between respondents and among copy executions is an important goal. With controls for extraneous influence, this simulated natural exposure environment condition seems to offer advertising researchers precisely what they are looking for.

Priemer (1989), speaking about the deficiencies of the artificial test environment and the obvious effects on advertising response scores, says,

A media person can alert a creative team about the environment for which they create their commercials. Commercials seem to be created without regard for the environment in which the consumer will see them. I've never seen a new commercial screened for approval under conditions comparable to what this commercial will encounter in the real world. The screening TV set is big, expensive, and kept in perfect working condition. The screening room is kept silent while the new commercial is being shown. No other commercial is shown before or after it. If anyone coughs or sneezes during a screening, the commercial is shown again, so it can be seen under perfect viewing conditions. (p. 230)

Media buyers and planners know that this is not the environment in which consumers view commercials. Priemer (1989) writes,

It isn't perfect. It's on a set of average size, of average quality, and in "working order." Conversation in the room where TV is viewed is never hushed by anyone when the commercials come on. Someone coughs, someone sneezes. The phone rings. Or the doorbell . . . Mr. Advertiser, your commercial is running while all this takes place! (p. 230)

Kover et al. (1995) state that the advertising agency creative department's posture is "no one wants to watch advertising" and provides an illustration of someone returning home from a hard day, "where nobody appreciates what he does, where his work is meaningless . . . and wants only the surcease and the balm that comes from watching television." The authors maintain that this viewer "does not want that flow broken by watching advertising." Kover et al. then go on to lay out a theory of advertising in which they argue that it is nothing more than an intrusion on the audience.

After maintaining that their statements follow on discussions with a number of people from the research end of the business, Kover et al. (1995) pose the question (here in their attack on copy-testing methods): why don't researchers allow for distractions in the test environments, so that the home viewing situation is more closely duplicated? Our research is not, of course, the first to use some form of natural test environment, as Chapters 2 and 3 have pointed out—day-after recall testing is a prime example.

Advertising executives Mark McNeely and Scott Marshall (1992) maintain that standard copy-testing practices are in large measure responsible for the "ho-hum" ads that have "diluted many peoples' beliefs in our product and contributed to the current state of doubt . . . [in] our business" (p. 18). Specifically,

There are a whole bunch of ancient research techniques, which many clients and agencies still use to measure the "effectiveness" of their ads, that rely on forced and artificial forms of exposure. These techniques inherently miss the new voluntary nature of the medium. (p. 18)

McNeely and Marshall's (1992) admonitions to the profession are in our view on target but border on hyperbole. Copy testing in our view plays only a modest role in the decline of television advertising effectiveness. As we stated in Chapter 1, most advertising campaigns do not appear to be based on either a clear targeting or positioning strategy.

> Managers find comfort in making decisions quickly using the same tried and true approaches that they've used over and over again.

Why, beyond the fact that they can save a relatively small amount of money, do marketers continue to use questionable testing procedures or, even worse, no research at all? We suspect that the reason has to do with tradition and the dizzying pace of business and personal lives today. Managers find comfort in making decisions quickly using the same tried and true approaches that they've used over and over again. They are not particularly interested in knowing whether the approach works or doesn't work. Consequently, advertising decisions based on intuition alone, preposterous research approaches such as four focus groups, or, a step up, highly artificial copy-testing methods continue untrammeled.

The moral? We have outlined what may become a more valid and discriminating approach to testing television commercials: Multiple measures of advertising response, simulated natural viewing conditions, and the means to control the influence of extraneous factors on copy-test scores. If television advertisers skip the testing function or stand by testing methods that do not acknowledge breaking developments in our field, it is inevitable that the decline in television advertising effectiveness will continue unabated.

AREAS FOR FUTURE STUDY

Our research suggests numerous areas for future investigation, both from the applied and theoretical perspectives. Although the authors have initiated additional research in some of these areas—the print advertising study described in Chapter 10, for example—more wide-ranging research efforts could prove beneficial for testing, refining, and extending the potential value and usefulness of the findings reported here. Here are descriptions of a few such efforts.

A similar study among additional target groups. In light of the dramatic changes occurring in the demographics and purchase patterns of Americans, any future research into television advertising along these lines should include both men and consumers 50 years old and older. (Our study of print advertising includes men and women.) Although females 18 to 49 or 18 to 54 have traditionally bought most packaged goods, increasingly men are buying them as well, due in part to the increase in single-male households and changes in roles among married couples. Among married men, a significant percentage always or frequently shop for grocery and other household items. Although females represent a majority of those shopping for household goods, the importance of males in the market makes it important to examine the relationships between program involvement and advertising effectiveness for them, as well. Then, too, as the baby boomers age and Americans are living longer, it is increasingly important to understand the effects of television—the effects of television programming in particular—on older consumers.

Measure attitudes toward the advertising. A 5-year, multimillion-dollar study of copy research measures and methods, sponsored by the Advertising Research Foundation, reached some surprising conclusions: Within each category of copy test measures, from persuasion to recall, individual measures (also used in this study) were found to predict sales response. Most surprising was that the single most predictive measure of in-market success was "overall reaction to the commercial"—a likability measure consisting of scaled, multiple-item dimensions of commercial reaction. The measure had a predictive success ratio of 87% (Haley, 1990a, 1990b).

> It would seem quite probable that qualitative measurement in media research may be more important to measuring and predicting advertising effectiveness.

Unfortunately, time and financial constraints in this research prevented us from incorporating other measures—including attitudes toward advertising—but any future research should incorporate the advertising reaction measure into the dependent construct. There is every reason to believe, going by the Advertising Research Foundation's results, that this type of measure will significantly boost both the sensitivity and ability to discriminate of the advertising response construct in all areas of application. It is also of more than casual interest that this commercial reaction measure, like the program reaction (involvement) measure, is also a multi-aspect, content-reaction measure, tapping key dimensions of attitudes toward advertisements. To suggest a very general basis for future research, it would seem quite probable that qualitative measurement in media research may be of greater significance and importance to the measurement and prediction of advertising effectiveness than previously considered.

Include additional commercials for the analysis. While recommending additional advertising response measures, we also believe it is desirable to include additional commercials. Such a move would: (a) provide additional ads to potentially strengthen and extend our conclusion and knowledge concerning the tested, positive relationships between program involvement and advertising effectiveness; (b) test the enhanced validity, sensitivity, and ability to discriminate of the simulated natural test environment; and (c) allow more "robust" testing of the potentially different relationships between program involvement and ad response across the levels of the various control variables we examined in Chapter 7. Some of these tests were problematic for various reasons, making it difficult to draw confident conclusions.

Considering the program reaction or involvement measure used in this research, we noted that the weaker factors extracted from the program involvement item inventory, Values Incongruency and Mood Enhancement, satisfied statistical tests for factor retention (and in the case of the former, proved generally reliable) but to a considerably weaker degree than the Involvement factor (see Figure 5.1 in Chapter 5). We showed, however, that these weaker factors provided clear evidence of what may be called latent dimensions of television program content reaction. But due to the comparatively few items loading strongly and exclusively on the factors, among other statistically based reasons, we excluded them from the analysis. As it turned out, the Involvement factor scale, with its own clear multidimensionality, was more than adequate for all hypotheses tests. Nevertheless, in light of new research on program environment effects and broadcast communications, and in the interest of increasing the explained variability in program involvement to the highest possible level, further content analysis and item development and testing is appropriate.

Explore the relationship between program involvement, program/commercial attention, and advertising effectiveness. Given the close, almost overlapping association theorized to exist between attention and involvement in this context, it is of more than casual interest to pursue insights into the nature of relationships between self-reported viewer attention, program involvement, and the dimensions of advertising effectiveness. Questions include whether attention and program involvement have separate and independent or interactive effects on advertising response and, if the latter, what insights can be provided into the nature of the causal ordering between these variables?

Beyond the theoretical appeal of an analysis into these issues lies a practical rationale. If we find self-reported viewer attention to have a significant effect on some dimension of advertising response—either independently of that produced by program involvement, or in interaction with program involvement—researchers should incorporate measures of viewer attention into any future qualitative measurement approach.

Many in the industry consider the simple attention measures that syndicated services provide to give adequate insights into the qualitative domain of viewership, considering involvement superfluous. Our preliminary research has shown attention and involvement to be related, but quite different constructs, however. In the simulated natural exposure environment, the bivariate correlation coefficient between self-reported attention to programming and program involvement was found to be .65, significant at the $p < .000$ level. This finding could be said to be consistent with the theory that involved viewers are motivated to attend to program material and minimize distracting influences. Further bivariate correlations showed attention to have statistically significant effects on both higher order response dimensions (persuasion, interest, etc.) as well as on recall.

After a simple, exploratory exercise, removing the effects of program attitudes from the relationships between attention and higher order commercial response by means of partial correlation analysis, the adjusted simple correlation between attention and behavioral intentions became completely nonsignificant and that between attention and purchase interest became negative and nonsignificant. Thus, in this preliminary look, it would appear that attention has little direct effect of its own on higher order advertising response and that the significant, uncontrolled relationships observed were spurious due to the impact of attention on program attitudes. This was substantiated by partial correlation coefficients computed within the levels of program attitudes. Furthermore, the independent effect of attention on these higher order commercial effectiveness dimensions is at its lowest—virtually zero—among those most involved in programming.

In the case of advertising recall, the role of attention was dramatically different. Unadjusted bivariate correlations between attention and both recall measures were highly significant, a condition that remained unchanged controlling for the effects of program attitudes in the case of proven recall and weakened to a minor extent in the case of aided recall. The effect of attention on the ability to recall commercial content was, therefore, positive, highly significant, and for the most part uncontaminated by the effects of program attitudes. Among those with the highest level of program involvement, once again, this did not appear to be the case, however, as the adjusted independent effects of attention no longer achieved statistical significance. Thus, it would appear that under simulated natural viewing conditions, program attention does not contribute significantly to advertising effectiveness, independently of program attitudes, among those with highly favorable attitudes toward the program.

> In a simulated natural test environment, attention and program involvement merit further investigation via path-analytic modeling.

Overall, this preliminary look at the role of attention and its effects on advertising response allows us to suggest that in a simulated natural test environment, attention and program involvement—as well as interrelated patterns of response effects—merit further investigation via path analytic modeling, perhaps by including more state-of-the-science, objective attention measures.

Understand the role of unaided proven recall. An intriguing discovery in both our television and print studies is that unaided proven recall stands alone as a variable insensitive to differences in television or print involvement. Stated differently, as the level of media involvement increased in both studies, a variety of advertising response measures increased as well—save one, unaided proven recall. This is puzzling to us for many reasons, only one of which we'll discuss here.

In the simulated natural exposure environment in which we conducted the print study and where we focused the bulk of our analyses in the television study, one would think that recall of the advertising, especially recall of the demanding, proven variety, would presage the other measures of advertising effectiveness. Inquiries about purchase interest, as an illustration, were asked after people were questioned about their recall of an advertisement on an unaided basis. We assumed that differences in product interest between highly involved and less involved consumers would follow from differences in attentiveness and recall. But there were no differences in recall, not just in purchase interest, but in our three other measures of advertising response as well. Thus, it is not clear what is going on with the unaided recall measure.

This finding, we should add, is totally consistent with observations we have been making of data from advertising tracking studies undertaken by some of the largest, most sophisticated advertising tracking companies in the world. Over and over again, we see examples of campaigns that produce negligible levels of unaided proven recall but that produce sizable changes in brand attitudes and sometimes in behavior as well. Does this portend the return of a literature on subliminal effects? We doubt it. But someone needs to study this phenomenon in more detail.

This study has shown that as involvement with program material increases, so too does the effectiveness of advertising carried by the program as measured by standard industry criteria. It therefore follows that advertisers and agencies that want to improve their media buying and copy testing will embrace the concept of the CPMI. Buying media on the basis of the target audience's involvement with the programs and publications can only improve the advertising's effectiveness and ultimately the advertiser's bottom line.

The predicted mean advertising effectiveness index for programs in the top quartile according to CPMI was a full 23% higher than when calculated on the basis of CPM. Programs appearing in the top quartile, as calculated by CPMI, produce a significant boost in effectiveness and cost savings.

Given all the issues advertisers confront today—media fragmentation, advertising clutter, rising costs, and more—the fact that we have solved a 30-year mystery and pointed the way to improved advertising effectiveness should be a cause for joy. We have, after all, discovered the hidden power of television programming and print editorial.

Appendix

N*otes to Chapter 5, pages 98-102, Item Analysis and Validation:* With the confirmation of Hypothesis 1, we conducted detailed item analyses within each of the resulting factors to yield scales of maximum reliability and validity.

This involved, in the case of reliability, standard tests for internal consistency associated with conventional factor structure analysis and the computation of Cronbach's alpha and related internal consistency statistics. Efforts to demonstrate the validity of the scales involved the computation of correlation coefficients between each scale and alternative measures of program content reaction (convergence), and difference-of-means t-tests on each scale between viewing conditions (ability to discriminate). After these tests, factor scale scores for the sample were divided into low, moderate, and high program involvement levels on each dimension to facilitate testing of the remaining hypotheses.

This primary analytical stage involved detailed examination of the nature of the relationship between the program environment and commercial effectiveness. Although a variety of analytical models could form the basis of this analysis—from separate regressions of the advertising response criteria on the program environment variables to canonical correlation of the criterion and predictor variable sets—multivariate analysis of variance (MANOVA) was the most logical and appropriate analytical model to employ for several reasons:

1. To assess the impact of the program environment on advertising effectiveness more completely, multiple commercial response measures are used. As each of these response criteria is a component aspect of the underlying composite construct, advertising effectiveness, however, the individual measures can be expected to interrelate to some extent. Under these circumstances, test results obtained for each criterion separately, as in univariate analysis of variance or regression, are not strictly correct. Univariate approaches ignore any effect of such interrelation on overall response and assume that each criterion represents an independent source of variation. This could substantially alter the

results and conclusions drawn from the analysis (Berkowitz & Walton, 1980; Bray & Maxwell, 1985; Leckenby, 1978; Wind & Denny, 1974).

2. There are a number of advantages to the use of the MANOVA routine. Chief among these is the unique multivariate test of factor effects, which permits tests of factor-level differences on the overall response construct. Conclusions regarding overall commercial performance (in this case) based on statistically accurate testing can be easily drawn, therefore, and need not be inferred from univariate analyses on each criterion individually and in isolation. In testing the significance of differences between levels of a factor, the MANOVA model considers the direction and magnitude of correlations between the individual criteria within the levels of a factor rather than simply testing mean differences between levels on each criterion separately. This involves creating a new variable that, for each respondent, represents a weighted, linear combination of the original criteria. The weights associated with each criterion variable are determined from the nature of the intercorrelations between them. This new multivariate criterion then maximizes mean differences among groups relative to the within-groups variance on this variable (Bray & Maxwell, 1985). These manipulations are important because they provide maximum group separation on the overall response construct for the testing of factor effects. These properties of the MANOVA model enhance the interpretability of analysis results.

3. Additional advantages to MANOVA include reporting closely related analyses and statistical tests; for example, univariate test results for each member of the criterion set and canonical discriminate function analysis results for each significant effect. Both are very useful in appraising the importance or contribution of the individual criteria to the significant factor-level differences observed. These analyses provide insights into the specific nature of program involvement effects on the different dimensions of advertising response, as Chapter 7 demonstrated and explained.

The analyses were performed with separate MANOVAs, one for each of the program involvement dimensions emerging from stage one of the analysis. Assuming, for example, that three program involvement scales were retained for this stage of the analysis, the resulting four-way (with the viewing conditions factor), full-factorial model would be inappropriate on statistical as well as theoretical grounds. Simultaneous analysis of all attitude factors in this case would involve an analytical design consisting of 81 cells. Even with the large sample this study employed, this translates to an average cell frequency of about five respondents. Statistical tests would be meaningless, and results could not be generalized.

Beyond the obvious statistical reasons for separate analyses is an equally compelling theoretical rationale. It is considered more desirable to examine the importance of each program involvement element separately and unadjusted for the presence of the remaining elements. Part of the reasoning behind this position is that if any of the attitude elements fail to demonstrate significance separately (i.e., a main effect, or at the very least, a significant interaction with the viewing condition factor), the logic of pursuing the role of such a factor in the present analysis would be questionable. Furthermore, the presence of any significant interactions involving two or more attitude factors would present additional problems. Interpretation would be, of necessity, highly conjectural.

Although a summary program involvement scale scored across the individual attitude dimensions would perhaps resolve the primary cell frequencies problem, this approach is inconsistent with the logic and objectives indicated in Point 2 above. First, preliminary interest is focused on the relative explanatory importance of each involvement dimension separately. Second, each factor scale retained for this stage of the analysis will represent a somewhat related, but unique and separate dimension of program involvement. Constructing a factor scale combining these independent subdimensions in such a way as to facilitate meaningful interpretation of subsequent factor effects clearly is not a straightforward task.

The primary multivariate test of significance for Hypotheses 2 through 4 was the Pillai-Bartlett trace (Bray & Maxwell, 1985). This test statistic represents a multivariate generalization of the univariate F ratio and is computed with explicit consideration for the nature and magnitude of criterion variable intercorrelations. A significance level of $p < .05$ is required for confirmation of each hypothesis.

We also examined univariate F ratios in the case of each significant effect. Computed separately for each of the five criterion variables, these statistics aid in the determination of the relative contribution of each criterion to the significant multivariate differences observed between levels of the factor. Further insights into the underlying dimensionality of significant factor-level differences will be provided by canonical discriminate function analysis for each significant effect.

Following the results of this analysis, we tested Hypothesis 5, the hypothesis that the multidimensional, multi-item approach to measuring program involvement more completely assesses the nature of viewers' program involvement than single-item affect scales. Comparative explanatory significance was assessed initially by computing simple bivariate correlation coefficients between each of the program content reaction measures and each of the advertising effectiveness criteria.

Next, separate MANOVAs were performed for the IPSOS-ASI 5-point Favorites measure and the 11-point, 0-10 Liking Scale (divided into three) using the original set of five advertising effectiveness criteria. The same multivariate and univariate analyses, test statistics, and significance levels employed in testing the significance of the multidimensional program attitudes measure were used.

Finally, the observed effects for each of the unidimensional measures were subjected to the same MANCOVA analysis described above for the multidimensional program attitudes measure. Hypothesis 5 was confirmed when the results of these analyses demonstrated that the covariance-adjusted effect of the multidimensional measure exhibits a higher level of explanatory significance on the effectiveness criteria than the similarly adjusted effects of each of the unidimensional measures.

TABLE A.1 Item Analysis Results: Program Involvement Factor Scales

		A. Factor 1: Program Involvement	
Factor Loading	*Item-Total Correlation*	*Correlated Item-Total Correlation*	*Item Description (Abbreviated)*
.82	.78	.72	Characters true-to-life/believable
−.81	.82	.77	Never got involved
.80	.82	.77	Parts touched my feelings
.78	.83	.78	Felt same things as characters
.73	.81	.76	Really involved in program
−.71	.78	.72	Didn't relate to characters
.68	.72	.65	Really made me concentrate
−.67	.71	.63	Didn't affect my feelings
.59	.71	.64	Understood how character felt
−.54	.59	.49	Interested at first, not after

B. Scale Reliability Test Results (n = 451)	
Aggregate level reliability (split-sample, mean item score correlations)	.98
Total scale alpha	.92
Split-halves alphas	
Form 1	.88
Form 2	.82
Correlation between alternative forms	.82

NOTE: Mean factor loading = .71. Mean interitem correlation = .52. Mean item-total correlation (corrected) = .69.

Tables A.1, A.2, and A.3 indicate the results of this first stage of the item analyses. For those who may be unfamiliar with some of the tests employed, definitions and the levels of significance associated with these test results appear following the tables.

To test for internal consistency and reliability, we computed the mean factor loading for each item combination. This is a basic indicator of the strength of association between the underlying factor and the items used to explain that factor.

We used the mean interitem correlation to indicate both the homogeneity of the items used to define a factor and their combined explanatory strength.

We computed item-total correlations within each combination. These are simple bivariate correlations between individual item scores and the total score, summed across the component items. These correlations, as well as their mean value, provide yet another indication of the extent to which the items defining each factor hang together. Individually, they demonstrate the strength of the relationships of the parts to the whole. For proper interpretation, however, these correlations must be corrected: Each will be inflated

TABLE A.2 Program Involvement Factor Scales

			A. Factor 2: Values Incongruency
Factor Loading	_Item-Total Correlation_	_Corrected Item-Total Correlation_	_Item Description (Abbreviated)_
.87	.85	.77	So much sex and violence in program that I wouldn't want children to watch it
−.84	.82	.73	Language acceptable even for children
−.82	.78	.66	If this were a movie, it would receive a G (general audience) rating
.75	.77	.66	Too much adult material for a prime-time show
.62	.72	.59	This show teaches young people poor values
.58	.68	.54	Some of the humor a bit tasteless

B. Scale Reliability Test Results
Factor Scale 2 (n = 457)

Aggregate level reliability correlation coefficient	.99
Total scale alpha	.86
Split-halves alphas:	
Form 1	.70
Form 2	.75
Correlation between alternative forms	.82

Mean interitem correlation = .51. Mean item loading, factor 2 = .75. Mean item-total correlation (corrected) = .66.

because each is a component of the total with which it is correlated. We removed the resulting upward shift from each correlation by a shrinkage formula recommended by Nunnally (1978), where:

$$r_{1(y-1)} = \frac{r_{y1-y} - -1}{\sqrt{\dfrac{2}{-i} + \dfrac{2}{-y} - 2_{-1-y} \; r_{y1}}}$$

r_{y1} = the correlation of item 1 with total scale score y

$-y$ = the standard deviation of total scale scores

-1 = the standard deviation of item 1

$r_{1(y-1)}$ = the correlation of item 1 with total score y, exclusive of item 1

Finally, at the bottom of Table A.1 (Factor Scale 1), Table A.2 (Factor 2), and Table A.3 (Factor 3) are the remaining tests of reliability.

TABLE A.3 Program Involvement Factor Scales

	A. Factor 3: Mood Enhancement		
Factor Loading	Item-Total Correlation	Corrected Item-Total Correlation	Item Description (Abbreviated)
.72	.61	.33	This was one of the funniest shows I've ever seen
.67	.83	.66	Programs like this put me in good spirits and make me laugh
.53	.78	.58	This is one of those uplifting programs that helps people forget their problems
.47	.74	.51	Part of fun in watching a show like this is to imagine self in same situations

B. Scale Reliability Test Results	
Factor Scale 3 (n = 438)	
Aggregate level reliability correlation coefficient	.99
Total scale alpha	.73
Split-halves alphas:	
Form 1	.39
Form 2	.68
Correlation between alternative forms	.61

Mean item loading, factor 3 = .60. Mean interitem correlation = .40. Mean item-total correlation (corrected) = .52.

We obtained an aggregate-level indicator of the reliability of each item combination by randomly dividing the sample into equal halves and computing, within each half, the mean score on each item. We then used the corresponding means on each item to compute a correlation coefficient for each combination.

We computed Cronbach's alpha and related reliability statistics for each item combination. Coefficient alpha provides a unique and conservative estimate of the reliability of a scale without requiring repeated applications. It can be interpreted as an estimate of the expected correlation of a multi-item measure with a hypothetical alternative form of the measure containing the same number of items (Nunnally, 1978). As Churchill (1979) states, "Coefficient alpha absolutely should be the first measure one calculates to assess the quality of the measurement" (p. 64). We also computed split-half alphas for each item combination. These coefficients result from randomly dividing each set of items into equal halves or alternative forms and computing separate alphas for each half. These statistics, together with the correlation between the alternative halves of the scales, are augmenting reliability indicators. They demonstrate the extent to which random halves of the items produce equivalent results and hence, with what level of reliability they measure the same concept.

Parallel with internal consistency tests, we computed bivariate correlations between each item and each of the criterion variables as a measure of the predictive validity of the items to be used in the construction of final scales. These tests significantly altered the factor item composition of the dominant first factor only. In this case, a 10-item scale was the result, exhibiting improved internal consistency, criterion validity, and measurement efficiency over the original 17-item scale. Although the items deleted from this first scale were usually only weakly correlated with the criterion measures, this was not the only reason we removed them. They also exhibited one or more additional undesirable characteristics, such as a lack of independence evidenced by secondary loadings on other factors and comparatively low correlations with key items in the factor. In the latter case, removing the offending items significantly improved reliability tests. The resulting 10-item scale demonstrates a high degree of reliability, while the average correlation of component items with criterion variables exhibits significance at the .01 level (see Table A.1).

In the case of Factor Scale 2 (Values Incongruency), both adding to, as well as deleting from, the original six items negatively affected internal consistency test results. The original scale does, however, perform quite well in this regard, as Table A.2 suggests. This is not the case in terms of item correlations with the dependent variables. None of the items in Factor Scale 2 exhibit the strong relationships to the advertising response measures evident in the case of Factor Scale 1, (Program Involvement).

Factor Scale 3 (Mood Enhancement), as we observed earlier, may represent an incompletely revealed program involvement dimension suffering from an inadequate number and range of emotive and affective items or from an original content analysis that tapped only a portion of the relevant and true domain (or both), and hence, the comparatively weak factor structure (see Table A.3).

Following the results of the item analysis, we evaluated a variety of alternative item-weighting schemes to construct the three program involvement scales. In this context, we note Nunnally's concisely stated rationale against using differential weighting schema: First, with most attitude scales, it is difficult to defend the superiority of any particular weighting approach over a simple sum of the unweighted item values; and second, weighted and unweighted summed scores are usually highly correlated. As evidence for this latter point, Nunnally cites results obtained by Likert (1932), who, although using a complex weighting scheme, correlated scores from the same scales and found that they correlated .99.

Consequently, although it may be reasonable to argue against this rationale in other applications, we deemed the use of the unweighted summed approach to be adequate in the present research.

Notes to Chapter 6, pages 109-110, Program Involvement Effects Vary by Viewing Condition: Although one can use univariate test results to identify the relative contribution of each of the individual criteria to the overall factor-level differences observed, canonical discriminate analysis reveals more precisely the underlying dimensionality of factor-level differences. This statistical model is closely related to MANOVA and has been described as a typical one-way multivariate analysis of variance "in reverse": The criterion set functions as predictor variables, and the levels of a factor function as groups of a discrete dependent variable (Berkowitz & Walton, 1980; Leckenby, 1978).

For each significant effect, canonical discriminate analysis reveals the number and nature of discriminating dimensions underlying factor-level differences on the composite response variable. The relative contribution of each criteria to the discriminating functions, as well as their relationship to one another in the discrimination provided, is reflected in (a) the discriminate weights calculated for each criterion, and (b) the correlation of each with each of the significant discriminate functions (canonical variate correlations). We use these correlations as the basis for conclusions concerning the underlying dimensionality of factor effects because they are less likely than the discriminate weights to be influenced by intercorrelations among the criterion variables.

A particularly useful statistic provided in the course of this analysis is the canonical correlation of the criterion and predictor sets for each dimension underlying a significant factor effect. It is well known that in large-sample studies, a statistically significant result may not necessarily be a practically important one. Thus, a strength of association measure, independent of sample size, can be useful in assessing the practical significance of findings. In univariate analyses, researchers frequently choose the eta statistic for this purpose. The multivariate counterpart of eta is the canonical correlation coefficient. When squared, this statistic reflects the proportion of variability between levels of a factor explained by the criterion, or dependent variable set, or vector.

As Table A.4 shows, the discriminate function analysis for the first program environment factor reveals two significant dimensions underlying treatment differences. As is usually the case, the first function is by far the more important and is seen by standardized discriminate weights and canonical variate correlations to be associated with commercial recall. The second, marginally significant discriminating dimension is associated not with copy-point credibility, as suggested by univariate test results, but rather with purchase interest and, perhaps, behavioral intentions change. This result, although of limited practical importance, is of interest, nevertheless. It lends a bit of credence to the age-old contention between proponents of recall versus those of persuasion (by simply substantiating the fact that the two categories of copy-test measurement are different, and do, indeed, tap into different dimensions of advertising response) as the better category of copy-test measurement for predicting ad performance. Together, the two underlying dimensions account for a substantial 36% of the variability in advertising response between viewing environments, but of this total explained variation, only 2% is attributable to the discrimination provided by the second dimension.

Thus, it may be said that differences in external conditions surrounding television viewing produce the greatest effect on responses to advertising in the area of commercial recall. The effects on other higher order dimensions of ad response, although generally significant, are of comparatively minor importance to the overall discrimination between levels of this factor.

TABLE A.4 Canonical Discriminant Analysis Results

	Viewing Condition				Program Involvement One Significant Dimension		Interaction One Significant Dimension	
	Dimension 1		Dimension 2					
	SDW[a]	CCVC[b]	SDW	CCVC	SDW	CCVC	SDW	CCVC
F ratio	21.33***		2.39*		2.50**		1.55**	
Behavioral intentions change	-.10	-.07	-.36	-.66	-.52	-.70	-.23	-.34
Copy-point credibility	.39	-.32	.17	-.27	-.37	-.76	.27	-.55
Purchase interest	.16	.06	-.82	-.93	-.12	-.47	-.09	-.27
Aided message recall	-.77	-.78	-.23	-.23	-.48	-.69	-.96	-.93
Unaided proven recall	-.61	-.83	.12	-.03	-.27	-.12	-.24	-.62
Canonical correlation	.5825		.1460		.2155		.2341	
Squared canonical correlation	34%		2%		5%		5.5%	

a. SDW = Standardized Discriminant Weights.

b. CCVC = Criterion Canonical Variable Correlations.

$*.05 \leq p > .01; **.01 \leq p > .001; ***p < .001.$

217

Table A.4 further shows that discriminate analysis on the program attitude factor results in one dimension significant at the $p < .01$ level associated with behavioral intentions change, copy-point credibility, and aided message recall. This substantiates the univariate test results and suggests that differences in program attitude or program content-involvement levels primarily affect higher-order response to advertising messages. This effect, considered across viewing environments, appears modest in comparison to that of viewing conditions as about 5% of the variability in advertising response between attitude levels is explained by this primary dimension. At the same time, however, it must also be considered that

1. This represents a generalized effect of program attitudes observed across different exposure conditions

and

2. In any event, even a 5% improvement in the efficiency of a $50 million television advertising schedule translates to a substantial $2.5 million.

(As we noted in the earlier discussion of discriminate analysis in this chapter, the canonical correlation, when squared, reflects the proportion of variability between the levels of a factor explained by the criterion set in multivariate analysis of variance.)

Discriminate analysis results for the interaction term conform to univariate analysis of variance test results revealing an underlying dimensionality similar to that observed for the main effect of viewing conditions.

References

Aaker, D. A. (1996). *Building strong brands.* New York: Free Press.

Aaker, D. A., & Bruzzone, D. (1981). Viewer perceptions of prime time television advertising. *Journal of Advertising Research, 21,* 15.

Aaker, D. A., & Myers, J. G. (1987). *Advertising management* (3rd ed.). Englewood Cliffs, NJ: Prentice Hall.

Achenbaum, A. A. (1966). Knowledge is a thing called measurement. In L. Adler & I. Crespi (Eds.), *Attitude research at sea.* Chicago: American Marketing Association.

Appel, V. (1987, August/September). Editorial environment and advertising effectiveness. *Journal of Advertising Research,* p. 11.

Arnold, S. J., & Bird, R. (1982). Recall of television commercials. *Journal of the Professional Market Research Society, 1,* 18.

Axelrod, J. N. (1963, April). Induced moods and attitudes toward products. *Journal of Advertising Research, 3,* 19.

Axelrod, J. N. (1968, March). Attitude measures that predict purchase. *Journal of Advertising Research, 8,* 3.

Bartos, R., & Dunn, T. F. (1976). *Advertising and consumers: New perspectives.* New York: American Association of Advertising Agencies.

Baumgartner, H., Sujan, M., & Padgett, D. (1997). Patterns of affective reaction to advertisements: The integration of moment-to-moment responses into overall judgments. *Journal of Marketing Research, 34*(2), 219-232.

Benton & Bowles, Inc. (1970, April). Untitled internal report. New York: Author.

Berkowitz, E. N., & Walton, J. R. (1980, August). Contextual influences on consumer price responses: An experimental analysis. *Journal of Marketing Research.*

Beville, H. M., Jr. (1988). *Audience ratings: Radio, television, and cable.* Hillsdale, NJ: Lawrence Erlbaum.

Blair, M. H. (1987, December/January). An empirical investigation of advertising wearin and wearout. *Journal of Advertising Research,* pp. 45-50.

Bloch, P., & Richins, M. L. (1983, Summer). A theoretical model for the study of importance perceptions. *Journal of Marketing, 47,* 69.

Bogart, L. B. (1986a, February/March). The future of advertising research. *Journal of Advertising Research,* p. 99.

Bogart, L. B. (1986b). *Strategy in advertising* (2nd ed.). Lincolnwood, IL: NTC Business Books.

Bogart, L. B. (1989, February/March). What forces shape the future of advertising research? *Journal of Advertising Research,* p. 89.

Bogart, L. B., Tolley, S., & Ornstein, F. (1970, August). What one little ad can do. *Journal of Advertising Research, 10,* 3.

Bray, J. H., & Maxwell, S. E. (1985). *Multivariate analysis of variance.* Beverly Hills, CA: Sage.

Brock, T. C., & Shavitt, S. (1983). Cognitive response and advertising. In L. Percy & A. G. Woodside (Eds.), *Advertising and consumer psychology.* Lexington, MA: Lexington Books.

Callcott, M., & Phillips, B. J. (1996). Observations: Elves make good cookies: Creating likable spokes-character advertising. *Journal of Advertising Research, 36*(5), 73-79.

Cannon, H. M. (1982). A new method for estimating the effect of media context. *Journal of Advertising Research, 22*(5).

Celsi, R. L., & Olson, J. C. (1988). The role of involvement in attention and comprehension processes. *Journal of Consumer Research, 15*(2), 23-33.

Churchill, G. A. (1979, November). A paradigm for developing better measures of marketing constructs. *Journal of Marketing Research, 16,* 64.

Clancy, K. J. (1990). The coming revolution in advertising: Ten developments which will separate the winners from losers. *Journal of Advertising Research, 30*(1), 47.

Clancy, K. J., & Kweskin, D. M. (1971, April). TV commercial recall correlates. *Journal of Advertising Research, 11,* 18.

Clancy, K. J., & Lloyd, D. W. (1988). A study of the effects of program involvement on advertising response: Implications for copy testing. In *Transcript Proceedings of the Fifth Annual ARF Copy Research Workshop.* New York: Advertising Research Foundation.

Clancy, K. J., & Ostlund, L. E. (1976, February). Commercial effectiveness measures. *Journal of Advertising Research, 16,* 29.

Clancy, K. J., & Shulman, R. S. (1991). *The marketing revolution: A radical manifesto for dominating the marketplace.* New York: HarperBusiness.

Clancy, K. J., & Shulman, R. S. (1995). *Marketing myths that are killing business.* New York: McGraw-Hill.

Clancy, K. J., Shulman, R. S., & Wolf, M. (1994). *Simulated test marketing.* New York: Lexington Books.

Cohen, J. B. (1983). Involvement and you: 1000 great ideas. In R. P. Bagozzi & A. M. Tybout (Eds.), *Advances in consumer research* (Vol. 10, pp. 325-328). Association for Consumer Research.

Comstock, G. (1977). Television's four highly attracted audiences. *New York University Education Quarterly.*

Comstock, G. (1980). *Television in America.* Beverly Hills, CA: Sage.

Crane, L. E. (1964, January). How product, appeal, and program affect attitudes toward commercials. *Journal of Advertising Research, 4,* 15.

Cronin, J. J., & Menelly, N. E. (1992). Discrimination vs. avoidance: "Zipping" of television commercials. *Journal of Advertising, 21*(1), 1.

Dunn, T. (1984, May). *An overview of copy research today.* Paper presented at First Annual Advertising Research Foundation Copy Research Workshop, New York.

Eastman, S. T. (1979, Fall). Uses of television viewing and consumer life styles: A multivariate analysis. *Journal of Broadcasting, 23.*

Eastman, S. T., & Newton, G. D. (1995). Delineating grazing: Observations of remote control use. *Journal of Communication, 45*(1), 78-96.

Edmondson, B. (1997, October). TV execs to Nielsen: Get SMART. *American Demographics,* p. 10.

Engel, J. F., Warshaw, M. R., & Kinnear, T. C. (1983). *Promotional strategy* (5th ed.). Homewood, IL: Richard D. Irwin.

Ernst, O., & Verlag, A. S. (1978, February). New evidence on how advertising works: Theories and results. *Admap,* p. 80.

Fall TV report (1991, June 10). *AdWeek,* p. 4.

Festinger, L., & Maccoby, N. (1964). On resistance to persuasive communications. *Journal of Abnormal and Social Psychology,* p, 68.

Fitzgerald, N. (1997, August 11). Moral prescriptions: Congress adds sex, language and violence to the TV ratings system. *AdWeek,* p. 16.

Gardner, D. M. (1970). Distraction hypothesis in marketing. *Journal of Advertising Research,* p. 10.

Gelb, B. D., & Pickett, C. M. (1983). Attitude-toward-the-ad: Links to humor and advertising effectiveness. *Journal of Advertising,* p. 12.

Gibson, L. D. (1983, February/March). Not recall. *Journal of Advertising Research, 23,* 39.

Goldman, K. (1994, May 13). Industry warned to heed new technology. *Wall Street Journal,* p. B5.

Goldman, K. (1995a, April 2). Sprint chief lectures agencies on future. *Wall Street Journal,* p. B4.

Goldman, K. (1995b, May 4). Agencies found to favor ads for the young. *Wall Street Journal,* p. B4.

Greene, W. (1984). External factors which affect TV commercial performance. *Transcript Proceedings of the First Annual Advertising Research Foundation Copy Research Workshop.* New York: Advertising Research Foundation.

Grunert, K. G. (1996). Automatic and strategic processes in advertising effects. *Journal of Marketing, 60*(4), 88-101.

Haley, R. I. (1990a, July 11-12). *The ARF Copy Research Validity Project: Final report.* Paper presented at Seventh Annual Advertising Research Foundation Copy Research Workshop, New York.

Haley, R. I. (1990b). *The ARF Copy Research Validity Project: Final report.* New York: The Advertising Research Foundation.

Haley, R. I., & Baldinger, A. L. (1991, April/May). The ARF Copy Research Validity Project. *Journal of Advertising Research,* pp. 11-32.

Haley, R. I., & Case, P. B. (1979). Testing thirteen attitude scales for agreement and brand differentiation. *Journal of Marketing, 43*(4), 20.

Haskins, J. B. (1964, March). Factual recall as a measure of advertising effectiveness. *Journal of Advertising Research, 4,* 2.

Herbig, P., & Milewicz, J. (1995). The relationship of reputation and credibility to brand success. *Journal of Consumer Marketing, 12*(4), 5-10.

Home Testing Institute, Inc. (1968). *Summary of fourteen studies dealing with the concept of favorites.* New York: Author.

Horn, M. I., & McEwen, W. J. (1977, April). The effect of program context on commercial performance. *Journal of Advertising, 17,* 23.

Houston, M. J., & Rothschild, M. (1978). Conceptual and methodological perspectives in involvement. In S. Jain (Ed.), *Research frontiers in marketing.* Chicago: American Marketing Association.

It's official: Some ads work. (1995, April 1). *The Economist,* p. 52.

Jensen, E. (Ed.). (1994, September 9). Still kicking. *The Wall Street Journal Reports: Television,* p. R3.

Kamp, E., & MacInnis, D. (1995). Characteristics of portrayed emotions in commercials: When does what is shown in ads affect viewers? *Journal of Advertising Research, 35*(6), 19-28.

Kanner, B. (1995, February 20). Standing by their brands—well, some of them. *Advertising Age,* p. 28.

Kennedy, J. R. (1971, February). How program environment affects TV commercials. *Journal of Advertising Research, 11,* 33.

King, T. R. (1994, September 9). Keeping track. *The Wall Street Journal Reports: Television,* p. R11.

Korgaonkar, P. K., & Bellenger, D. (1985, August/September). Correlates of successful advertising campaigns: The manager's perspective. *Journal of Advertising Research, 25,* 34.

Kover, A. J., Goldberg, S. M., & James, W. L. (1995). Creativity vs. effectiveness? An integrating classification for advertising. *Journal of Advertising Research, 35*(6), 29-40.

Kroeber-Riel, W. (1979, March). Activation research: Psychological approaches in consumer research. *Journal of Consumer Research,* p. 240.

Krugman, H. E. (1965). The impact of television advertising: Learning without involvement. *Public Opinion Quarterly,* p. 29.

Krugman, H. E. (1967). The measurement of advertising involvement. *Public Opinion Quarterly,* p. 30.

Krugman, H. E. (1983, February/March). Television program interest and commercial interruption. *Journal of Advertising Research, 23,* 21.

Krugman, H. E. (1988, October/November). Point of view: Limits of attention to advertising. *Journal of Advertising Research, 28,* 43.

LaTour, M. S. Snipes, R. L., & Bliss S. (1996, March/April). Don't be afraid of using fear appeals: An experimental study. *Journal of Advertising Research 36*(2), 59-67

Laurent, G., & Kapferer, J.-N. (1985, February). Measuring consumer-involvement profiles. *Journal of Marketing Research, 22,* 41.

Leach, D. (1981). *The reliability, sensitivity, and validity of Burke day-after-recall.* Paper presented at Advertising Research Foundation Key Issues Workshop on Copy Research Validation, New York.

Leavitt, C. (1968). Response structure: A determinant of recall. *Journal of Advertising Research, 8,* 3.

Leavitt, C. (1970). A multidimensional set of rating scales for television commercials. *Journal of Applied Psychology,* p. 54.

Leckenby, J. D. (1978). An empirical approach to the multiple criteria problem in copy-testing research. *Journal of Advertising, 7*(Winter).

Lee, B., & Lee, R. S. (1995). How and why people watch TV: Implications for the future of interactive television. *Journal of Advertising Research, 35*(6), 9-18.

Levy, M. (1978). Audience for TV-news interview programs. *Journal of Broadcasting, 22.*

Liesse, J. (1991, December 2). Brands in trouble. *Advertising Age,* p. 16.

Likert, R. A. (1932). A technique for the measurement of attitudes. *Archives of Psychology,* No. 140.

Lloyd, D. W. (1987). *The impact of the television program environment on advertising effectiveness.* Ph.D. dissertation, Boston University Graduate School of Management, Boston, MA.

Lloyd, D. W. (1996). *Advertising and copy testing measurement.* Internal report. Chadwick Martin Bailey, Inc.

Lloyd, D. W., & Clancy, K. J. (1991, August/September). CPMs versus CPMIs: Implications for media planning. *Journal of Advertising Research, 31,* 34.

Lodish, L. M. (1986). *The advertising and promotion challenge, vaguely right or precisely wrong?* (p. 127). New York: Oxford University Press.

Lodish, L. M. Abraham M., Kalmenson S., Livelsberger J., Lubetkin B., Richardson, B., & Stevens, M. E. (1995, May). How T.V. advertising works: A meta-analysis of 389 real world split cable T.V. advertising experiments. *Journal of Marketing Research, 32,* 125.

MacDonald, G. (1986, September 29). Zapping the clutter. *Advertising Age,* p. 18.

Mackenzie, S., & Spreng, R. A. (1992, March). How does motivation moderate the impact of central and peripheral processing on brand attitudes and intentions? *Journal of Consumer Research, 18,* 519-529.

Mandese, J. (1994, July 25). Death knell for demo? Buyers set to move on. *Advertising Age,* p. S-2.

Mano, H., & Oliver, R. L. (1993, December). Assessing the dimensionality and structure of the consumption experience: Evaluation, feeling, and satisfaction. *Journal of Consumer Research, 20,* 451-466.

McNeely, M., & Marshall, S. (1992, January 13). Thumb wrestling. *AdWeek,* p. 18.

Mehrabian, A., & Russell, J. A. (1974). *An approach to environmental psychology.* Cambridge: MIT Press.

Milavsky, J. R. (1992, Spring). How good is the A.C. Nielsen people-meter system? *Public Opinion Quarterly, 56,* 102.

Mitchell, A. A. (1979). Involvement: A potentially important mediator of consumer behavior. In W. L. Wilkie (Ed.), *Advances in consumer research* (Vol. 6, pp. 191-196). Association for Consumer Research.

Mogelonsky, M. (1995, February). When stores become brands. *American Demographics,* p. 32.

Morgan, F. (1979, June). Students in marketing research: Surrogates versus role players. *Journal of the Academy of Marketing Science, 7,* 255.

Morris, J. D. (1995). Observations: SAM: The self-assessment manikin. *Journal of Advertising Research, 35*(6), 63-68.

Motavalli, J. (1989, September 11). Cable TV. *AdWeek Marketing to the Year 2000* (Supplement), p. 158.

Murry, J. P., Jr., Lastovicka, J. L., & Singh, S. N. (1992, March). Feeling and liking responses to television programs: An examination of two explanations for media-context effects. *Journal of Consumer Research, 18,* 441-451.

Myers, J. C. (1968). *Consumer image and attitude.* Berkeley: Institute of Business and Economic Research, University of California.

Naples, M. (1984, August/September). Electronic media research: An update and a look at the future. *Journal of Advertising Research, 24,* 39.

Nunnally, J. C. (1978). *Psychometric theory* (2nd ed.). New York: McGraw-Hill.

Park, C. W., & Young, S. M. (1986, February). Consumer response to television commercials: The impact of involvement and background music on brand attitude formation. *Journal of Marketing Research, 23,* 11-24.

Park, J.-W., & Hastak, M. (1994, December). Memory-based product judgments: Effects of involvement at encoding and retrieval. *Journal of Consumer Research, 21,* 534-547.

The party's over. (1992, February 1). *The Economist,* p. 69.

Poltrack, D. (1989). Good media planning will have to go beyond numbers to qualitative analysis. *Journal of Media Planning, 4*(2), 25.

Priemer, A. B. (1989). *Effective media planning* (p. 230). Lexington, MA: Lexington Books.

Rapaport, D. (1971). *Emotions and memory.* New York: International University Press.

Raymondo, J. C. (1997). Confessions of a Nielsen household. *American Demographics, 19*(3), 24.

Rogers, P. (1988, March 28). Food marketers: Slow the "frenetic" pace of new product introductions. *Marketing News,* p. 17.

Ross, C. (1996, August 5). JWT, Comedy Central study ad placement. *Advertising Age,* pp. 3, 37.

Ross, C. (1997, August 4). Media buying and planning (Ad Age Special Report). *Advertising Age,* p. S-2.

Ross, H. L. (1982, February/March). Recall versus persuasion: An answer. *Journal of Advertising Research, 22,* 13.

Rossiter, J. R., & Eagleson, G. (1994). Conclusions from the ARF's copy research validity project. *Journal of Advertising Research, 34*(3), 19-32.

Rothchild, M. L. (1979). Advertising strategies for high and low involvement situations. In J. Maloney & B. Silverman (Eds.), *Attitude research plays for high stakes.* Chicago: American Marketing Association.

Rubens, W. S. (1989, February/March). We don't care about research quality anymore. *Journal of Advertising Research,* p. RC-3.

Runyon, K. E., & Stewart, D. W. (1987). *Consumer behavior* (3rd ed.). Columbus, OH: Merrill.

Russell, J. (1989). Measures of emotion. In R. Plutchik & H. Kellerman (Eds.), *Emotion: Theory, research, and experience*. San Diego, CA: Academic Press.

Rust, L. (1987, April/May). Using attention and intention to predict at home program choice. *Journal of Advertising Research, 27,* 25.

Sawyer, A. G., & Howard, D. J. (1991). Effects of omitting conclusions in advertisements to involved and uninvolved audiences. *Journal of Marketing Research, 28,* 467.

Schlinger, M. J. (1979, April). A profile of responses to commercials. *Journal of Advertising Research, 19,* 37.

Schlinger, M. J. (1982). Respondent characteristics that affect copy-test attitude scales. *Journal of Advertising Research, 22.*

Schumann, D. W., & Thorson, E. (1990). The influence of viewing context on commercial effectiveness: A selection-processing model. *Current Issues in Advertising, 12*(1), 1-24.

Schwerin, H. A. (1960). Program-commercial compatibility: A summary of SRC's findings on the relationship that exists between the television commercial and its environment. *Schwerin Research Corporation Bulletin* no. 8.

Settle, R. B., & Alreck, P. L. (1988, May). Hyperchoice shapes the marketplace. *Marketing Communications,* p. 15.

Smith, D. C. (1956). *Television program selection, liking for television programs, and levels of attention given to television programs by housewives* (Radio-Television Audience Studies, New Series No. 3). Department of Speech, Ohio State University.

Soldow, G. F., & Principe, V. (1981, April). Response to commercials as a function of program content. *Journal of Advertising Research, 4,* 59.

Soley, L. C., & Reid, L. N. (1983, August/September). On the validity of students as subjects in advertising experiments. *Journal of Advertising Research, 23,* 57.

Stanton, J., & Lowenhar, J. (1977, Spring). Perceptual mapping of consumer products and television shows. *Journal of Advertising, 12,* 38.

Star Wars. (1997, March 22). *The Economist,* pp. 15-16.

Steiner, G. A. (1963). *The people look at television.* New York: Knopf.

Steiner, G. A. (1966, April). The people look at commercials: A study of audience behavior. *Journal of Business, 39,* 272.

Stewart, D. W. (1986). *Effective television advertising.* Lexington, MA: Lexington Books.

Stewart, D. W., & Furse, D. H. (1984-1985, December/January). Analysis of the impact of executional factors on advertising performance. *Journal of Advertising Research, 24,* 23.

Stipp, H., & Schiavone, N. (1990, September). Research at a commercial television network: NBC 1990. *Marketing Research.*

Stipp, H., & Schiavone, N. (1996). Modeling the impact of Olympic sponsorship on corporate image. *Journal of Advertising Research, 36*(4), 22-28.

Tannenbaum, P. (1980). Entertainment as vicarious emotional experience. In P. Tannenbaum (Ed.), *Entertainment functions of television.* Hillsdale, NJ: Lawrence Erlbaum.

Tavassoli, N. D., Shultz, C. J., & Fitszimons, G. J. (1995, September/October). Program involvement: Are moderate levels best for ad memory and attitude toward the ad? *Journal of Advertising Research*, p. 64.

Times Mirror Center for the People and the Press. (1994). *The role of technology in American life*. Washington, DC: Author.

Tooley, J. A. (1989, May 15). Talk, talk, talk. *U.S. News & World Report*.

TV ad effectiveness declines. (1993, September 27). *Marketing News*, p. 1.

Twyman, W. A. (1974). Setting TV advertising in context. *Journal of the Market Research Society of London, 16*.

Tyebjee, T. T. (1978). Cognitive response and the reception environment of advertising. In S. C. Jain (Ed.), *Research frontiers in marketing*. Chicago: American Marketing Association.

Un-seamly. (1997, February 3). *Advertising Age*, p. 26.

Venkatesan, M., & Haaland, G. A. (1968, May). Divided attention and television commercials: An experimental study. *Journal of Marketing Research*.

Walley, W. (1989, September 28). Media is key to successful ads. *Advertising Age*, p. 47.

Webb, P. H. (1979, December). Consumer initial processing in a difficult media environment. *Journal of Consumer Research, 6*, 225.

Wells, W. D. (1964). EQ, son of EQ, and the reaction profile. *Journal of Marketing, 28*.

Wells, W. D., Leavitt, C., & McConville, M. (1971). A reaction profile for TV commercials. *Journal of Advertising Research, 11*.

Wind, Y., & Denny, J. (1974, May). Multivariate analysis of variance in research on the effectiveness of TV commercials. *Journal of Marketing*.

Wright, P. L. (1973, February). The cognitive processes mediating acceptance of advertising. *Journal of Marketing Research, 10*, p. 53.

Wright, P. L. (1974). Analyzing media effects on advertising responses. *Public Opinion Quarterly, 38*, 192.

Young, S. (1972, February). Copy testing without magic numbers. *Journal of Advertising Research, 12*, 3.

Yuspeh, S. (1979). The medium versus the message. In G. Hafer (Ed.), *A look back, a look ahead: Proceedings of the Tenth National Attitude Research Conference*. Chicago: American Marketing Association.

Zachary, G. P. (1995, May 17). NBC to produce programming for new Microsoft electronic network. *Wall Street Journal*, p. B-6.

Zaichkowsky, J. L. (1985, December). Measuring the involvement construct. *Journal of Consumer Research, 12*, 341.

Index

Aaker, David A., 55, 61

Achenbaum, Alvin A., 151

Advertising:

  and attitudes, 204-205

  and creativity, 10

  and line extensions, 144, 146

  and new products, 5, 129, 146

  and performance, 8

  and persuasion, 61, 87, 105, 146, 192

  and recall, 5, 12, 17, 20, 24, 26, 30, 32, 35, 42, 56, 61, 72, 74, 87, 89, 104, 117, 124, 132, 136, 146, 157, 179, 190, 204

  and sales, 6, 8, 87, 189

  and shift to promotion, 11

  and stimuli, 33, 43-45, 50, 57-59, 74, 152

  and testing, 9, 12-13, 17

  commercial placement decisions, 31-32, 165-169, 200

  content, 69

  contextually similar to program material, 30-32

  decisions, based on tried and true approaches, 203

  effect on sales, 8-9

  effectiveness and program carrier, 5, 12, 15, 24, 30, 35, 39, 57, 60, 72, 103

  efficiency value, 173

  engaging, 166

  exposure, 112

  factual vs. image, 147

  for established test brands, 144

  for new test brands, 144

  in-market, 182

  involving, link with involving programming, 41, 61, 162, 165, 169-170

  measurement of attitudes toward, 55, 205

  pods, middle, 3

  positioning penetration, measurement of, 6

  reach and frequency, 11

  receptivity, 54, 116

  relationship to attention and involvement, 206

  response, effect of program environment, 22

  television, adding to clutter, 3

  television, decline in effectiveness and efficiency, 1-11

  See also Campaigns; Commercials

Advertising effectiveness, 39, 40 (figure), 87

  and cost efficiency, 168

  and environmental conditions, 60

  and high involvement programming and viewership, 29, 42, 66, 130, 162, 169

  and involvement, 16, 23, 40, 122, 194

  and print media involvement, 175-187

  predictors of, 57, 172

  scores, calculating predicted, 35,79, 120, 150, 155, 160, 172

Advertising response:

  and environmental conditions surrounding exposure, 16, 18-19, 42, 103, 150

  and print media, 179, 183-184

  and program involvement, 13, 26, 43, 58, 61, 101, 104, 107-109, 130, 150, 168, 192-194

  and viewing conditions, 18, 36, 41, 59, 105-106

forced, 24, 32, 34, 61, 69
opportunity, 162
program and commercial, 3, 16
Exposure environment, 23, 150, 155, 200

Filters, intervening, 39
Focus group research, 9, 200
Foote, Cone & Belding, 25
Fouriezos, N. T., 26
Fragmentation of media, since mid-1960s,
    2-5
Frank, Betsy, 12, 166

Gallup and Robinson, 26
Gardner, David M., 61
Grazing, with less involving programs, more
    prone to, 53, 167-168
Greene, Jerome D., 31

Haaland, Gordon A., 61
Halo effect, 28
Hand-held meters:
    to register viewer reactions, 45, 63
    in experimental environment, 45, 77
Hastak, Manoj, 18
Hayes, George, 11
Hollingshead, A. B., 135
Home Testing Institute, Inc., 26, 27
Hooper, L. E., 26
Houston, Michael J., 48

Informercial, 31
Information load, 43
Involvement:
    ad-related, 49
    and audience counts, 172
    construct with full range of emotional and
        affective dimensions of attitude, 48
    definitions, 17-18, 19, 32, 47, 56
    differences in level of and type of, 49, 56
    feelings and liking as elements of, 19, 49-50
    index value, 67
    measurement of, 44, 48, 178-179
    multidimensional scale predicts advertising
        effectiveness, 48

print media involvement and advertising
    effectiveness, 175-187
program, and advertising effectiveness, 15
See also Program involvement
Index value, 67, 172
IPSOS-ASI, 27, 72, 82, 87, 100, 123-124, 211
    trends in ad recall scores, 5

J. Walter Thompson, 26

Kapferer, Jean-Noel, 47
Kennedy, John R., 21, 23
Kinnear, Thomas C., 166
Korgaonkar, Pradeep K., 144
Kover, Arthur J., 202
Krugman, Herbert E., 27, 30, 47, 165
Kweskin, David M., 27

LaTour, Michael S., 86
Laboratory conditions, 61, 76, 193
Lastovicka, John L., 27
Laurent, Gilles, 47
Leavitt, C., 56
Lee, Barbara, 53, 85
Lee, Robert S., 53, 85
Levy, M., 85
Lodish, Leonard M., 67, 87, 163

Mackenzie, S., 56
Mano, Haim, 43, 56
Market share, growth in, 9 (figure)
Markets:
    fragmented, 2-3, 156
    mass, and television networks' share, 3
Mini-mass, 140
Marshall, Scott, 202
McCann-Erickson Worldwide, 3, 11
McCollum/Spielman approach to commercial
    testing, 152
McNeely, Mark, 202
Measures, IPSOS-ASI, Inc. favorites, 27, 72,
    100, 124, 211
Media:
    and fragmentation, 1-3, 208
    and media plans, 67, 133, 163, 165, 168
    and ratings, 164-165

About the Authors

Kevin J. Clancy is a graduate of The City University of New York and earned a Ph.D. in social psychology and research methods from New York University. He taught marketing and sociology at the Wharton School, and is an adjunct professor of marketing at Boston University.

In 1982, he and his partner, Robert Shulman, formed Clancy Shulman Associates, which was acquired by Saatchi & Saatchi, then the largest advertising agency in the world. The marketing consulting firm ultimately became Yankelovich Clancy Shulman, with Clancy as chairman.

In 1993, he formed Copernicus: The Marketing Investment Strategy Group, headquartered in Westport, Connecticut, where Dr. Clancy is chairman and chief executive officer. Copernicus, a marketing, consulting, and research firm, is one of the world's pre-eminent research organizations, with an international clientele.

Dr. Clancy is co-author of *The Marketing Revolution: A Radical Manifesto for Dominating the Marketplace* (1991), *Marketing Myths That Are Killing Business* (1994), and *Simulated Test Marketing: Technology for Launching Successful New Products* (1995).

David W. Lloyd was educated at Gettysburg College and Boston University's School of Management where his doctoral dissertation, which represents the foundation for the work reported in this book, won the Kearny Fellowship award. He has held faculty positions at the University of New Hampshire, Boston University, and Boston College, where he taught graduate courses in marketing research, consumer behavior, and advertising.

In 1990, Dr. Lloyd formed his own consulting practice, consulting primarily to marketing and advertising research companies on measurement design and analysis, as well as new product and service development. Much of his work has involved three companies, Chadwick, Martin, Bailey, Inc., a marketing consulting and research firm in Boston; the Yankelovich Organization, a global marketing and public opinion research company; and Copernicus: The Marketing Investment Strategy Group.

Dr. Lloyd has worked extensively on some of the more fundamental problems facing advertising today. The author of a number of published articles on the hidden power of television advertising and related topics, he has spoken frequently at domestic and international conferences on improving advertising copy-testing methods and about his proprietary model for enhancing the efficiency and effectiveness of media buys.